T0283340

Grandmothering

Grandmothering

Building Strong Ties
with Every Generation

Kathleen Stassen Berger

ROWMAN & LITTLEFIELD
Lanham • Boulder • New York • London

Published by Rowman & Littlefield
An imprint of The Rowman & Littlefield Publishing Group, Inc.
4501 Forbes Boulevard, Suite 200, Lanham, Maryland 20706
www.rowman.com

86-90 Paul Street, London EC2A 4NE

Copyright © 2019 by Kathleen Stassen Berger
First paperback edition 2023

British Library Cataloguing in Publication Information Available

Library of Congress Cataloging-in-Publication Data available

9781538133132 (cloth)
9781538185407 (paper)
9781538133149 (electronic)

Grandmothers are older women who care deeply about the young. Some such women are not biological grandmothers, and some older women are grandmothers only in the genetic sense. This book is dedicated to all older women with vision, hope, and power.

Contents

Preface

$\mathcal{G}$randmothers make the gears of a family machine mesh and move, clicking together in harmony. They help babies sleep, toddlers eat, preschoolers read, school children study, adolescents find themselves, and young adults become happy and successful.

Smooth clicks are not automatic: some grandmothers are uninvolved, others destructive. But most older women are wiser and happier than their younger selves, more sanguine, more patient, and more willing to sacrifice for the younger generation. Grandmothers are designed to be pivotal family members, to oil the family machine and support every member.

Why grand*mothers*, not grand*fathers* or grand*parents*? Some children need grandfathering more than grandmothering, and some men are great caregivers. But this book focuses on grandmothers not only because I am one but also because they generally provide more care and intimacy than grandfathers do. This gender difference might be nature (brains, genes, and hormones) or nurture (cultural norms and personal history)—probably both. But whatever the reason, women and men are not interchangeable; grandmothers merit a book dedicated to them.

Of course, what I have written is limited by my perspective. But our common humanity allows each person's experiences to help others. All grandmothers seek the sweet spot between intrusive and distant; all want to strengthen their grandchildren; all hope political leaders and younger family members respect their role.

Sadly, this may not occur. Modern families are often fractured, with gaps where grandmothers belong. Increases in troubled children, broken relationships, and economic pressures make grandmothers more important than ever; yet old stereotypes echo in empty chambers. Many grandmothers are neglected, absent, or excluded.

I am a developmental psychologist. For decades, I have studied, taught, read, and written about families. Research guides me in being the grandmother I want to be. So do strangers and students, as well as my friends, my children, and my grandchildren. I am still learning. But the combination of science and experience gives me joy that I want to share with you. The goal is a better life for all of us . . . elders, children, and everyone in between.

Part I

GET UP FROM THE FLOOR

THANKSGIVING

Admirable, but long gone. This buxom woman, with apron, rolling pin, granny glasses, and white hair in a bun, trimming a homemade pie crust, is unlike the grandmother of any current wide-eyed grandson.

Similar *Saturday Evening Post* cover, Thanksgiving, 1908, by the same artist, J. C. Leyendecker.

• 1 •

Excluded and on the Floor

I am lying on a hard, hospital floor at 4 a.m., trying to sleep. Down the hall is a miracle, or maybe a death.

My left shoulder aches on the tile. I roll over: my right hip hurts. The crumpled jacket is no pillow; measured breathing does not quiet me. My own bed—soft, empty, and waiting—is a twelve-minute walk away.

Why am I here, in this waiting room? To help Elissa, my daughter, who has been laboring for thirty hours to deliver my first grandchild.

She does not need me. Oscar, her husband, and Chris, her midwife, are with her. Since early evening, when Chris deftly deflected a Cesarean, no one has told me anything. I am excluded, ignored, forgotten.

"We should go home," says Rachel, another daughter, my only companion here with the hard chairs, harder floor, and colorful brochures about cord blood. "We are useless."

Rachel's right. We've been here all night, of no use, with no word of Elissa. We should go home. Will someone, some time, remember us and be surprised to find us gone? I should tell them we are leaving. I run my fingers through my hair, slap my cheeks, find my shoes, walk down the dark hall to the brightly lit nurse's station. Two nurses are chatting happily.

"Any word on Elissa?" I ask.

"Yes, there is word," a nurse replies. "Go back and wait."

I rush to tell Rachel. "'Word,' she said, and 'wait.' Smiling."

We watch the door. It opens.

"You can see her now," a nurse says.

We speed to the only lit room, way down the hall. Elissa is beatific, mostly covered with a crisp, white hospital sheet, nursing a tiny creature, born at 3:46 a.m. Oscar and Chris stand nearby, beaming.

We are told that the baby is perfect and technically not tiny: he has already been taken elsewhere to be checked and weighed: 10 pounds, 2 ounces. Oscar went with him, having been warned in prenatal class, "Never lose sight of your newborn."

I congratulate Elissa. She apologizes: "I asked them to tell you right away, but they said I must be cleaned up first."

I learn his name, Asa, for A. Philip Randolph. I kiss my cleaned-up daughter, admire Asa, thank the midwife, and hug Oscar. He has already phoned his parents, three thousand miles away.

WHAT IS WRONG?

A survey of more than a thousand grandmothers reports that "the arrival of a grandchild" often results in an "instantaneous . . . unbounded . . . magical love."[1]

Another grandmother wrote about her daughter's long labor, "My daughter was struggling in this wild current . . . braving those rapids, alone in the frail craft of her own body."[2] That grandmother's fears vanished when she saw her moments-old grandchild, who, "radiant and glowing, is the future."

Not my words, not my feelings. Something's wrong. Not with Asa, Elissa, or Oscar. Something is wrong with me, or the hospital, or the century.

I went home, slept fitfully until noon, and woke up troubled.

Why was I kept ignorant and distant while waiting for my child to give birth? She was my little girl. I diapered her for years, sponged her when she threw up, bathed her after she played in mud, picked lice from her hair, hour after hour. Now "wait until she is cleaned up"? I am her mother, not some formal visitor. I am now a grandmother, a crucial part of her family.

I thought of Elissa's birth, thirty-three years ago. Midwives were banned from my world-class hospital.[3] Fathers were forbidden at deliveries as my husband, Martin, had been for our first two. Newly inspired by feminism, I convinced my board-certified obstetrician to let Martin witness Elissa's arrival. He wept when he held her, wet and wide-eyed, moments old. I reached out; they did not let me touch her. Germs, they said. With gloved hands, they wiped, weighed, wrapped, and whisked her away.

The hospital kept us apart for twenty-four hours. They said that I had no milk, that I needed rest, that she was tired, too. Grandmothers were also shut out. That didn't bother my mother. She was heavily sedated when I was born; she was horrified that I planned a natural birth.

"Don't let her do it," Mom had told Martin, about my birth plans. He smiled. He knew he couldn't stop me.

When she was one day old, Elissa was wheeled to me, asleep. I woke her, got her to suck.

The day after that, Martin brought our two older daughters, Bethany and Rachel. Children were not allowed on the maternity floor; my little girls could not view their new sister, even through the nursery glass. But I could hobble down to the elevator to a special room to see them. That was an innovation; formerly, no visitors under age twelve could set foot in the hospital.

On day three, I was breastfeeding and talking on the phone when an aide came to take Elissa back to the nursery. She scolded me: "Hang up. When you nurse, you must give your baby undivided attention."

Wrong. Old-fashioned. I knew better. I had suckled Bethany and Rachel while setting the table, stirring a pot, turning pages, and, of course, holding a phone. I was a pioneer. I was riding the wave of liberation, with millions of my sisters, toward a brighter, fairer, future.

Hurrah for the past half century. Now men routinely witness their children's births; midwives deliver babies; mothers feed life-sustaining colostrum to their minutes-old newborns. We rock the cradle *and* rock the world. We became doctors, lawyers, CEOs, prime ministers, presidents. Strong. Invincible. Women! Helen Reddy belted it out; we sang along, loud and victorious.

Decades passed. Victories improved our lives. But liberated boomers grew old. Age sneaked up on us. We did not anticipate reading glasses, gray hair, stiffness, grandchildren asking whether telephones were invented when we were girls, or teenagers sending us texts. Few of us burned bras, broke ceilings, or led nations, but we all crossed barriers. Now we must cross another one.

Some in our culture equate grandmotherhood with disability and death, but most of us are vital for decades after the first grandchild, who arrives, on average, when the woman is fifty years old. Most new grandmothers see, hear, and move well; they can be energetic playmates. A survey of 1,205 grandmothers found that only one in five felt that their health interfered with grandmothering.[4] Their most common health problem—less energy. One said, "I do find that I'm a little bit more tired now than when Steven was little. I would play ball with him in the garden when he was two and three and four, and now that he's going on nine, I do notice that I don't have the same amount of energy to run around that I used to."[5]

As grandchildren grow older, grandmothers grow older, too. If a second, third, or fourth grandchild arrives when a grandmother is sixty, seventy, or eighty, she is less able chase, play ball, or swing a grandchild around. But she still can be a vital force.

We do not deny aging; we deny incapacity. Grandmothers might wish for the body of a twenty-year-old, but age need not stop us, even when the oldest grandchild reaches adulthood, and new grandchildren or great-grandchildren are born. *Selective compensation with optimization* is a cliché for gerontologists. Disabilities can be selectively overcome, and better actions can replace difficulties.

- My third grandson, at age three, asked me to carry him down the stairs, as his parents do. But I feared he might wiggle, and then we might both fall. Instead, we bumped down the stairs together on our butts—to his delight.

- My eight-year-old grandson wanted me to play soccer. Again, no. But together we read, play cards, do homework, and make pancakes.
- My grandchildren ask questions so softly that I cannot hear. That reminds me to check with my audiologist; if I need hearing aids, I will get them.
- My grandchildren ask me to read to them. I try to remember to keep my reading glasses in my pocket. Is it time to wear them on a chain?

COHORT AND CULTURE

Back to the hard floor. Why didn't I stay home as my mother did, waiting by the phone, visiting in a day or two? Why didn't a *granny* deliver my grandson at home, as was true for my grandmothers?

The answer is evident in those questions: every era perceives birth in its own way. *Cohort differences*, as social scientists call them, mean that we all are influenced by our political, historical, and cultural zeitgeist. Cohort is historical, not generational. If my mother, my daughter, and I had all given birth at the same chronological age, our experiences would nonetheless differ radically.

But there is a deeper reason I was at that hospital, a reason that transcends history. My mother waited by the phone, my grandmother labored at home, billions of women helped other women give birth in jungles, shacks, yurts, tents, igloos, and bedrooms—we all were responding as our cultures permitted to a universal mandate. Age brings awareness of mortality and immortality, and older women everywhere are driven to help younger women. I was at that hospital because I felt compelled to be nearby in case my daughter needed me.

My mother, in her nineties, with her dying words, expressed joy at seeing me and my children. No matter what our cohort or context, my foremothers and I want a better world for our descendants; we strive to bring that about; we fight the cultural barriers that keep us away.

Fighting for recognition is the history of my cohort. A revolution transformed me, my daughters, and everyone else. We barrier-smashing women became educated, employed, and independent, not docile like grandmothers of yore. They stayed home wearing faded, flowery, house dresses; we went to work in pants suits. We dismissed them, proclaiming, "Don't trust anyone over thirty."

But now we are long past thirty. We have gotten older, but we are still strong, invincible. Our culture, and that hospital, is stuck in the past, clinging to the limits imposed on past generations of women. Another revolution is needed.

Or maybe not. Perhaps grandmothers were never docile, except on *Saturday Evening Post* covers.

Perhaps the sweet, housebound, pie-baking grandmother is a mirage that shimmers, never real. Perhaps strong grandmother instincts and emotions have always been part of women's experience, hidden because history was written by men. I was taught more about U.S. Civil War battle strategies than about the struggles of the suffragettes. But many individuals have told me of their powerful grandmothers.

Recently I learned that the first Mother's Day, in 1908, was instituted to honor a grandmother who opposed war because it killed her sons and grandsons. Perhaps past grandmothers shared our deepest hopes—healthy and happy grandchildren in a peaceful world. Were their passions not recorded because men did not want women to think or vote?

We share many impulses with those grandmothers of old. But the *demographic revolution* is recent and real, as the following six statistics prove. That's why being forgotten in that tiny hospital room was so troubling. Grandmothering endures, but families changed and grandmothers changed. The culture and that hospital did not.

1. We have had jobs; many grandmothers still do. In the 1950s, most women were *housewives* (married to houses!), but beginning in the 1970s, millions of mothers joined the workforce.[6]
2. We are educated. My cohort has far more high school graduates and college degrees (including JDs, MDs, and PhDs) than our foremothers.[7]

3. We live longer.[8]
4. We live healthier.[9]
5. We are mentally more alert.[10]
6. We had fewer babies. Our children have even fewer (and have them later), often only one.[11]

These six put me on that hard floor. I *never* stayed home while men did the world's work; I am educated and healthy and expect to live to a hundred. It is odd that I bore four children, but I have a grandmother excuse: my role model was my maternal grandmother, who lived with us. She bore sixteen infants. My four adult children are typical. My mother's mother had twenty-two grandchildren; my mother had seven; I have three.

Am I the odd one, unlike grandmothers in other ethnic groups, other social classes, other cultures, other nations? I am privileged in many ways; does this make my experience irrelevant for most grandmothers?

No. Everyone is unique, but I am not that odd. The statistics above refer to *all* U.S. women, of every ethnicity. Over the past half century, education has increased, and fertility has fallen faster for Latino and African Americans than for European Americans. Similar data could be compiled from every nation, even those at the bottom of the economic ladder. Bangladesh, for instance, may be the poorest nation in the world. The United Nations estimates that the average Bangladeshi woman had 6.91 live births in 1975 and 2.22 in 2015.[12]

Some people assume that nonwhite U.S. grandmothers are more involved with their families and more respected within their communities than white grandmothers. That assumption might be racist. Or elitist. Or ageist. It is not accurate. Involved grandmothers are not exclusive to any group.

Indeed, in the United States, rates of grandmother caregiving and financial support are similar among African American, Latino, and European American grandmothers.[13] There are some ethnic differences, detailed later, but grandmothers of all backgrounds are caught in the same demographic riptide.

That does not mean that every grandmother is the same. Some women were *not* housewives fifty years ago, some women are *not* now employed, some current grandmothers are respected matriarchs, some die young. But the demographic revolution affects us all, with new grandmothers unable to fit into the old wineskins that society fashioned a century ago.

There are many more grandmothers, and many fewer grandchildren, than in prior generations. Consider both the facts and the implications. As recently as 1970, half of the world's population was under age twenty-two.[14] Every older age group was notably smaller than the next younger one, creating a "demographic pyramid" when the population is stacked by age group. The shape of the stacks was like a wedding cake, large at the bottom and tiny at the top.

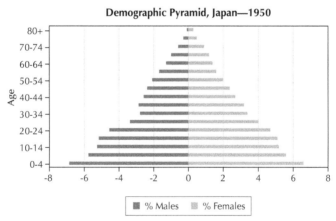

The demographic picture is changing from a pyramid to a rectangle or even toward an inverted pyramid. Shown here are Japan, the world leader of the demographic revolution, and the United States, which is moving in that direction. (The low bars in the late 20s of the 1965 U.S. chart reflect the low birth rate during the Great Depression.) Other nations show similar changes.

Data from Statistics Bureau, Ministry of Internal Affairs and Communications, Population Census of Japan, Table 2.2: Population and Japanese Population by Age and Sex: 2010, 2015. http://www.ipss.go.jp/p-info/e/psj2017/PSJ2017.asp; https://factfinder .census.gov/faces/tableservices/jsf/pages/productview.xhtml?src=bkmk.

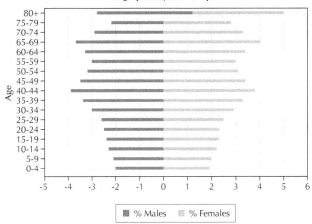

Demographic Pyramid, Japan—2015

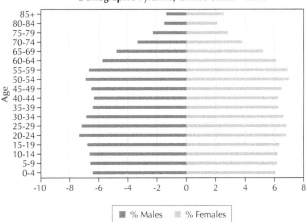

Demographic Pyramid, United States—2015

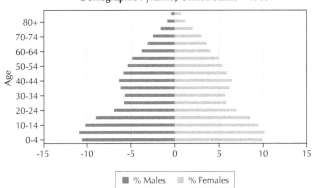

Demographic Pyramid, United States—1965

A high birth rate was one reason for the pyramid; ageism was another, causing premature deaths, shrinking each older cohort. When people hit middle age, they expected cancer, lung disease, deafness, and *senility* (a word that literally means *old* but became a synonym for dementia).

Elders were told to stay quiet, lest their hearts fail. In part because of that bad advice, hearts did indeed fail, and many (twice as many men than women) died before age sixty-five.[15] Widows often moved in with their children, sat in rocking chairs, and watched the grandchildren. That was a hundred years ago.

A demographic flip began in the second half of the twentieth century. Immunization, contraception, clean water, and sanitation led to child survival, while new drugs and better surgery meant that more people grew old. For a brief moment, around 1960, most grandmothers had many grandchildren. No longer. The pyramid has become a rectangle; an inverted pyramid is projected.

New crisis: *grandmother glut and birth dearth*. The world has more adults over age fifty than children under age fifteen.[16] In the United States, the ratio of *women* over sixty to children of *both* sexes under fifteen is about 1:1.[17] An average grandmother eventually shares two or three grandchildren with another grandmother and often with a step-grandmother, a childless great-aunt, or a great-grandmother. But society has not yet adjusted. As one observer notes, "we are still immersed in cultures designed for lives half as long as the ones we are living."[18]

Grandmother glut and birth dearth, glaring in North America and Europe, is coming to every nation. Fertility in Brazil, Mexico, Egypt, Iran, and Thailand was more than six children per woman in 1960; now it is two in those five nations and below replacement level (2.1) in eighty-two others.[19]

GRANDMOTHERS AND FAMILIES

Too many grandmothers? The notion that we have more grandmothers than we need arises from an ageist assumption that the purpose of grandmothers is to devote themselves to grandchildren. If that were so, the new demographics render many grandmothers superfluous. But people of all ages and relationships need grandmothers; more grandmothers are good for everyone because older women are needed by every society.

Consider one example in detail—the increase in disasters, defined as a natural event (flood, fire, earthquake, etc.) that causes more than ten deaths and affects more than one hundred people.[20] Disasters are increasing worldwide. In the Americas, for instance, there were about thirty disasters per year in the 1980s, but now there are about one hundred. Population density (demographic revolution again) is the reason: more people are nearby to suffer from each calamity.

The extent of harm correlates less with the strength of the event (i.e., the intensity of a hurricane) than with the knowledge of the women.[21] Wise women stockpile supplies, develop plans, interpret warnings, guide families. That is exactly what older women do if they are nearby and heeded. But many are missing in action. Social mobility separates generations, ageism devalues elders' wisdom, the young take risks, disasters kill.

Ageism is endemic, undercutting grandmothers. A 2014 analysis of all two hundred picture books published in the United States that included images of grandmothers found an ethnic improvement over the past decades: more nonwhite grandmothers were depicted.[22] However, virtually no grandmother in any current book was employed. Almost all of the illustrations showed a shortish old woman, often wearing an apron, with gray or white hair, sometimes in a bun. This image is contrary to what children themselves experience: most preschoolers (the audience for these books) have employed grandmothers with stylish hair and clothes. The authors note "a collective nostalgia that is shared by the full range of adults who are involved in the process of the publishing, marketing, and distributing children's picture books."

Ageist stereotypes are everywhere, and grandmothers are favorite targets. Here are a dozen examples; every astute observer can find many more.

- Thousands of people are murdered or murderers, drug addicts or drug sellers. Yet if one of those people is a grandmother, that becomes news.
- A headline in *People* magazine: "Grandmother, 63, Accused of Smuggling 500K in Cocaine through Detroit Airport." The judge scolded her for not growing up (i.e., not acting as grandmothers should).[23]
- A front-page banner headline in the *Daily News* was "Granny Gotti Begs for Baby," mocking the gangster's widow for asking a Brooklyn judge to set bail for her convicted grandson, age twenty-four: "He is my baby. I adore him and pray he will have the opportunity to be a productive member of society again." Other members of that Mafia family also wrote letters, but the newspaper did not highlight them.[24]
- When Hillary Clinton first became a grandmother, some speculated that she would no longer want to become president. (In fact, the opposite was more accurate.)[25] That was sexist as well as ageist. Would anyone expect a male candidate to quit when he became a grandfather?
- When Nancy Pelosi maneuvered President Trump to postpone his State of the Union address, commentators noted with surprise that a grandmother could be so powerful.
- The entire culture forgets that grandmothers might be vital family members. A search for "family" photographs in Google Images finds that 93 percent are of mother, father, and children; no grandmothers present.[26]
- Social scientists overwhelmingly assume that "family" means parents and young children.
- Many people equate family with *household.* Since most grandmothers do not live with their grandchildren, does this mean they are not part of the family?
- Some psychologists became "family therapists." They specialize in parents and young children; they almost never include parents and adult children, or three generations of the same family.
- Adults are expected to escape from their parents: A leading text on family therapy, now in its ninth edition, praises a ther-

apist who "helped the daughter detach from her grandmother, creating a more appropriate hierarchical structure."[27] Why is that appropriate?

- Many grandmothers advise each other to stay distant, good advice to counter overinvolvement. But the "norm of non-interference" may keep grandmothers from intervening even in cases of domestic violence.[28]
- One summary says that traditional psychoanalytic writing "mentioned . . . grandmother . . . mostly unfavorably . . . the noxious influence of the grandmother on the child."[29]

Even worse, the laws of the land and the attitudes of the middle generation may marginalize the cogent, active grandmother, who is by far the more common type of grandmother. Consequently, when legislators consider older women, they usually bemoan the burden of caring for them. But the facts are the opposite: grandmothers provide more money and care to younger generations than vice versa.[30]

When new mothers try to figure out the grandmother's role, they assume the worst. One grandmother wrote, "I felt as though I was auditioning for the role of grandmother: Did I hold Isabelle properly? Was I capable of changing her diaper? Didn't I know that you never put a newborn down on her stomach. . . . And that was just the beginning."[31]

For all our social ills, families need grandmothers more than ever. And yet statistics, reports, and studies suggest that grandmothers (and probably grandfathers as well) are sidelined at best, forgotten at worst. But grandmothers can provide much more than a warm lap when Mom or Dad is busy. Nostalgia and inertia exclude contemporary grandmothers and harm families.

Time to fight back. I began by rising from a hard floor in a dark hospital. The rest of this book contains weapons and strategies for every grandmother: why grandmothers are needed; when grandmothering is too much and when not enough; how changing times have rendered some grandmother advice irrelevant and other grandmother help crucial for grandchildren of every age—from before birth to adulthood.

Why Grandmothers?

$\mathcal{T}$he night sky lightens; early birds sing.

Someone wakes. An old woman rises, stiff and bent, grabbing her digging stick, setting forth before her grandchild stirs. She is joined by seven others, all long past menopause, walking toward the hard ground where tubers are buried. They will unearth that nutritious root all day, later joined by younger women and children.

As the sun sets, those eight are the last to quit, each with food for herself along with a thousand calories for nursing mothers or a newly weaned toddler. In this community, every woman with a babe at the breast has an aged helper, either a genetic grandmother (including one maternal great-grandmother) or another older woman. Because of them, children survive.

This is documented.[1] A team of anthropologists chronicled the actions of these eight as part of an intense study of one group of Hadza, a hunter-gatherer tribe in East Africa. Their published research was the first in a string of studies to shed light on a dark mystery that bedeviled biologists for decades—why menopause? And then, why old age? Shouldn't *sterile* old women die?

THE PARADOX OF MENOPAUSE

That question bothered me, too. What are grandmothers for? What is the purpose of life, when menopause makes birth impossible? Grandmothers are often pushed aside. Instead of pushing back, should I accept that I am a sterile old woman who should quietly disappear?

As George Williams (a scholar whose insights changed the social sciences for generations) expressed it, "The paradox about human female menopause is that evolutionary theory predicts that there should be no selection for any post-reproductive life-span. The reason is that sterility is—in principle—the selective equivalent of death."[2]

Figuring out this paradox requires understanding human biology over hundreds of thousands of years. That makes research on the Hadza relevant. In a small region in northern Tanzania, the Hadza cluster into groups of 6 to 139, living as nomadic hunter-gatherers, as did all humans before agriculture required settlement about eleven thousand years ago.[3] Social scientists hope that Hadza life patterns reflect inborn human nature.

Each Hadza group relocates every few weeks when nearby food is depleted. Everyone hunts or gathers. Men hunt at night, using arrows to fell impala, eland, zebra, or giraffe. The researchers reported that one time the hunters returned sorrowful, empty-handed. Fortunately, the women gather the community's main sustenance, tubers, nuts, and honey, so no one starved.

Food is shared when needed. After this failed hunt, a nearby Hadza group sent scraps from a dead giraffe. The Hadza consider themselves all one people; individuals move freely from one group to another.

The eight senior women spent more time gathering than did the younger women. Nursing mothers, particularly, foraged less. Newly weaned children gathered almost nothing: they lost or gained weight depending on the grandmothers.

The basic premise of evolution is that every characteristic of all living creatures serves survival or reproduction. Peculiarities, such as the peacock's feathers, the giraffe's neck, the salmon's death swim, promote life. Extinction occurs when too few survive to reproduce. That was the fate of 99 percent of all the species that ever lived, including more than a billion kinds of fish and insects, every type of dinosaur, and all of the human species save one—*Homo sapiens.*[4]

Our species is unusual, not only for survival but also for proliferation. *Homo sapiens* multiplied and spread from East Africa to all corners of the earth, the only species to thrive on every continent. Because humans are one species, a Zulu warrior could marry a Siberian woman, and they could have many fine children. Their cultural differences might cause friction, but their biology would not.

How did *Homo sapiens* survive, when an estimated five billion larger and smaller species died? Possibilities abound, including digits, diet, language, fire. Might grandmothers be the reason?[5] Could midlife menopause—halting motherhood and allowing grandmotherhood—be life sustaining rather than "the selective equivalent of death"?

Ancient teeth and bones reveal that extinct hominids and other early mammals had few grandparents. Ancient burying grounds for those long-gone species find that almost no one survived past age thirty.[6] Suddenly, at about the same time that *Homo sapiens* first appeared, the proportion of grandparents in the population almost tripled. Did grandparents transmit vital knowledge (such as where to dig for tubers and how to survive climate change) that prevented extinction? Does longevity allow transmission of technology, social organization, and values that aid the entire species?

The possibility that aging women increased survival is buttressed by studies in the animal kingdom. Among Asian elephants, compared to newborns without a grandmother, a newborn with a grandmother nearby is eight times less likely to die young.[7] Unlike elephants and humans, most mammal grandmothers are pre-menopausal, busy with new babies because they are young and fertile.

You might be confused if you have learned that, in past millennia, human life was "solitary, poore, nasty, brutish, and short,"[8] with survival until age thirty or so, on the average. However, that average is an arithmetic mean reflecting many dead infants and young children. Our fortunate foremothers who survived infancy, childhood, and childbirth usually reached grandmotherhood, menopause, and then old age. That is dramatically true now; worldwide, the average woman lives three decades after menopause (four decades in Japan).

Genes sometimes change over time, via selective adaptation if a mutation benefits survival and reproduction. But that has not happened with the genes for menopause at about age fifty and survival for decades beyond that. Those genes have been transmitted from the first women to walk the African soil, long before modern medicine. That fact buttresses the case that menopause aids species survival. Further evidence comes not only from archeology but also from the Hadza: "Many women live . . . into their 80s," never seeing a doctor.[9]

This aspect of human biology is peculiar. Even with excellent medical care, death comes quickly to virtually all post-reproductive mammals, from aardvarks to zebras. Some other primates experience menopause, but their lives end soon after that.[10] Menopause *plus* longevity is unique to human females, elephants, and two species of whales (*Orcinus orca* and *Globicephala macrorhynchus*).

The more biologists learn about other species, the more bewildering this is. Many creatures die before the next generation is born. The female praying mantis eats the male while he impregnates her, biting off his head before copulation is complete. This aids species survival; his body nourishes the pregnancy. Many fish and insects die after laying eggs, as Charlotte did soon after her triumphant, Wilbur-saving web.

That is never the case for mammals: until recently, newborns starved without breast milk, which, to begin, requires pregnancy. (Mammals are named for mammary glands that produce milk.) Most primates nurse their babies for years. Not until baby gorillas, baboons, orangutans, or chimpanzees are finally weaned (age four or later for chimps) do the mother's pheromones broadcast that she is fertile, which alerts every male. In some primate species, receptive females display another come-hither signal: their buttocks turn bright red.

If female primates are not cycling, gestating, or nursing, they are dying; no male is interested. Human primates are an exception; sexual attraction is disconnected from fertility, and life continues decades after menopause. Why? A clue comes from those two species of whales. Postmenopausal whales help their grown offspring find food and avoid predators: adult whales are more likely to survive if their postmenopausal mother is nearby.[11]

After Charlotte died and baby spiders began to hatch, Wilbur said, "I shall always treasure her memory. To you, her daughters, I pledge my friendship, forever and ever."[12]

I cried when I read that: it is touching that Charlotte died for her children and that her sacrifice is memorialized by her friends, pledging to love her progeny.

But that is neither my plan nor my fate, unlike virtually every other species and unlike human men. The male example is instructive. Why can men father children in old age? One man holds the record: Ramajit Raghav, from rural India, claimed to father one baby at age ninety-four and a second at age ninety-six. That brought him fame but not happiness. His first son disappeared at age two, and his wife (in her early fifties) left with the second at age one.[13]

Even if his wife and children had stayed, Ramajit was unlikely to be an active father throughout their childhood. That would be his loss as well as theirs because men who become active caregivers tend to be happier and healthier than other men their age. Hundreds of studies leave no doubt that children benefit from involved fathers and grandfathers. Nonetheless, childbearing stops in midlife for women, not for men.

The reason is the nature of human mating. Although it is possible for an old man to become a father, men usually stop fathering children when their wives stop bearing children. Humans tend to notice unusual cases, which is why people are aware of men's midlife divorce, remarriage, and late fatherhood. But that pattern is relatively rare.

To be specific, contrary to the impression from headlines, most men marry women only a few years younger than they are, most divorces occur in the first five years of marriage, and only one newborn in a hundred has a father older than age fifty.[14] These rates have increased in the past decades, but almost all older husbands stay with their post-menopausal wives.

Indeed, late fatherhood may be destructive, not only because women often choose children over men, as Ramajit's wife did, but also because advanced paternal age at conception correlates with problems in the fetus and child.[15] Rates of autism, particularly, rise when the father is over age forty-five.[16]

How might long life after midlife menopause benefit the species? Research led primarily by women (Kristen Hawkes on the Hadza, Sarah Hrdy on allomothering, Rebecca Sear in West Africa, Ruth Mace on cooperative breeding, Jan Beise on Germans and Québécois) developed the *grandmother hypothesis.*

Grandmothers are ideal *allomothers*, or people who care for children but are not their biological mothers. Young mothers need allomothers; raising children alone is arduous. Fathers often help, but not always, and even with two involved parents, childrearing is difficult.

Throughout the millennia, grandmothers have often been allomothers. When older women no longer bear children, they help their grown daughters with pregnancy, birth, and child care, allowing young women to become pregnant again. A new pregnancy soon after giving birth is biologically impossible for other primates; they are infertile unless their infants die or are old enough to care for themselves.

Allomothers are essential for *Homo sapiens* because lengthy brain development (unlike in every other creature) makes human children and adolescents vulnerable to starvation, predators, raging rivers, speeding cars, and many other killers for decades before neurological maturation allows self-preservation. For survival, "each new human being [needed] protectors—people who make sure that the child can thrive, learn, and imagine in spite of being so vulnerable. . . . Those protectors are parents, of course, but they also are grandparents."[17]

Grandmothers kept infants from wandering off into jungles, in much the same way that they now keep children from running into traffic. Historically, childbirth was the leading cause of female death between ages fifteen and thirty-five. It was essential that lactating and loving caregivers be available to nurse and nurture motherless children.

Over two hundred thousand years, because of grandmother al-lomothering, more offspring were conceived, more newborns survived, more toddlers were protected, and more children became educated adults. Humans multiplied; other primates did not.

Menopause kept older women from the demands of their own infants. Those ancient, protective, genes and habits have endured. Modern humans still need allomothering.

I observed that myself. On a crowded subway, I sat in front of a standing young woman, balancing an infant and several packages, pre-cariously grasping a pole. I offered to help, expecting to hold her pack-ages, but she handed me . . . the baby. I sang quietly to the infant as the train hurtled through the tunnel. I should not have been surprised at the mother's trust: our genetic mandate includes shared child care.

Human allomothering is in stark contrast to chimpanzee mothers who hide their infants from other chimps, fearing poking fingers and infanticide (a realistic fear; newly dominant males kill newborns).

Older female humans have always been fiercely protective, as well as caring, not only of their own descendants but also of other infants. This is an inner compulsion, far beyond rational. Seeing, touching, and caring for an infant unlocks a flood of hormones; we care for babies not our own.

When my pediatrician was examining Bethany, my firstborn, I asked, "Isn't she one of the cutest, smartest babies you have ever known?" He responded with a twinkle, "Yes, and my patients are cuter and smarter than the patients of other pediatricians."

Caregiving fuels allomothering; logic and inheritance are not required. Five of those early-rising Hadza crones were genetic grand-mothers, but the other three were not. They had no grandchildren who needed them, but each dedicated herself to another family. Likewise, in the twenty-first century, children have a host of allomothers: teach-ers, doctors, nurses, babysitters, neighbors, and more. If our early care depended solely on our mothers, most of us would be dead.

Menopause, long life, and allomothering are factual, but not every scientist accepts the grandmother hypothesis.[18] Two other ideas have been proposed:

1. The *good mother hypothesis.* Older children need motherly attention; good mothers should not be torn between caring for infants and older children.
2. The *resource competition hypothesis.* Men can continue their genetic legacy with a new wife and children, but human babies need resources to survive, so they need mothers to provide for them.

Neither of these theories contradicts the grandmother hypothesis. Good grandmothers are good mothers, and resource competition increases the need for grandmothers.

EVIDENCE FOR GRANDMOTHER HYPOTHESIS

Scientists seek data before they accept hypotheses. Historical birth and death records in many nations (including Germany, Gambia, Canada, Japan, and India), before the widespread use of contraception, immunization, and safe childbirth, provide that data: fewer babies died and more were born when maternal grandmothers helped young mothers.[19]

Grandfathers on either side often had no impact, and sometimes the paternal grandmother was no help. Indeed, in one region (Krummhorn, Germany, in the eighteenth century) young wives typically lived with their mothers-in-law, and that *increased* fetal and newborn death (but not toddler death). This was especially true if the young woman's natural protector—her own mother—had died.[20] Why? One explanation: young, pregnant daughters-in-law suffered from exhausting work, emotional stress, and poor nutrition, which harmed the fetus.

Why were those German mothers-in-law so demanding? Because "a daughter-in-law is, in principle, replaceable; a daughter is not."[21] Thus young women were pushed to work and reproduce. Young husbands, dependent on their mothers, did not protect their brides.

Later research focused again on the Hadza, with fifteen years of data on more than a thousand men and women over age forty.[22] Grand-

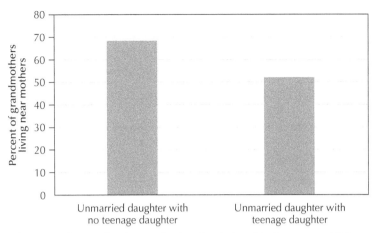

When a Hadza mother has no husband to help with the young children, a grandmother often lives nearby. The mother especially needs Grandma if she has no older daughters of her own to help her. This data is from the Hadza in the twentieth century. Are similar trends apparent in the United States in the twenty-first century?

Jones et al., "Hadza Gradmothers as Helpers," 2005.

mothers lived where they were needed, especially if fathers and older daughters were unavailable as allomothers. When grandmother care was needed, old women built a leaf-and-stick shelter near their grandchildren. When fathers and older children (especially girls) became allomothers, grandmothers more often lived with another Hadza group.

One scholar, a well-respected man, concludes:

> *Because a Hadza grandmother is so productive as a forager, and because she tends to reside in the same camp as her daughter, she is a reliable and important source of help for a woman who is raising a young child. With the Hadza as an example, the grandmother hypothesis is not only plausible but compelling.*[23]

Details from two other places drive home this point.

One research team examined records from Quebec between 1680 and 1750.[24] The average family had seven children, causing a population explosion: in 1650, Montreal had about one thousand inhabitants;

in 1750, fifty-five thousand. Having all four grandparents improved grandchild survival. When neither grandmother was alive, 29 percent of the newborns died; when both grandmothers were alive, the death rate was 24 percent. Thus, for one in every twenty Montreal infants, life itself depended on grandmothers.

The second example is from the Mandinka, in the west African nation of Gambia, in the twentieth century.[25] Before massive immunization, more than a third (35 percent) of the children died before age five, typically of childhood diseases that were lethal because of malnutrition. Death came only half as often if the maternal grandmother lived within walking distance.

Many other examples prove that grandmothers aided survival in past centuries and in poor nations. They helped toddlers gain weight and young women have babies.

STILL TRUE?

But what about today? Newborn deaths, childhood starvation, and childbirth fatalities are rare. Are grandmothers now superfluous? Current hazards—obesity and population explosion—are opposite to those that past grandmothers mitigated. Might modern grandmothers, with their traditional drive to feed children and promote fertility, be destructive?

One older woman laughed as she praised her grandmother: "She would cook for us, you know stuff food down our faces, all the wrong food but you know she was a full-on stay-at-home grandmother."[26]

Her laugh masks a hard truth: that grandmother increased her grandchildren's risk of stroke, heart disease, and diabetes. Overall, children raised by grandmothers are more often overweight than other children.[27] Why? Don't grandmothers know the dangers of sweets? Are they trying to buy love? Do they "spoil" children, ignoring what the parents say?[28] There are other possibilities as well, but no matter what the explanation, a grandmother's digging skills no longer aid grandchildren survival.

Not only do some contemporary grandmothers overfeed infants and encourage births, but they may also be directly destructive of a marriage. Some mothers criticize their grown child's partner. Some demand intensive attention. One reason for marital friction in middle age is disagreement about the care of elderly parents,[29] who may use guilt to claim time, money, and attention.

But a human failing is to focus on exceptional cases (the serial killer, the fatal plane crash, the welfare cheat, the self-absorbed grandmother) and to ignore the more common ones. Although selfish, destructive grandmothers exist, if you know such a woman, think of all the benevolent grandmothers you know. Most grandmothers neither interfere with marriages nor demand care.

Is there evidence that most contemporary grandmothers are helpful, not harmful? Yes. Children do better in school, are more compassionate toward other people, and have fewer emotional problems when their grandparents are supportive.[30] A study of twenty-three European nations found that many parents prefer grandparent care for their children because they judge such care to be best.[31] In thirty-three African countries, children who lived with their grandmothers were more likely to attend school than other children.[32]

Some advanced nations provide extensive, excellent child care for very young children. That does not stop the grandmothers. In fact, in those places, grandmothers are *more* likely to help with grandchildren, adding to the national care network.

Scholars who study human development have long understood that "grandparents are particularly valuable when social forces threaten to weaken the fabric of family life."[33] For example, most women in Scandinavian nations are in the labor market, which might interfere with child care. That is one reason that those nations subsidize excellent and extensive early child care. Yet two-thirds of the Danish grandmothers also provide regular care for young grandchildren.[34]

That contrasts with Italy, with no public infant care because most government officials think families need mothers to stay home with their children. Many Italian women believe they must choose between employment and motherhood. That is one reason Italy has one of the lowest birth rates in the world. That also is why fewer Italian grand-mothers provide child care than Scandinavian ones. However, the minority who are caregivers tend to put in more hours per week than the Scandinavian grandmothers because their daughters have jobs. Apparently, no matter what the national policies and attitudes about mothers, grandmothers everywhere contribute to family life.

Consider overpopulation, a new and serious worldwide problem, straining the global supply of food, fresh water, and renewable energy. Contemporary grandmothers more often limit the population explosion than worsen it. For example:

- The nations with the most grandmothers and great-grand-mothers (Japan, Singapore, China) are among the nations with the lowest birth rates.
- A large study in England found that having paternal grand-parents made it more likely that a couple with one child would have a second one, but having maternal grandparents made it less likely that they would have a third.[35]
- In France, Germany, and Bulgaria, family pressures are likely to limit fertility.[36]
- A large survey in Europe (SHARE) found that couples were less likely to become pregnant if no grandmother was available.

As for childhood deaths, twenty-first-century newborns rarely die unless they are born several months premature or have a severe disability. However, for North American fifteen- to twenty-four-year-olds, violent deaths (accidents, suicide, and homicide) are three times higher than mortality from all diseases combined. Even in poor nations with horrific public health, children and young adults are far more likely to die violently than from malnutrition or any disease.

Grandmothers to the rescue. They reduce the risk not only by providing a watchful eye but also indirectly by being a reason to avoid danger. One specific is that rates of accidental death and homicide are reduced with education. Grandmother involvement improves the likelihood that a child will graduate from high school and attend college because grandmothers express interest, help with homework, and pay for school expenses.

Regarding suicide, grandmothers provide hope and social support, the key antidotes to depression. One study of suicide risk among young adults from rural Alaskan villages (they have the world's highest rates of youth suicide) noted protection from elders. That study quoted an Alaskan college student: "I was pretty much raised by my parents and my grandparents, my maternal grandparents, we would go camping every August for a week, pick berries, and while we're picking berries the men would trap, we'd eat fish and drink tundra tea, and just living, the way our ancestors did."[37]

Dramatic data of grandmother protection is found during national tragedies.

- When HIV/AIDS killed tens of thousands of young parents, especially in Africa, grandmothers often cared for children. That increased survival.[38]
- In Argentina, when many adults "disappeared" between 1976 and 1983, a group called Grandmothers of the Plaza de Mayo marched in defiance of the government, calling attention to their abducted grandchildren. One grandmother leader was captured, killed, and dumped in the Atlantic, but other grandmothers kept marching. International journalists rated them a major force in deposing the regime.[39]
- In developed nations, including the United States, when children are removed from their parents because they are severely maltreated, they are often placed in kinship care with a grandmother. There are many problems with custodial grandmothering (discussed in chapter 5), but to the surprise of skeptics, foster children are more likely to thrive with grandmothers than with strangers.[40]
- When parents divorce, die, enter prison, leave home to find work, or are sent away for military service, grandmothers step in. Their care rescues children despite circumstances that can be devastating.

Overall, grandmothers are "public health assets."[41] Demographic and political shifts unsettle children, but grandmothers are an "anchor" providing "ties of trust and moral obligation [and] significant intergenerational support."[42]

As anecdotal evidence, consider four famous Americans:

- Oprah Winfrey, one of the richest and most admired women in America, credits her success to living with her grandmother, Hattie May, until she was six years old. Hattie May taught Oprah to read at age three and encouraged her first public performance: preaching to the crows on the backyard fence.
- Michelle Obama relied on her mother to care for her daughters, making it possible for Barack to become president and then for Michelle to be an active first lady for eight years. Her mother did not want to move to the White House, but she agreed to do so for her granddaughters.
- J. D. Vance, in *Hillbilly Elegy*, chronicles his journey from poverty, as a child of a drug-addicted mother who remarried five times, to graduation from Yale Law School. When he was thirteen, his mother was arrested for trying to kill him. He wanted her jailed so he could live with his grandmother. But a social worker told him that his grandmother would not qualify for providing foster care, so J. D. lied to the judge. His mother was acquitted; his grandmother took over. He credits her "saving grace of a crazy hillbilly" for his success.[43]
- Supreme Court justice Sonia Sotomayor suffered from maternal neglect and paternal alcoholism. Her father died when she was nine; her mother then locked herself in her room for weeks. But Sonia had Abuelita (Grandmother Mercedes):

> *I loved Abuelita totally, and without reservation, and her apartment on Southern Boulevard was a safe haven from my parents' storms at home. Since those years, I have come to believe that in order to thrive, a child must have at least one adult in her life who shows her unconditional love, respect, and confidence.*

For me it was Abuelita. I was determined to grow up to be just like her, to age with the same ungraying, exuberant grace. Not that we looked very much alike: she had very dark eyes, darker than mine, and a long face with a pointed nose, framed by long straight hair—nothing like my pudgy nose and short, curly mop. But otherwise we recognized in each other a twin spirit and enjoyed a bond beyond explanation, a deep emotional resonance that sometimes seemed telepathic. We were so much alike, in fact, that people called me Mercedita—little Mercedes—which was a source of great pride for me.[44]

Hundreds of thousands of less famous Americans of all ethnic groups credit their grandmothers for their emotional health. Experts suggest that "in many families of Western societies, the grandparent–grandchild relationships is more important than ever before."[45]

Secure attachment between a child and a grandparent is protective lifelong. Even after a grandparent dies, memories continue to sustain the grandchildren.[46] All the evidence suggests that the grandmother hypothesis is as valid today as in earlier centuries, no longer measured by infant life or death, but by children who become happy, accomplished adults.

Deep within, on the Floor Again

*E*xalted, not excluded, for my second grandchild. Bethany honored me; she asked me to be her birth partner. I was welcomed to prenatal classes, medical check-ups, the labor-delivery room. They even let me stand in a corner of the newborn nursery, witnessing neonates being checked for infections, heart health, genetic diseases, and organ functions. I watched my minutes-old grandson intently; a wet diaper meant he could be brought to his mother.

All these externals were grandmother friendly. Unlike with my first grandchild, I found no reason to fight cultural myths and antiquated practices. But internal forces attacked.

I held a bent right leg in place with all my strength, fighting against strong muscles to move it. A nurse strained as she held the left. The midwife commanded, "Push . . . push . . . push." Bethany's arm muscles bulged as she pulled a sheet tied to a mental stanchion above her. A circle of fetal skull visible, then larger, then crowning. Tissues tore, Bethany pushed once more.

"Yes! Yes! Yes!" the midwife shouted. A head emerged, quickly followed by all 4139 grams of Caleb. His Apgar score was a stellar 9; every other number was good.[1]

Bethany, smiling, began to nurse. Four professionals looked on, relaxed now. This is grandmother bliss. Decades of praying, studying, teaching, and mothering led me to a miracle, 6:11 a.m., my firstborn with her firstborn. Celestial music rang in my ears.

The ringing grew loud, a buzzing, roaring crescendo. Bethany shimmered, overhead lights became stars, flashing bright. Then dark. I was flat on the floor, looking up at four faces staring down. I had fainted.

Stop staring, I wanted to say. *Look at Bethany; look at Caleb. They need you.* I scrambled onto the pallet where I spent the night, and mumbled

"I am fine."

"You need to go to triage."

"No, I am fine, sorry I fainted."

"Hospital policy. Triage."

"No. I belong here."

"You cannot stay."

"I'm fine. I have never fainted before."

A frowning nurse responded, "That's worse; I would be less concerned if you fainted often."

I was confused, angry, searching for magic words. Please? Pretty please? I wanted to stay. I wanted everyone to forget about me and attend to Bethany.

A younger nurse told me, "You can refuse treatment."

Saving grace, I remember now, God bless you.

I knew my priorities, I had a strategy. I rose quickly, the sooner to return.

They stopped me. "Hospital policy, you need a wheelchair."

Wheeled down the hall, waited for an elevator, wheeled to Admitting, explained that I was with my laboring daughter all night, without food, drink, or sleep.

"I refuse treatment."

The triage nurse scanned my face, took my blood pressure, and checked with her supervisor. I repeated my new mantra: "I refuse treatment."

"You can go back."

I stood up, smiling. Stopped again.

"Someone must wheel you back."

My priority was Bethany and Caleb; I obeyed. Back in time to witness delivery of the placenta. All well with mother and babe, with doctors and nurses. But not with me. What happened?

I know about birth, personally and professionally. I interpret numbers and jargon; I analyze monitors and body language; I evaluate doctors and nurses; I assess hospitals, noticing stray paper on floors, sharp voices in corridors, faded pictures on walls. Nothing here amiss; this hospital was excellent.

I also know Bethany: strong, healthy, drug free. All through the night—indeed, all through the nine months—I followed this pregnancy. I expected Caleb to be well formed and Bethany okay. I was relieved and happy, but not surprised, when my almost perfect daughter began nursing my quite perfect grandson.

Then why did I faint when all the drama was over? Indeed, why faint at all? I told the triage nurse that I had neither slept nor eaten all night. She accepted that; I do not. I have often been tired and hungry; I have never fainted. Something snapped, cracked, flooded my brain, flung me down. Grandmotherhood?

Bethany had labored and moaned for hours as Pitocin dripped into her veins. I had rested, quietly crying in a dark corner, watching the doula (a woman who helps with the entire birth process) massage her back, adjust the IV, support her in the shower. About every half hour, a midwife entered to check on progress. All was well. After four hours of hard labor, Bethany asked for an epidural. The two professionals exchanged glances. The midwife spoke: "You can have an epidural, but the fetal position means that if you can't push, you might need a Cesarean."

Bethany responded immediately, words from a new maternal brain that I never knew: "No epidural."

More hard labor. The doula gestured to me to help. I shook my head and pointed to silent tears on my cheeks. Unbidden, unwanted, I could not stop them. I did not want Bethany to know. The doula nodded, understood. I watched wordlessly in the dark periphery until summoned to hold a leg.

Primordial bonds must have been tightening all night long. At Caleb's arrival, they snapped, a seismic release from an underground fault. Earthquake. Tsunami. Shimmering. Darkness. Unconscious. On the floor.

Anne Lamott wrote, "This is the one fly in the grandmother ointment—the total love addiction—the highest highs, and then withdrawal, craving, scheming to get another fix. . . . But it's not my fault—we're wired to be delighted, obsessed; we're engineered that way."[2]

Wired for grandchildren? Sounds like new-age nonsense. Until the current comes on.

One woman, Janet, was aghast when a longtime friend insisted on shopping for her grandchild on their way to a lunch date. Her "once glamorous friend who now smelled of spit-up and stumbled tiredly though the store misty-eyed with joy . . . had become a grandmother."[3]

At the restaurant, Janet's friend spread photos on the table, expecting to hear that this "bald-headed tyke with the toothless smile" was cuter than all the millions of other babies in the world. Why didn't the friend know that a two-dimensional image of a distant small creature was insignificant compared to the vibrant, immediacy of Janet, ready to laugh about life?

A few months later, Janet's daughter phoned to announce that she was pregnant. Janet "imagined trundling after an infant who needed smelly diapers changed" and burst into tears, grateful that the call was voice only.

But when that grandchild was born:

"Let Grandma hold her" I shouted, almost knocking my poor son-in-law off his feet as I snatched my new granddaughter out of his arms. . . . Over the next few days I fought like a dragon to hold her, feed her, change her. . . . Until the day she had come into the world, I had been blind. The miracle of her birth had wrought a miracle in me, one I could not get enough of.

"All of those in favor of looking at pictures of grandchildren
before we discuss *Feminist Theory* say aye."

Does becoming a grandmother change priorities?
Martha Gradisher, CartoonCollections.com.

This snatching dragon joined millions of women eager to sacrifice time and money for tiny immobile creatures. They call it joy, not sacrifice.

Deep fears may vanish. One mother of an unmarried college student told her daughter to avoid motherhood, to avoid the poverty that burdened her mother to a lifetime of paid housework. "I did not approve that my daughter was pregnant. . . . But once the child was born, I take back all that I said . . . because my grandchild changed my life. . . . Even on my worst day, she just makes me happy."[4]

Another grandmother also works full time, yet cares for her grandchildren forty hours a week.

I never imagined this. I imagined I was going to be a Hollywood starlet. The only thing that kept me from posing for Playboy was I didn't have large breasts. I thought I would be lounging by a pool. But I don't wish I could quit, nah, not really. In all honesty, if I won the lottery. . . . And if I had houses all over the country, I would still expect my grandchildren to be there.[5]

She babysits by choice and works by necessity, to support herself and to buy gifts for her grandchildren.

At the other end of the economic scale, an oft-published, award-winning author writes that grandmother love is "scary in its irrationality."

There's something suspiciously viral about the condition, relentless, forceful, and all consuming. . . . Before it struck me, I'd listened—patiently, indulgently—to others in their blithe affliction. I'd never be susceptible, I thought. I knew love—infatuation, passion, devotion, the whole business—inside and out; I wrote the book—lots of them actually, about the ways we link or entwine or hook up. No variety of attachment could subjugate me. That it could was something I didn't know.[6]

Insightful authors describe frightening love addiction: a proper lady grabs a newborn from the father, old women continue backbreaking work, millions of grandmothers claim that grandchildren are the "enriching, fulfilling, even transcendent . . . joy of their lives."[7] Something powerful and mysterious threw me on the floor. What?

Before answering, we must acknowledge that not every grandmother is smitten. Some are indifferent, even angry, at a grandchild's arrival. Human brains are *plastic*, which means that experiences and cultures mold them lifelong, and that may undercut any biological force. Grandmothers who complain that their new grandchildren are demanding, squalling creatures are clear headed and honest.

Love may develop slowly. Something unexpected—a sudden laugh, a moment of danger—might astonish a woman to realize that she does, indeed, care deeply about a grandchild. Caring itself triggers love—another miracle.[8]

Every neuroscientist knows that nurture is essential for nature to develop. A person may have the genetic potential to be six feet tall, to be a musical genius, or to be a loving grandmother, but realizing that potential depends on childhood, experience, and culture.[9] Some brains wither, others expand; some genes are silenced, others explode; some hormones are quiet, others spread through every organ.

You will soon read about three explanations for the biological force of grandmotherhood—brains, genes, and hormones. Each is persuasive, based on evidence, although as an explanation of grandmother emotions, none is accepted by every scientist. As you read about these three aspects of human biology, remember that nature never acts alone. Some women are not besotted.

EVERY PART OF THE BRAIN

The drive to care for the young arises from deep in the brain; it has been lodged there for hundreds of thousands of years, not just in one region but throughout the world. The sound of a baby's cry, the sight of an infant face, even smell and touch—all the senses are attuned to child care, which means that every lobe is primed for grandmothering. Strong caregiving impulses, beyond the most advanced computer, are in every mammal.

Grandmother love begins deep within the brain, and is common in all mammals, who instinctively protect their young. Those deep impulses are sent to the prefrontal cortex, where people anticipate what might happen in a newborn's future, connect that future with past history, and add cultural goals and religious values.

Thus, the entire human brain is involved in care and adoration, with deep impulses that, for humans, join prioritizing, anticipating, philosophizing. We call babies *gifts from God*; we surround them with rituals (thought to distinguish humans from other mammals). They are circumcised, baptized, fed honey, washed, shaved, named, and so on, in sacred ceremonies. Grandmothers connect each baby with an entire family, clan, and ethnic group with "Grandpa's nose" or "my mother's eyes" or "black hair like Daddy." Since the prefrontal cortex connects each birth with the past and future, no wonder grandmothers are overwhelmed.

To fully appreciate this neurological impact, understand that humans have two modes of thought, called "intuitive" and "analytic" (or also called emotional and rational or hot and cold or instinct and reason). Following Kahneman, here we refer to that same pair as *System 1* and *System 2*, respectively.[10]

System 1 is the emotional default; it is instantaneous. It comes from deep within, from the amygdala, pituitary, and hypothalamus, said to arise "from the gut." System 2 is slower, with analysis and reflection, lodged primarily in the frontal lobe. System 2 is underdeveloped at first and advances with maturation over the first twenty-five years of life, as the prefrontal cortex expands and links to deeper parts of the brain. Humans need both systems; it is pathological to function with only one.

System 1 hijacks logic. That is why teenage love is sometimes called a *crush*, why we speak of *falling* in love: reason plummets when emotions rise. System 2 accumulates knowledge, makes plans, coordinates conflicting goals, and evaluates possibilities. The prefrontal cortex is not fully functioning until adulthood.

Both processes were evident in Caleb's birth. I had prepared with System 2 and was ready: I had practiced massage, learned about Pitocin, and met the midwife. But System 1 brought unwanted tears to my eyes, dropped me to the floor, and led me to insist that I belonged in the delivery room. Thankfully, System 2 awakened again and let me listen to the nurse, weigh priorities, and obey instructions. As in this example, System 2 sometimes reigns in System 1. I wanted to argue, fight, and yell, but logic quieted me. Once reminded of my legal right to refuse treatment, I climbed into the wheelchair.

For everyone, System 1 causes an emotional rush. Grandmothers have no choice, just like anger, fear, or lust that arise suddenly, catching a person off guard. But then System 2 is crucial. Ideally, grandmothers have learned to balance emotions and reason, and the entire brain cares for each grandchild.

That balance extends to caregiving of other people as well. That is why a white grandmother welcomed a young black stranger to dinner.[11]

An Arizona matriarch mistakenly texted a Thanksgiving invitation to a stranger, seventeen-year-old Jamal Hinton. He didn't recognize the number. He replied, "Who are you?"

"Your grandma."

Puzzled, he asked for a screen shot. She sent back a grandmother emoji and a selfie. He wrote back, "You not my grandma," with a surprised emoji and his own selfie, adding, "Can I still get a plate tho?"

She responded, "Of course you can, that's what grandmas do . . . feed everyone."

He came to dinner, welcomed not only by the grandmother but also by all her kin. The following Thanksgiving, she invited him back, and he came again. It became a tradition; he came to the third Thanksgiving.

GENES, SELFISH AND NOT

Some scientists believe that genes themselves seek survival. They perpetuate themselves via miosis and mitosis, being transmitted from one carrier (a parent) to the next (a child). With each birth, half of a person's genes live on. Thus, people choose expensive, frustrating, exasperating burdens—aka children—because their genes demand it.[12]

This *selfish gene* hypothesis might explain why grandmothers sacrifice time, resources, food, and life itself for every grandchild, who carries one-fourth of her genes. That may also explain wars: people fight other tribes, races, or nations that ostensibly have fewer of their genes and defend their own group, even when they should not. This impulse is evident in children; they believe that their particular religion, nation, gender, or whatever, is better than all the other religions, nations, and so on. Of course, we know that religion is not inherited genetically, but the selfish gene impulse is not rational and therefore seeks similarity even when it is not directly genetic. If their parents express prejudice against another group, children readily agree.[13]

One amusing example of this inborn instinct to defend one's own kind occurred when preschoolers were asked to explain why one person would steal from another, as occurred in a story about two fictional tribes, the Zaz and the Flurps. Even at that early age, the children assumed tribal loyalty.[14] "Why did a Zaz steal a toy from a Flurp?" "Because he's a Zaz, but he's a Flurp . . . They're not the same kind . . . "

Then they were asked about a more difficult case, when genetic loyalty could not explain stealing. The children were forced to find another explanation, and they chose character: "Why did a Zaz steal a toy from a Zaz?" "Because he's a very mean boy."

Many social scientists, including me, hate the selfish gene hypothesis, in part because it discounts altruism and demeans grandmother love.[15] Could my care for my children and grandchildren be a self-serving compulsion, not commendable self-sacrifice? With my own children, I changed an estimated sixteen thousand dirty diapers, read twenty thousand boring books out loud (most of them repeats), paid more than four hundred thousand dollars for college classes. I am doing the same for my grandchildren. (Diapers and boring books are immediate; education for the grandchildren is via 529 bank accounts because my prefrontal cortex anticipates college for my genetic progeny.)

Is that admirable? I would like to think so, but maybe this is merely selfish genes. Why do I care for my own grandchildren but not for other children, even those next door or down the block, and certainly not children in Yemen, Bangladesh, or elsewhere who desperately need food and protection, never mind a college education? Selfish genes?

I proudly extend my love for my own grandchildren to other children, but in much smaller increments. For example, my political activity centers on public education and immigrant families, but that takes an hour or so a week, compared to twenty hours for my grandchildren. With my children, when it was my day to help at the parent-cooperative daycare center, I changed diapers on all the other babies so I could change my own daughter's without seeming to favor her. I fooled no one, including myself. Selfish genes? Maybe. I hope not.

Selfish genes are used to explain another fact: in every nation, the average grandmother devotes more time, money, and worry to grandchildren than the average grandfather does. Why? Some scholars advance a *paternal uncertainty* explanation. Men cannot be certain that their children carry their genes because another man might have impregnated their wives. Women know their babies are theirs, because they carried them for nine prenatal months and then gave birth. Paternal uncertainty unconsciously compels men to harbor doubt, some say.

Men's wish to promote their genes with certainty is thought to explain the extreme sexual jealousy that many men—and not as many women—express.[16] Thousands of people in many nations have been asked, "Which would trouble you more, if your romantic partner had sex with someone else or was in love (no sex) with someone else?" Generally, men say *sex* and women say *love*.

Paternal uncertainty is also cited to explain why paternal grandparents provide less grandchild care than maternal grandparents.[17] Almost always, maternal grandmothers are most closely connected to their grandchildren and paternal grandfathers the least, perhaps because they are doubly uncertain.[18]

But blaming selfish genes for male/female patterns of caregiving seems too narrow. Culture may be more important than biology.[19] Genes encourage parental commitment: parents invest most heavily in the children who look and act like them,[20] but genes do not determine caregiver dedication.

I prefer the evidence contrary to the selfish gene hypothesis. For one thing, genes do not always produce caregiving: some fathers deny paternity despite evidence; some new mothers reject their own newborns. Furthermore, nongenetic caregiving abounds: some adoptive fathers and mothers are more dedicated to their children than some biological parents; many stepparents and "social fathers" nurture children who are not, genetically, theirs.[21]

For another thing, some children are said to fall far "from the tree," with genetic oddities (such as the extra chromosome of a child with Down syndrome, or the double recessive of a child who will never grow tall) that make them look or act quite unlike either parent. Some

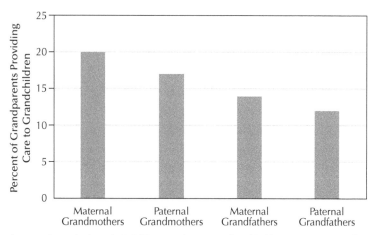

A massive study of 8,667 grandparents in 13 European countries (SHARE) found that whether the grandparents provided daily or almost daily grandchild care depended on everyone's age, health, residence, culture, and, as shown here, gender. (They were asked if they currently provided care. More had earlier cared for grandchildren who were now teenagers.)

Data from Danielsbacka et al., "Grandparental Child Care in Europe," 2011.

children can never have children, so their parents know that their own selfish genes will not continue. Nonetheless, many parents and grandparents are devoted caregivers when they bear an infertile child who does not look like them.[22]

Indeed, humans do many things that are contrary to genetic survival. They seek dangerous sexual partners, eat foods that shorten their lives, take life-threatening risks. Genes do not rule us, which makes me hope that love for grandchildren is not determined by selfish genes. I prefer the third biological explanation for grandmother love.

OXYTOCIN AND OTHER HORMONES

Hormones push all of us to be anxious, lustful, sleepy, hungry, fearful, depressed, sexy, and happy and to make some of us homicidal, suicidal, anorexic, or schizophrenic. None of this is solely hormonal, but hormones are one reason for human behavior, including grandmothering.

Hormonal effects vary by age, dose, sex, experience, and species. Social hormones—vasopressin, testosterone, oxytocin among them—are especially complicated. Social hormones pulse through the veins of men as well as women, babies as well as elders. Everyone responds to the hormones of other people, especially if that other person is a sexual partner or one's own child. Hormones may explain why attachment and caregiving are evident in families across the generations.[23] For men particularly, testosterone is reduced and oxytocin increased by infant care.

Scientists do not yet know all the effects of the social hormones, especially in humans. However, scientists agree that these hormones propel caregiving. We focus here on one hormone, *oxytocin*, which may be especially crucial. Several experts, reviewing the biology of love, write that "it is highly likely that oxytocin plays a role in grandparenting and bonding between grandparents and grandchildren."[24]

Oxytocin is "best known as 'the love hormone'" among the general public, called "the paramount social hormone" by scientists, and considered "a parenting hormone" by some developmental psychologists.[25] A rush of oxytocin might cause grandmothers to be enraptured by their newborn grandchildren.

The best understood role of oxytocin is in birth. Labor begins because oxytocin naturally triggers contractions. Ancient mammals, half a million years ago, first produced that hormone to aid birth and breastfeeding. Obstetricians have used artificial oxytocin (Pitocin) for decades to strengthen contractions if they are weak and to start labor if continued pregnancy is harmful or the due date is past. Bethany's labor was accelerated by Pitocin, as is the labor of about three thousand women every day in the United States.

Over the millennia, oxytocin has developed many other uses, including fostering social bonding, decreasing anxiety, and increasing trust. With humans, oxytocin increases parent-child affection, loyalty among friends, and caregiving by relatives. It cements the bond between lovers, promotes trust and generosity between strangers, aids emotional comprehension in old men, buttresses the immune system, and reduces fear, especially fear of social rejection, in everyone.[26] No wonder it increases love.

But not always. Oxytocin may increase aggression, especially in defense of one's family and friends. Research finds that the effects of oxytocin (and, indeed, of all the social hormones) are not simple, not straightforward, not universal. One detailed (103 pages) review concludes that there is "a high level of uncertainty" regarding the connections between oxytocin and "various behavioral traits . . . including . . . loneliness . . . emotional withdrawal . . . empathy . . . maternal sensitivity . . . aggression and antisocial behavior."[27]

Research on voles (a mouse-like wild creature) has led to understanding of oxytocin. Montane voles, with very little natural oxytocin, are selfish and promiscuous. They are neglectful parents; their offspring sometimes starve for lack of parental care. Prairie voles (another species) have abundant oxytocin. Even virginal prairie voles have oxytocin; when they mate, their oxytocin rises. That causes the impulse to devote themselves to their partners and, soon, to their offspring. Both male and female prairie voles mate for life, tending to their offspring with admirable, cooperative solicitude.[28] Credit oxytocin.

Scientists blocked oxytocin in some prairie voles.[29] Bonding and caregiving disappeared. The opposite worked, too: adding oxytocin to montane voles increased caregiving. Thousands of experiments on many mammals led to the conclusion that oxytocin induces maternal behavior, changing the brain as well as behavior.

What does this have to do with grandmothers? Fortunately, humans are more like prairie than montane voles. Deep within every human brain are genes and receptors that produce and distribute oxytocin, signaling the hypothalamus to produce the hormone and then the pituitary to spread it throughout the body and brain, especially the amygdala and prefrontal cortex.

Oxytocin may function differently in humans than in other mammals. Scientists find it very difficult to assess exactly how much natural oxytocin circulates in the human brain or how many receptors there are or how this relates to caregiving motivation, experience, or quality. Blood oxytocin is easier to measure but may not accurately reflect brain oxytocin.

However, some functions of oxytocin are known. Research has established that oxytocin increases with physical touch: having sex, holding a baby, experiencing a massage, hugging a stranger, even petting a dog—all increase oxytocin as long as those events do not provoke stress (such as a growling dog might). I am not the only scientist who now readily hugs friends and acquaintances, nor the only dog owner often asked by strangers on the street, "Can I pet your dog?"

As for grandmothers, it is known that chronological age and personal experience affect oxytocin. Infants produce it, which enhances their attachment to their caregivers. Women experience a surge at birth, and then more oxytocin as they care for their infants. That may prime them for another surge later on, when grandmotherhood begins.

Given that older people have higher rates of illness, pain, and death of close friends, researchers in life-span development were initially surprised that elders tend to be happier and less stressed than younger adults. Collectively, the psychosocial changes of aging are called the *positivity effect*, with elders more optimistic, more trusting, and less worried.[30] Increased oxytocin, as well as decreased testosterone and cortisol, might undergird the positivity effect. This is logical but not proven, although it is known that many grandparents are more nurturing than they were as parents.

One grandmother writes that when she was a new mother, if she had to fly somewhere without her daughter, she "gripped the armrests with white-knuckled fingers," wondering how her child would survive if she died in a plane crash. But about her granddaughter she wrote:

She's my retirement gift, the platinum gold watch for being a mother. Here is a baby for whom you don't have to grip the armrests, whom you can adore without being responsible for everything that goes wrong. You aren't in charge, so nothing will be your fault. It's like being told you no longer have to eat vegetables, only dessert—and really only the icing.[31]

In a study of new parents, oxytocin was at similar levels in both partners (some couples high, some low), increasing over the first six months, presumably because their "relationship with the infant evolves."[32] For both sexes, those high in oxytocin were more responsive to their infants. Presumably, grandmothers experience the same effects as their grandmothering relationships evolve. Again, caregiving increases the love hormone.

Oxytocin is a "particularly promising candidate" for research on socio-emotional behavior among older people.[33] Oxytocin strengthens the immune system: that may explain why caregiving grandparents live longer and are healthier than other people the same age.[34]

Experiences shape genetic expression, and vice versa. Being cherished, giving birth, and loving others primes the oxytocin producers and receptors, flooding the body and brain.[35] Once that happens, oxytocin is likely to surge again when a grandchild appears. The opposite occurs: parents who neglected their babies, and children who themselves experienced early maltreatment, have reduced oxytocin years later.[36] Some grandchildren greet their grandmothers with shouts of joy as they run into their arms—that is high oxytocin in everyone.

Indeed, whenever an infant nuzzles in a grandmother's arms, or a young grandchild grabs her hand, or an older grandchild cups her ear to whisper a secret, oxytocin rises. No wonder Janet fought "like a dragon" to diaper her granddaughter; her hormones overwhelmed System 2.

Since neurons that fire together wire together (a basic law of neuroscience, famously penned by Donald Hebb), repeatedly touching babies—diapering, bathing, carrying, feeding—increases brain responses and oxytocin. Once triggered, oxytocin-producing events continue lifelong: mothers comfort sad or frightened children by rocking, cradling, and so on; parents hug their adult children; lovers hold hands, touch each other's feet under the table, kiss. I was pulling Bethany's leg before I fainted—maybe oxytocin overwhelmed me.

This suggests another explanation for the finding that grandmothers everywhere do far more grandchild care than grandfathers do. The rigid gender division in caregiving of fifty years ago, when mothers cradled infants hour after hour and fathers rarely did, may have primed oxytocin. Future grandfathers may provide more care for their infant descendants since current fathers provide more care.

It is quite plausible that past oxytocin now produce grandmothers' "total love addiction," with a craving for a fix, or that an older woman's brain is genetically primed to love grandchildren. Most scientists, including me, seek more research before we can be convinced that neurons or genes or hormones compel grandmother reactions. But I do not need to be convinced that something biological, not logical, made me faint.

Too Little Grandmothering

$\mathscr{T}$he demographic revolution reconfigured families, rattling their cages without creating new, solid structures. What should grandmothers do? Spoil or discipline? Pay doctors, tuition, mortgages? Babysit 24/7 or never? Tell teenagers about sex, or drugs, or diet? Move in or move away?

None of these is recommended. But some, sometimes, are best. Families are molded by past history, current circumstances, culture, personality, religion, and everyone's age—elders, parents, and children. Grandchildren are shy, bold, needy, independent, cheery, adorable, dirty, difficult, and destructive. Roles vary accordingly; grandmothers adjust, seeking a spot between never and always.

Somewhere between the extremes is "good enough," as Winnicott famously explained for mothers.[1] Precise prescriptions are impossible because families are diverse. Good-enough grandmothering takes between 50 and 1,600 hours a year; financial support ranges from baking a cake to buying a house; talk with grandchildren can be stock pleasantries or deep discussion.

SOME CARE IS ESSENTIAL

However, although tactics must vary, *never* is never good. Supportive involvement is always best. The goal doesn't change, either: grandchildren thrive because Grandma is part of their lives. This chapter is about one extreme: the estimated 10 percent who almost never see their grandchildren. The next chapter describes the opposite danger. Both miss the mark.

A sixteen-year-old boy still mourns because his grandparents left their home in Boston when he was five.[2]

I'll never forget the day they left. I hid and wouldn't say goodbye. They lived three houses down from us. I saw them every day of my life before they moved, and I loved to be with them so much. Then they just up and left me, my brother and sister, my mother and her brother, everyone. And life was never the same. I see them once in a while, and I remember the old days, but those grandparents from the old days are dead. These grandparents are just the same nice old people, like ghosts of the others. They act nice to me, like they never moved, like time has stood still for them, but I don't have very much to give them. . . . I would have died for those other grandparents.

His grandfather said, "He was such a cute, wonderful boy. . . . We were so close, but now it's like he's a stranger. The spark we used to have is gone."

His grandmother misses that spark, but she doesn't realize that she extinguished it. According to a survey, "it is difficult for devoted grandparents to accept the reality, reported by many children . . . that they are hurting their grandchildren when they move away."[3]

That boy is a warning: keep embers glowing. Everyone—all three generations—suffers when the spark is gone.[4] A study of five thousand grandmothers in ten nations found that those who sometimes babysat were healthier because of it.[5] Of course, causality flows in the other direction as well: young and healthy grandparents are more likely to be active caregivers. But these researchers controlled for age, prior health, and income. The results were clear: caregiving promoted health, not just vice versa. The old and sick grandmothers who sometimes took care of their grandchildren became happier and healthier than the equally old and sick grandmothers who did not.

Another study found that active grandmothering increased language skills without decreasing any other intellectual abilities.[6] How can that be? Providing care is stressful, time-consuming, and tiring, requiring long hours with children who have small vocabularies and immature minds. That should deplete the intellect, not the opposite. Eight reasons:

- less loneliness;
- a feeling of usefulness;
- closer human relationships;
- better communication with the middle generation;
- more intellectual challenge;
- more exercise;
- a reason to stay healthy; and
- other adults (the parents) who monitor health, getting medical care for the grandparents when needed.

Notice that only the last reason involves doctors. In this and many other studies, the primary defenses against fading intellect and physical illness involve cognition, social interaction, and perception long before the medical establishment does their part. Grandmother-grandchild relationships are life giving; uninvolved grandmothers risk illness.

One grandmother who no longer sees her grandchildren says, "It was so enjoyable and now to think about it brings me to tears. . . . I have had anxiety and depression, none of which I had previously and now I have been diagnosed with a severe heart problem, cardiomyopathy. This is more than I can bear—it breaks my heart to think of them."[7]

Illness is one consequence of a lack of social support; death is another. National analysis of the 22,618 suicides and homicides of people of all ages concludes that the best prevention is "safe, stable, nurturing relationships."[8] Involved grandmothers live longer, and in the United States in the twenty-first century, lonely elders are more likely to die (of disease or suicide) than elders who are connected to their families.

WHO IS TO BLAME?

Since caregiving benefits all three generations, why do some grand-mothers never do it? Wealth is not the reason. Grandmothers with more education and money, who can afford to travel the world or buy theater tickets, are *more* likely to babysit (although less likely to live with their grandchildren).[9]

Illness is not the reason, either. A longitudinal study of U.S. grandmothers found that having chronic health problems (such as heart ailments, diabetes, and cancer) did *not* diminish the likelihood of providing care.[10] Sick grandmothers still convey love. Several studies of older people with major disabilities report that they figure out how to cope and connect. They selectively optimize and compensate. In other words, they choose good activities (optimization), overcoming (compensation) disabilities. As one grandmother said, "There is still life beyond a funny knee."[11]

If neither money nor health impedes grandmother connection with grandchildren, what does? It is easy to blame the culture that leaves a concerned grandmother on a hard, dark floor until a grandchild is cleaned up, as chapter 1 describes. It is also easy to blame the middle generation: I have heard many sad stories—presents returned unopened, births not known until acquaintances congratulate the unsuspecting grandmother, and families relocating, with address unknown.

But some culprits are the grandmothers themselves. As in the opening example of this chapter, grandparents might move away. About one in ten (seven million) U.S. residents over age sixty-five has moved to another state in the past decade. Some were snared by glossy, multicolored ads or personal phone calls offering free dinners for po-tential customers of gated, child-free retirement communities in warm climates. Of course, every decision to move is complex, and sometimes becoming a snowbird makes sense, but movers often underestimate their need to be near friends and family.

Consider again the Boston grandparents who left that five-year-old "cute, wonderful boy." Why did they go to Florida? A review of retirement communities touts Boston: "Its downtown is walkable, safe, and interesting. There are many parks and every kind of urban amenity—museums, shopping, restaurants, mass transit, and theatre. Friends and grandchildren will beat a path to your door."[12]

Not every grandmother wants people to "beat a path to your door," and few elders outside of New England choose to retire in Boston. But these grandparents were already there, near children, grandchildren, and lifelong friends, in a city with good public transportation, many free lectures and senior activities, and the Boston College Center for Retirement Research.

Then why did they relocate a thousand miles to the South? Did they feel overwhelmed by their grandson's daily visits? If so, why not set boundaries (perhaps only on Saturday, or never before noon or after 5 p.m.)? Did they want to avoid icy winters, forgetting about hurricanes and hot, humid summers?

No matter where a person lives, psychologists advocate staying near family, friends, and familiar places. Grandparents in a large suburban home might buy a smaller, city apartment in walking distance of stores and public transit, but moving to a distant retirement enclave is shortsighted, unless the grandchildren are already nearby.

Consider the results of a U.S. survey of almost two thousand grandparents.[13] Most wished they saw their grandchildren more often, and only 4 percent wished they saw them less (mostly those who lived with them). Wishing for more contact was highest among those responding about how often they saw the grandchild who lived farthest away: only 2 percent said "too much," 36 percent said "the right amount," and 61 percent said not enough. What stopped them? Most of them gave several reasons:

> distance—67 percent
> grandchild's busy schedule—64 percent
> grandparent's health problems—43 percent
> grandparent's busy schedule—42 percent
> lack of money—41 percent
> lack of energy—39 percent

difficult relationship with grandchild's parents—22 percent divorce or separation of grandchild's parents—21 percent

Reasons or excuses? Distance is the most common. Why didn't they travel? "Lack of money," "too busy," and "grandparent health problems" are all possible impediments, but most grandparents with little money and impaired health nonetheless prioritize grandchildren. They visit and host.

Am I unfair? Every grandmother must decide for herself, but illness that truly prevents contact is unusual: less than 3 percent of all North American grandparents and great-grandparents are stuck in nursing homes or hospitals, and many of them already were alienated from their family. Another small group, maybe 4 percent, are seriously ill or infirm enough to be homebound. That leaves 93 percent able to travel.

"Too busy" is the worst excuse. Grandmothers who blame their own busy schedule have wacky priorities. Those who say their grandchildren are too busy (school, sports, socializing) need to be more creative and accommodating with what they do (e.g., help with homework, take the child to the doctor, watch a school game) and not simply pine for more connection.

One grandparent complained about a teenage granddaughter:

We'll come for Thanksgiving, she'll have dinner with us and then she'll say "I gotta go meet my friends." Well, your grandparents just drove 400 miles, we haven't seen you since whenever, would it be so wrong for us to expect that you could stay for a little bit longer after dinner and inquire about our life. . . .[14]

Do you see what is wrong with this complaint? These grandparents expected their granddaughter to inquire about *their* lives. What about inquiring about *her* life? Grandparent connections are reciprocal: some grandparents connect with busy teenage grandchildren, and others complain. Many older children are caught up in their social lives with friends, but that doesn't prevent a relationship (see chapters 13 and 14). Ideally, before adolescence, grandmothers are already integral

to their grandchildren's lives, and, ideally again, parents facilitate interaction. But if grandchildren are "too busy," grandmothers need to take
genuine interest in the grandchild's activities. Should these grandparents offer to drive their granddaughter to her friend's house? Offer to
take them all out? Perhaps not. But criticizing her does not strengthen
the relationship.

Another problem traced back to grandmothers may be an obses-
sion with looking young. Grandchildren can be collateral casualties in
this battle with age. The culture may connect age with ugly, so some
women call themselves *glammas*, a term first used by Goldie Hawn. She
said that "grandmother" had "so many connotations of old age and de-
crepitude" that she was happy to avoid it.[15] There are glamma pillows,
mugs, T-shirts, bibs, and posters.

A glamma Twitter hashtag has a thousand tweets a year. But
discarding the word "grandmother" implies agreeing with biased connotations. At least one grandmother thinks that *glamma* reflects old
stereotypes: "Glamma, to me, sounds fake, pretentious and desperate.
It smacks of someone who is terrified of aging, of being old enough to
have grandchildren. A panicked, desperate grab for some semblance of
youth. To not be the stereotyped old lady in the rocker, wrapped up in
a shawl."[16]

One new mother said her own mother was caught up in that illusion.[17] When invited to come and see her newly born granddaughter,
Mum said she couldn't that day.

"Why not?"

"I have a wax appointment."

The daughter suggested she come after waxing. That grandmother
said no because she had an appointment for a pedicure. Are toenails
more important than newborns? Can cosmetic appointments be can-
celed for a birth?

Another underlying problem that might keep grandmothers away
from granddaughters is the fantasy that close relationships are conflict
free. In fact, many family relationships are *ambivalent*, with both positive and negative aspects.[18] An intimate relationship that never includes
disagreements is either superficial or suppressive. In healthy families,

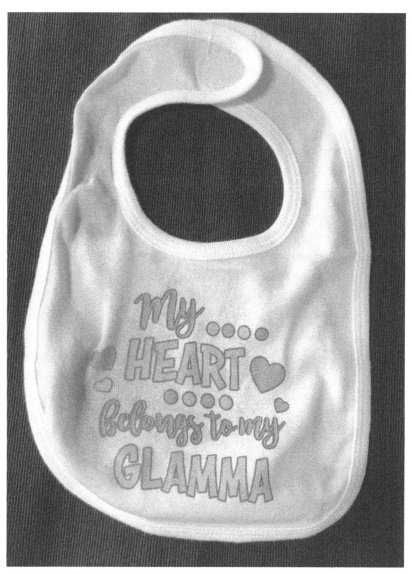

Who would buy this? Do babies still need bibs?
From Walmart, and many other stores.

disagreements lead to compromises, changes, or acceptance of differences, not to anger and pain.

I know this personally with my husband, my four daughters, and my three grandsons. I lived with one of my daughters, her husband, and two children for six months (because my apartment had a fire). We disagreed about small aspects of daily life, such as about the proper placement of sponges, the barking of my dog, when to close the microwave door. Our relationship during those months was close and loving, but our mutual admiration was sprinkled with conflict. Ambivalence. I finally accepted my insurance adjuster's offer of a replacement apartment to protect that mother/daughter relationship, which is still strong.

To avoid conflict, some family members never mention politics, religion, food, habits, appearance, or sports. That might preclude all emotional talk. Some families use distance and disengagement to avoid friction, but that also avoids connection. A study of Thanksgiving visits in 2016 (after the Trump/Clinton election) found that many grandparents and parents spent less time together than the year before because they disagreed about the election.[19]

I hope your family is like mine: we argue about many things, from whether the U.S. military belongs in Afghanistan to whether peanut butter belongs in the refrigerator. After my daughter drove us both on a long road trip, frustration erupted when the car door didn't open quickly. Soon I accused her of being too sure of herself, and she retorted that I didn't realize how selfish I was.

We fumed silently for several hours and spoke tersely the next morning. Two days later, we had a long conversation, acknowledging that we both had been stressed. Neither said the other was right. No backing down, but much warmth. That is much better for the psyche than peace via disengagement.

Worse than prioritizing comfort, appearance, or harmony over grandmotherhood is abandoning the role completely: never care providing, game playing, dinner fixing, book reading. Some grandchildren are rarely seen except as trophy photographs on the mantle.

That harms everyone. Lonely elders have higher rates of mental and physical problems, including clinical depression, heart disease, fibromyalgia, dementia, insomnia, and stroke.[20]

I do not mean to imply that selfish grandmothers are the only reason for those 10 percent who never see their grandchildren; the middle generation sometimes erects barricades. One in five of the grandparents in the study above noted difficult relations with adult children.

When such difficulties arise, about half of the time, the middle generation cuts off contact. One grandmother who never saw her grandchildren said that her daughter told her, "You've never been a good mother, only when I was little . . . you be quiet and listen to what I have to say, what I have to tell you now . . . I never want to see or hear from you the rest of your life."

How should the mother respond? She was angry and defensive, saying, "Now that is ridiculous and you know that is ridiculous. . . . I have fought hard. I have provided for both of your children. I've done all that I can to help you and [son-in-law]."[21]

Anger provokes anger. The daughter was cruel, but when the grandmother said "ridiculous," that shut down discussion. "Provided for both of your children" might be heard as criticism of the parents' provisioning. Implications, accusations, and misperceptions across generations cause the middle generation keep grandparents away.

The solution is to respect boundaries and overcome barriers—not to fortify one's own side. It does not help to justify one's own perceptions; what is needed is acknowledgment that an adult child might have been hurt accompanied by genuine apology. Grandmothers need to anticipate assumptions and expectations, lest a surprise explosion slams the gate shut. (Specific landmines are described in later chapters.)

SUING FOR VISITATION RIGHTS

Ideally, both generations work to understand each other. However, since parents arrange the social interactions of their young children, they sometimes cut off contact. What should grandparents do? Sometimes they sue.

Consider two famous court cases. In both, the middle generation shut out the grandparents. Tragic and wrong, I blame those parents. But in both cases, the grandparents ignored the parents' wishes, precipitating the break, and then sued for visitation. The middle generation fought back. That decision increased hostility between the adults, with grandchildren caught in crossfire.

The tragedy of banned grandparents became a national issue in the divorce boom of the 1970s, when about half of all marriages ended in divorce, often with children and grandchildren involved. Typically, custody was granted to the mother. Millions of paternal grandparents found their link to their grandchildren broken. Many of them convinced state legislators (often grandparents themselves) in all fifty U.S. states to enact laws granting grandparent rights. By the end of the twentieth century, thousands of grandparents had obtained court orders to allow them to see their grandchildren.

Few such court orders have been issued since 2000. The reason is one case decided by the U.S. Supreme Court. It began with two little girls, Isabelle and Natalie, born to Brad Troxel and Tommie Granville, near Seattle. After several years together, the parents separated in 1991. The mother, Tommie, had the girls during the week; Brad brought them to his parents' home with him every weekend. The paternal grandparents adored Isabelle and Natalie, providing music lessons, inviting cousins over to play, and setting aside a bedroom for them.

Two years after the separation, Brad killed himself. At this time, Tommie halted the long weekend stays. Instead, she offered monthly visits for a few hours. Brad's parents sued for more time, contending that the girls would benefit from ongoing relationships with their grandparents and cousins in a music-filled home. A local judge agreed. He set a schedule: every other weekend, two weeks in the summer, and extra time for grandparents' birthdays.

Later, Tommie married Kelly Wynn, who adopted Isabelle and Natalie. He and Tommie wanted their daughters with them, not with Tommie's deceased lover's family. Tommie appealed the above decision.

The Washington Supreme Court reversed the lower court, ruling that unless they are unfit, mothers can decide what is best for their children. One factor was the law: Tommie's marriage to Kelly and his adopting the girls were legally recognized, unlike the cohabitation of their biological parents.

The grandparents appealed to the highest court of the land, the United States Supreme Court. In a 2000 decision, the judges ruled six to three for the mother. They agreed that the grandparents provided good care but ruled that Tommie had a fundamental right "to make decisions regarding the care, custody, and control of her two daughters."[22]

This decision changed state laws and judicial decisions. Courts now almost always rule against grandparents, unless the mother is "unfit."

In one example, in Iowa, Joe and Lois Santi provided extensive care for Taylor, the infant daughter of their young son, Mike, and his wife, Heather. Mike and Heather were grateful for help when Taylor was an infant, but soon problems appeared. Contrary to the parents' wishes, the grandparents let Taylor eat food that Heather forbade; they bought Taylor her first shoes; and they took her to see Santa Claus so she could request gifts that the grandparents would buy because the parents could not afford them.

Mike and Heather decided that they and Taylor, now a toddler, would spend Christmas with Heather's parents. Mike's parents were livid, expressing such fury that Mike and Heather decided to ban their contact with Taylor completely. The grandparents sued.

In *Santi v. Santi*, the local judge agreed with the grandparents that denying visitation was unreasonable, not in the child's best interest. Nonetheless, citing *Troxel v. Granville*, he ruled against them. They appealed; the Iowa Supreme Court upheld the lower court: "We are convinced that fostering close relations between grandparents and grandchildren is not a sufficiently compelling state interest to justify court-ordered visitation over the joint objection of married parents in an intact nuclear family."[23]

In many legal rulings, as in both of these examples, judges enshrine the "intact, nuclear family" and the primacy of motherhood, ignoring grandmotherhood. This is another example of an institution (here the courts, not the hospitals) stuck in 1960, with the myths that parents are always legally married, that mothers are always wise about child care, and that grandmothers therefore can be ignored. The truth is otherwise: about 40 percent of all U.S. newborns have unmarried mothers,[24] almost all young adults cohabit,[25] and when children are neglected or abused, the most common perpetrator is their mother.[26] When judges hark back to old ideas, grandmothers and grandchildren suffer.

But it is more complex than that. Another toxic wedge between generations is money. Unlike in the 1960s, the older generations generally are richer than the younger ones. That fuels resentment. Almost all (96 percent) grandparents buy presents for their delighted grandchildren, but only 23 percent help with medical or dental expenses.[27] Grandchildren are thrilled; parents are not.

Resentment about money was a factor in both of these legal decisions. The Troxel grandparents had a larger house than Tommie Granville, a single mother, which is one reason why the granddaughters enjoyed coming every weekend, and one reason those grandparents assumed they had the right to extensive time with the girls. The Santi grandparents offered a paid cruise to Mike and Heather but reneged when Heather chose someone else to care for Taylor during the cruise.[28]

The grandparents in both cases hired lawyers to appeal, requiring the parents to pay for defense. Judges thought that unfair: the Santi judgment specified that grandparents reimburse the parents for legal expenses.

In these cases and thousands more, U.S. norms enshrine parental rights and expect grandparents to defer. Parents decide their children's education, diet, religion, discipline, and medical care, even when contrary to grandparents' wishes or community standards.

The government can intervene only if harm is unmistakable, such as if a child's life is at stake, if a child is never taught to read, or if the health of other people is threatened. Even those reasons are open to interpretation. For example, half the U.S. states allow parents to refuse to immunize their children against contagious diseases that might jeopardize the health of other people. Grandparents are almost never permitted to intervene, even in health or education. The only exception is when maltreatment is unmistakable (only a fifth of all reported cases of maltreatment are substantiated). Then the government can designate the grandparents as custodial parents, sometimes mandating that the biological parents stay away.

Since *Troxel*, thousands of grandparents have sued because they were shut out. Usually they lose. They win only in unusual circumstances, such as when the grandchildren lived with the grandparents for years before the parents took them back and shut out the grandparents. Even then there is no guarantee.

Each state has its own code, and each code is interpreted in many ways.[29] Lawyers develop plausible, opposing, arguments, and the judges rule, influenced by their own biases, as are we all. There is no legal or social consensus as to when parents can forbid grandparent contact.

However, the psychological consensus is often ignored. Judges, lawmakers, grandparents, and parents need to recognize grandparents as part of the family; grandchildren and grandparents benefit from warm and supportive connections. This psychological consensus leads to two conclusions, often ignored.

1. Grandmothers should not abdicate, using their own comfort, busy schedules, or vanity to rationalize a self-centered distance.
2. Parents, judges, and laws should not exclude grandparents, except in rare circumstances.

Too little grandmother care hurts everyone. The next chapter explores the opposite extreme, too much care.

Too Much Grandmothering

$\mathscr{A}$ grandmother got a surprise phone call: her grandchild was neglected. Her response: "Immediately I was just like 'Ok, we're taking the baby. We've got to raise him. We're his family, we're this, and we're that.'"[1]

Her reaction is not surprising. Family members everywhere and forever care for each other, simply because they are family. That basic impulse is understood and echoed by every group: nations glorify "founding fathers" and "foremothers," adults revere "ancestors," politicians address "my brothers and sisters," religious people pray to "Our Father" and "Holy Mother."

Family values are enduring and powerful, arising from the depths of the limbic system, from the brain's System 1.[2] Older women, particularly, have strong caregiving impulses: they are the most common caregivers for the frail elderly, and they are the first relatives to respond when a grandchild needs special help.

Wonderful.

But dangerous.

Family protection shelters criminals; family feuds kill babies; family loyalty lets child abuse fester; family secrets destroy adults. Grandmothers need System 2 to join System 1. Sometimes (always?) criminals should be reported rather than sheltered, sometimes (always?) children should be shielded from adult disputes, sometimes (always?) victims need nonfamily help. Family bonds are wonderful, but they can become too tight, harming grandmothers instead of helping grandchildren.

The possibility of too much grandmothering is not usually recognized by the public, the press, the political leaders, or the grandmothers themselves. The impulse of the woman above (*we're taking the baby*) arose from admirable System 1 thinking, from that powerful grandmother impulse that has sustained families for two hundred thousand years. But System 2 is also needed, an analysis of the assumption that grandmothers provide all necessary care. In this case, the grandfather expressed some System 2 thoughts.[3]

> *Well, immediately my husband and I didn't agree on this at the start. . . . And my husband's opinion, you know, was that she [the child's mother] needed to come get him. It's her responsibility. It's her child. If she can't raise him then, you know, then what about the father? And the other grandparents and whatever. I just couldn't imagine . . . she's not going to raise him and I don't even know about these other grandparents. I know I can at least take care of him and keep him safe.*

He was overruled. This woman became a custodial grandmother, defined as a grandmother who lives with a grandchild without either parent present. She is unusual: among all the grandmothers in the United States, only one grandmother in two hundred is custodial. Overall, the United States Census Bureau reports that only 4 percent of households include grandmothers and grandchildren living together.[4] Most of those households are not custodial, because they include the middle generation as well.

Grandmothers living with grandchildren (with or without other family members) is a household type idealized and mythologized. We focus on it here because all grandmothers, living with their grandchildren or not, are vulnerable to System 1. The facts on multigenerational households are instructive for all. Every grandmother needs System 2 analysis to protect her health, sanity, and social relationships.

CUSTODIAL GRANDMOTHERS

A few grandmothers become *custodial grandmothers*, also called *surrogate mothers*, because they do everything mothers do, day and night. Their families are called *skipped-generation* families: the middle generation is absent (skipped) because the child's parents are neglectful, abusive, imprisoned, sick, addicted, or dead.

About half of the skipped-generation families are headed by a single woman who is a widowed, divorced, or never-married grandmother. In the other half, a grandfather is the head, with the wife as main caregiver and the husband as main income producer. Despite ideological and labor-force changes worldwide, current research reports the "persistence of a highly gendered division of labour among most grandparents."[5] When grandparent custody is needed, employed women are likely to quit work, while men tend to postpone retirement.

It is easy to criticize, or admire, the woman who impulsively agreed to "take the baby." Some people praise grandmothers who sacrifice themselves for their grandchildren; others pity them, blaming the birth parents. In both cases, the emotions of System 1 overwhelm the analysis of System 2.

In many circumstances (such as divorce or summer vacation) grandmothers and grandchildren live together without the parents, but most such households are temporary. Only about one household in four hundred has a grandmother who has been sole caregiver for five years or more.[6]

Do you doubt the data that finds custodial grandmothers rare? There are good reasons to question U.S. census data, especially in regard to skipped households. Such households are often low income and nonwhite—exactly the kind of households that the census undercounts.

But similar conclusions can be drawn from a detailed longitudinal study involving a dozen scholars in twenty cities throughout the United States.[7] This study began with almost five thousand births to low-income mothers and followed those "fragile families" for fifteen years. Three-fourths of the mothers were unmarried, half were African American, and almost a third were Latino.

That background is relevant because, compared to the national average, rates of long-term custodial grandmotherhood are higher in such families.[8] Poverty, not ethnicity, is the usual reason, although cultural values matter as well.[9]

Despite their low income, the most common family structure of those five thousand fragile families was two generational (mother and child, sometimes with the father); the second most common was three generational, (grandmother, mother, and child). Skipped-generation households were rare.

The frequency of skipped-generation households rose over the first decade after the birth, but even when the children were nine years old, only 3 percent of them lived with their grandmothers while their mothers lived elsewhere. The other 97 percent of the nine-year-olds lived with their mothers, usually without their grandmothers.[10]

As already mentioned, one problem with skipped-generation households is that they are thought to be more common than they are. But there is a worse problem: they are thought to be better than they are.

In 2016 in the United States, 437,465 children were adjudicated to foster care because child protective workers concluded that their parents were woefully inadequate. Children removed from their parents have three possible placements: (1) an institution (such as a hospital or residence), (2) home care from a stranger, or (3) home care from a relative ("kinship care"). The first of those three may permanently harm a young child's brain and emotions,[11] so only 5 percent of all foster children (mostly teenagers) are in group care. Of the other 95 percent, almost half are placed with a relative, usually a grandmother. Originally, some feared that grandmother care would be inferior, but a careful review of 102 studies finds that children fare better with grandmothers than with strangers.[12]

Hundreds of thousands of other grandmothers are unofficial foster care providers. This is not necessarily wrong: sometimes the best caregiver for a mistreated, desperate child is Grandma. Kinship care also preserves some dignity for the middle generation. Compared to parents whose children are in an unrelated foster family, when grandmothers are foster parents, the biological parents are more likely to see their children occasionally and less likely to feel that they have failed entirely as parents. If the child is returned to their care in months or years (the "permanency plan" for about half the children), that does not disrupt the child and the foster grandparent as much as it does when the foster parent is a stranger.

Then why is custodial grandmothering "too much"? The most obvious reason is the effect on the grandmothers. Compared to other grandmothers of the same ethnicity, age, and income, the longer grandmothers have total responsibility for their grandchildren, the worse their health becomes. Custodial grandmothers have "generally poorer physical and mental health," "intense stress and depression," uncontrolled diabetes, and high blood pressure.[13] Vacations, nutrition, and sleep suffer. In the United States, these problems are particularly likely for nonwhite grandmothers, who often undertake kinship care.[14]

One reason for poor health is that, even compared to biological mothers, custodial grandmothers have less social support. Friends slip away, other relatives stay away or add to the burden.[15] In the fragile families study, 17 percent of the custodial grandmothers also sheltered their own aging mothers, great-aunts, or great-uncles.[16]

Poverty adds to the problem. Growing children are expensive to feed and clothe, but compared to the average grandmother, custodial grandmothers have less income. Unless they are official kinship foster parents, governmental support (medical insurance, food stamps, and so on) is hard to obtain for the grandchildren, causing "hardship even beyond that of poverty."[17]

Hospitals, community centers, and schools add to the stress. For instance, teachers ask children to make presents for Mother's and Father's Day; the PTA is the *Parent* Teachers Association; few schools send notices or reports to grandmothers unless they are legal guardians; hospitals may require permission from biological parents before treating a child.

Added to those practical problems are dashed expectations for "golden years." As one grandmother said, "I can't be a grandmother because I have to be a mother." Another asked, "How can you retire when you have a kid in school?"[18] A third complained when people told her to save money for her future: "I should not be forced to worry about my future. . . . I'm spending every resource to ensure that my granddaughter is being raised a certain way. And I'm spending my future."[19]

Another said:

> *It's not a place you expect to be at 55. At 55, you expect to be with your grandchildren that they come and play and that you're excited to see them and they're excited to see you and just all little bundles of cuteness, you know, and that they have a happy little home to go to and you're sharing things with your children and it's just not that at all. I mean, not that he's not a cute little bundle of cuteness, but there's sadness and then there's a responsibility. That's what I feel. Raising grandchildren becomes a full time job with no vacation time.*[20]

What about the children? Don't they benefit from having a loving and patient grandmother? Not necessarily. Children in custodial grandparent families are more likely to suffer than to thrive. The fragile families study found that, even though the grandmothers in skipped families were better educated than the mothers, the grandchildren were more often diagnosed with ADHD (attention-deficit/hyperactivity disorder) and achieved less in school than the children who lived with their mothers.[21]

The reasons may be that custodial grandmothers are less connected to the child's teachers, less likely to know the parents of the child's classmates, and less likely to understand homework, play sports, or otherwise engage with the children. Who is to blame for this disconnect? Schools? Parents? Grandparents? We do not know. But we know who experiences it: the children. They have more missed homework, they do not hand in permission forms for school trips, and they have fewer play dates.

Be wary of ethnic stereotypes here—positive or negative. Long-term custodial grandmothering is not the first choice of any ethnic group; it is a backup when parents are unable to be caregivers, a sign of family breakdown more than family unity. One custodial grandmother said, "I've had books thrown at me, chairs. I broke the blood vessels in my arms, but through it all, he always cried and said 'Nana, I didn't want to hurt you, I was so angry. . . . I don't think I'll ever forgive mommy and daddy.'"[22]

That grandmother says that she never thought of quitting her role. Why not? Indeed, why would any sane, mature women take on another child, especially an angry, difficult one?

Family values are part of it: many grandmothers feel duty bound to help their descendants, believing they can "at least keep them safe."

The same impulse leads grandmothers to rescue grandchildren before outsiders become involved. But it goes beyond duty. Remember that brains, genes, and hormones bind adults—especially older women—to new babies. That is how humans survived for two hundred thousand years.

One woman was raising two grandnieces when a third was born. She was determined *not* to raise that baby:

I'm not gonna take care of no more babies. . . . I'm too old. . . . But I was there when she was born. See, this is the thing that really hooked me. I was there when she took her first breaths. . . . She opened her eyes, looked at me, and started hollerin'. I was hooked like a fish. That was it.[23]

Grandmothers are hooked, and grandchildren have no choice, even though both may be harmed by the takeover. But what about the middle generation? If they are unable to parent, don't they benefit when their parents do? It saves them from the stress of child care, the guilt of child neglect, and sometimes from prison for child maltreatment. But many custodial grandparents resent that the middle generation has put them in this situation, which undermines the joy that the parents may feel.[24]

Some grandmothers keep the parents away, even adopting their grandchildren to protect them from their parents. One adoptive grandmother was asked by her grandson's mother if she could come back home.[25] The grandmother replied:

No. She can't. . . . I can't allow Porter to hear the woman he knows to be his biological mother shout "Don't cross me or I'll send you to hell. . . ." It's impossible to parent both my daughter and my son, and probably even crazy to try. Doing well by one often comes at the expense of the other—and Porter must come first, a call that's clear but excruciating to make.

She reached that conclusion after repeatedly sheltering her daughter and watching her grandson suffer. Her "excruciating" choice, as well as the work of parenting a difficult child, added unexpected problems to her life, but she felt not only duty bound but also delighted in her grandson. She was thrilled that he asked, "Mom, I've been wondering. Do you think I could use math to solve God?"

And then she writes, "Okay, this may not be how I planned to spend my life. Still, it is my life—and at moments like this I am blessed cell-deep by its surpassing perfection."

"Cell-deep" is accurate: caring for grandchildren goes far beyond duty. Some custodial grandmothers experience joy as well as a sense of purpose in their role.[26] But no one should idealize custodial grandmothers, considering them saints who gain from the sacrifice, bonding, and sense of purpose that surrogate motherhood provides. Those same benefits can accrue to all grandmothers, with less intensive caregiving. Custodial grandmothers deserve gratitude and respect, but they are the last resort when all else fails, not an easy solution to a hard problem.

Thus social workers, journalists, the general public, and grandmothers themselves need to know that all three generations are harmed by custodial grandmothering. Two other groups need a better understanding of custodial caregiving: political leaders who set immigration policies and the immigrants themselves. Many immigrants to North America or Western Europe leave their children behind with grandparents. They may think this is an expression of love, sending money to provide for their children. But many such children feel abandoned, no matter how loving their custodial grandmothers may be.[27] Sadly, "migration often transforms parents into relatively good providers of economic resources but relatively bad providers of emotional resources."[28]

If those distant parents send for their children in middle childhood or later, the children may long for their grandparents and rebel against their parents. All three generations may become angry and depressed.

Ideally, parents who work far from home are able to visit their children often. However, that may be legally impossible. Whether borders between nations are "blurred, brittle, or broken" depends more on international politics than on family needs.[29] System 1 emotionality among political leaders may enforce family separation; System 2 analysis of grandmothers and grandchildren finds that cruel.

Does custodial grandmothering ever benefit anyone? International research finds that the consequences depend partly on national culture, economic circumstances, and government policies.[30] Consider China. An estimated one in five Chinese grandparents heads a skipped-generation family, a dramatic contrast to the one in two hundred in the United States. They tend to be happier and healthier than other Chinese grandparents who have no grandchildren living with them.[31]

The reason for custodial grandparenting again springs from national policy, but Chinese culture and policy are unlike (not better than) those in the United States. In China, children must attend schools where their parents were born, but rural areas have few jobs. Consequently, many country-born parents travel to distant cities for work. According to the "China Labor Bulletin," more than 60 million Chinese children are "left behind," usually with grandparents.

Why is the experience of those grandparents so different from the U.S. experience? Attitudes, more than practicalities, seem crucial. Chinese culture respects custodial grandmothers, and parents phone, write, send money, and visit. Consequently, in those skipped families,

- children know they are loved by their parents;
- parents feel they are doing right by their children;
- elders feel appreciated by their descendants and their culture;
- parents are in frequent contact with their children (via mail, phone, or video) and visit on holidays (no borders, but often a long train ride); and

- custodial grandparents tend to be better off financially than other grandparents.

Could this occur in the United States? Might skipped families be a sign of family harmony rather than family trouble? Perhaps, if caregiving results from analysis and appreciation from every family member. But remember the grandfather's misgivings above. He thought the baby's parents and other grandparents should share responsibility before he and his wife "take the baby." He might have explained how the crisis could have been prevented and what community support might make custodial grandmothering easier. This provides direction for all the older women who care about children but who are not custodial grandmothers. They could change the policies and prejudices that are hostile to families, rendering custodial grandmothers less needed but more supported.

THREE-GENERATION HOUSEHOLDS

Now let us look at the second circumstance when American grand-mothers encounter unanticipated problems. Multigeneration households are idealized and mythologized.

Myth 1. *Three-generation families are formed to help a feeble, lonely grandparent.*

Not usually. More often, the middle generation is the needy one. In most three-generation families, grandparents are employed and pay expenses.[32]

Myth 2. *Shared living fosters close harmony among elders and adult children.*

Not usually. More often, whenever adults share living space, some conflict seems inevitable, especially when grandchildren are involved.

Myth 3. *Grandmothers are primary caregivers in three-generation homes.*

Not usually. When asked whether they or their spouse are primary caregivers of the grandchildren who live with them, less than a third say yes.[33] And when they say yes, the parents of the children might disagree.

To understand the myths surrounding three-generation families, we need to look closely at statistics. When you do, you read that only about 4 percent of all U.S. households include grandparents and grandchildren. Did those numbers surprise you? Whenever you see statistics, look closely.

- If you read that an increasing *number* of grandparents are living with grandchildren, remember that there are more grandparents alive than there once were, so an increase in numbers does not mean an increase in rate.
- If you read that 7 percent (not 4 percent) of grandparents live with grandchildren, remember that many households with one grandparent include a second grandparent, so more grandparents and grandchildren together does not mean more three-generation households.
- If you read that 6 percent of U.S. family households include grandparents and grandchildren, remember that about a third of households are not *family* households because many people (including many grandmothers) live alone.[34]
- If you read that the proportion of skipped-generation families is increasing, pay attention to the date because this kind of family is strongly affected by policies and practices regarding mistreated children. In fact, the number has gone down in recent years.[35]
- If you read that an increasing *proportion* of children live with grandparents, remember that most households have fewer children than in the past. Only about a third of all U.S. households include children under age eighteen. However, those households that include children *and* grandparents are more likely to have several children (siblings and cousins). That means that when all the children are counted, a greater proportion (in 2018 about 10 percent) of children live with grandparents.[36] The fact that more children live with grandparents does not mean that more grandparents live with children.

The most deceptive assumption is that grandparents in three-generation household provide full-time child care. Consider this passage from a national magazine in 2018.

In 2014, the Census Bureau reported that 6 percent of American households contained a co-resident grandparent and grandchild; in 1970, that figure was 3 percent. Sixty percent of those households were headed by grandparents, which translated to 2.7 million grandparents caring for grandchildren.[37]

The author misread the statistics. The source says that the percent of *children* in a grandparent household doubled from three to six, not the percent of co-resident households. As you just read, those statistics are already out of date. The economic recession of 2008 hit young families particularly hard, so a higher proportion of children live with grandparents.

But what about that word "translated"? All grandparents, no matter where they live, provide some grandchild care, but when grandchildren live in the grandparents' home, does that *translate* into primary care? No. Typically in three-generation households, the grandparents are employed homeowners. They make room for their adult children, who provides primary care for the grandchildren.

Many published reports misuse statistics. Now let us look closely at what really happens in three-generation families. First we need to undercut the benign racism that contends that some ethnic groups are to be admired because all generations of a family live together.

As shown in the graph on the next page, in every group, fewer than 30 percent of families are three generation. The most common group are Asian Americans, who are also most likely to include both parents and least likely to say that grandparents are primary caregivers.

Worldwide, when health and income permit, grandparents and parents prefer to live in separate homes. In fact, in the United States, some grandmothers spend thousands of dollars to maintain separate homes. For example, one may be jeopardizing her marriage by doing so:

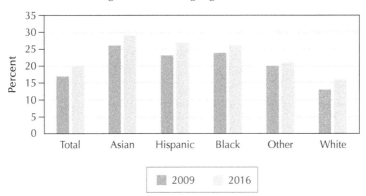

Two adult generations living together, United States

This increase in multigenerational households occurred because more young adults are living with their parents. Notice, however, that most older adults of every ethnicity live apart from their grown children.
From Pew Research, April 5, 2018.

When my daughter divorced, they nearly lost the house to foreclosure, so I went on the loan and signed for them. But then again they nearly foreclosed, so my husband and I bought it. . . . I have to make the payment on my own house and most of the payment on my daughter's house and that is hard. . . . I am hoping to get that money back from our daughter, to quell my husband's sense that the kids are all just taking and no one is giving back. He sometimes feels used and abused.[38]

Moving in with her daughter, or vice versa, was not the solution for her, although it is not clear why.

In another case, a grandmother adamantly resisted three-generation living. She said of her adult daughter and son, "The worst thing would be if she moved into my house. I would rather give them money than have her move in. Both of my kids would love to move into my house and have me take care of things. . . . That would wreck my life. I like a peaceful time, I like privacy."[39]

Traditionally, Asian nations value *filial* piety, which once meant that the oldest generation lived with their married sons, who cared for them. That custom is disappearing. Detailed studies in Indonesia, for instance, find that when three generations live together, it is more often because the elders need to take care of their needy descendants, not vice versa.[40]

In China, where skipped-generation families are common (as you just read), researchers asked grandparents whether they expected to live with their adult children when they were very old. All said no. One explicitly said she wanted to die in her own bed in her own house, and another (who was a custodial grandmother at the time) insisted, repeatedly, "I will not live with them, not live with them. I will live in my own hut. Even when I get older, I will not live with them."[41]

Worldwide, few older adults prefer three-generation households. Grandmothers without living partners often choose to live alone. The middle generation also seeks independence. One study began with 181 new mothers who lived with their mothers. Almost all were eager to leave. Almost half left in the first two years after the birth, although some returned reluctantly because they could not manage on their own.[42]

Some people who recognize that three-generation families decrease the privacy and independence of the two older generations nonetheless assume that children benefit. Unfortunately, that is not usually true.

It begins at birth. Every pediatrician now advocates breastfeeding, as breast milk contains substances that protect against disease and correlate with more intelligent, less obese, and healthier children. However, when three generations live together, new mothers are significantly less likely to breastfeed.[43]

Problems continue during early childhood. One study began with 194 young African American mothers of preschoolers.[44] Prior research had repeatedly reported stress and poorer health among grandmothers in three-generation households: these researchers were not surprised to find no benefits for the oldest generation who shared a home with their children and grandchildren. However, given "the enthusiasm of policy-makers for three generation households," they expected that the younger generations would benefit. Not so.

Compared to the mothers who lived apart from their mothers, young women in three-generation households were more often depressed, and the children were more often disobedient or with-drawn. The children also suffered intellectually: they were behind in language development. Worst of all, rates of mistreatment were higher when grandmothers and mothers were both caregivers. One suggested reason for this surprising outcome: grandmother criticism accompanied grandmother care. That reduced maternal pride and mother/child attachment.

Problems continue as children grow older. Some adolescents resent the space that the grandmothers take in the house and are angry because grandmothers express disapproval of clothes, neatness, and curfews. That is not always true, however. Much depends on the grandmothers' attitude, personality, and relationship with the teenager. One study found that when the grandmother/grandchild relationship was warm, teenagers were less self-absorbed, no matter where the grandmothers lived.[45] If grandmothers were uninvolved, no benefits were evident when they shared a home.

Why, then, are multigenerational families idealized? In theory, they save money, foster family relationships, and decrease child loneli-ness. Three-generation families are more common in traditional, non-Western cultures. Perhaps they succeed outside North America. One woman in India lived in a compound headed by her grandparents, with a total of forty-five family members. She wrote:

> *When I was a child, the only nuclear family I encountered was a fictional one in my kindergarten textbook. . . . I felt sorry for the girl child, who appeared to be my age in the illustrations, because she had to sleep in a bedroom of her own. How could you be happy if you didn't have scores of live-in cousins to play with?*[46]

However, her parents left that compound, partly because her mother resented her autocratic mother-in-law. Perhaps even in non-Western nations, women suffer when their home is not their own.

As a young woman, that girl left India to study in the United States, marry an American, and raise her children—far from their grandparents. Those children established nuclear families of their own, in the United States but distant from their mother, who is proud and happy to be an independent, dedicated grandmother.

FINDING THE BALANCE

A crucial issue in three-generational living is the independence of each generation. In traditional Africa, India, and China, wealthier families are more likely to be multigenerational because they can afford housing compounds that are designed to allow cousins to play together and adults to have privacy. Most homes in the United States are built for nuclear families, not for two independent generations living under one roof. However, some new homes have separate living quarters for grandparents and parents, or for parents and their adult children; often the assumption is that the oldest generation will need care from their children, not that they will be active grandparents.

If a grandmother believes the myths above, she may unwittingly find that she is expected to provide more grandmothering than she intends or that the middle generation resents her child care because they have their own routines and values regarding their children. Some written or televised accounts laud an idyllic case, misleading readers to believe it is far more typical (and benign) than it is. A common fallacy of human logic is that one memorable instance is mistakenly assumed to convey a general truth.

For example, the editor of a North Carolina newspaper wanted a story about a happy, intergenerational family. A reporter found one. The published article began, "Love, openness, and compatibility all figure into how the Merritts and the Borens of Wake Forest have built a happy multigenerational household."[47] This particular household had nine characteristics that made the arrangement work:

1. The Merritts were young grandparents (under age sixty).
2. The grandchildren were young (under age six).
3. The Boren mother worked full time outside the home.

4. The grandmother was the wife's mother (not her mother-in-law).
5. Both adult couples were married and in good health.
6. Both grandparents had retired.
7. The family shared strong religious values, praying together.
8. The adults met weekly to discuss and solve problems.
9. Each couple had separate quarters in a large house.

Only the first floor was common space. The middle generation (the Borens) had the second floor; the grandparents (the Merritts) had the basement, with their own bath, bedroom, and "man cave."

As in this example, three generations *can* live amicably in one home, especially when the nine circumstances above are in place. But that is unusual. As Amber Boren, the mother in the middle of that North Carolina household, said, "I would say 95 percent of people don't have the best relationship with their in-laws. . . . There are days when this house, as big as it is, it's very tight quarters. But then other days, we couldn't imagine life any other way."

This example is instructive. If a grandmother contemplates a three-generation household, instead of believing that it will benefit everyone, she should assess the nine circumstances above. A tenth should also be considered: The Borens and Merritts pooled their resources to buy a home together. More often, three-generation families begin because one generation cannot afford their own residence. That creates tension.

Typically, the oldest generation pays most of the bills, provides the space, and as a result, depletes their income. In every ethnic group, three-generation living depletes retirement income of the oldest generation.[48]

None of this is to deny that grandchildren *can* benefit when grandmothers are involved in their lives. One study begins, "Intergenerational relationships between grandparents and grandchildren can offer tremendous benefits to family members of each generation."[49] But custodial grandmothers should not be sanctified, and multigeneration living should not be idealized.[50] Both make grandmothers vulnerable to too much grandmothering, and both sometimes harm the younger generations as well.

The need to balance self-care and grandchild care is universally true, no matter who lives where. One grandmother learned this the hard way.

> *At the moment I'm happy to have a balance where I'm available to my daughter one day a week. Whereas the last few years she'd almost drop in at any moment and it was difficult for me to plan things. So I felt one day a week was the most I could cope with. . . . I'm also conscious of my own limits. I have to be careful not to overload myself because then everything crashes in a heap. I've had that happen before and I don't want to go there again.*[51]

All the foregoing warns grandmothers to avoid providing too much care and money. But each family is unique; crashing in a heap is not inevitable. Sometimes a grandmother needs to provide extensive care, whether she lives with her grandchildren or not. This chapter alerts everyone—grandmothers, parents, judges, lawmakers, and the general public—that too much grandmothering causes problems instead of reducing them.

Custodial care is a solution to a crisis that should have been prevented; multigeneration living needs to be entered warily, with boundaries set and privacy respected. Part II of this book suggests specifics to help grandmothers avoid doing too little and too much.

Part II

AT EVERY AGE

"*Of* all the peoples whom I have studied, from city dwellers to cliff dwellers, I always find that at least 50 percent would prefer to have at least one jungle between themselves and their mother-in-law."

That's from Margaret Mead (1901–1978), the brilliant anthropologist who was a heroine for many women of my cohort. Current researchers agree: intergenerational relationships are not always smooth.

When grandmothers overstep, young couples fertilize that jungle. Be grateful if they do not build a wall. A grandmother's offhand remarks, inadvertent facial expressions, or ingrained attitudes may have more power than her intentional actions, especially in the beginning.

To keep a path through the jungle, avoiding poisonous snakes and rushing water, accept some distance. Adult children are immersed in current culture. That clashes with grandmothers' long-standing roles, habits, and expectations. They told their children everything from "Drink your milk" to "Don't drink and drive"; they learned when to insist, cajole, and ignore, never abandoning the job. Dedication to caregiving never changes, with hard-won lessons of motherhood.

But some habits must be abandoned. Keep dedication to caregiving, but stop telling children what to do. Not that motherly advice is wrong (it's often right), but the goal is strong family relationships. Young adults do not take kindly to being told they are foolish, ignorant, or just plain wrong, especially by their mothers or mothers-in-law. Grandmothers must revise, retreat, reboot.

Each of the following chapters highlights three issues, with twenty-seven lessons in all. Circumstances have shifted; these lessons may keep grandmothers from stomping on a landmine because they know an explosive is nearby.

Of course, every family is unique. That renders some of these twenty-seven lessons obvious, some objectionable, some surprising. I hope that each, at least, provokes some System 2 analysis to add to grandmothers' instinctual, and laudatory emotions.

· *6* ·

The Loving Couple

*T*he grandmother journey begins before any children are conceived, when an adult child first finds a future partner. But the ultimate goal remains the same: thriving grandchildren and strong relationships. To achieve that, work is required before any wedding, pregnancy, or birth.

LESSON 1: KEEP COMMENTS TO YOURSELF

The stereotype of the intrusive mother-in-law arose for a reason: older women have spent decades telling their children how to behave. Future grandmothers might not realize that any comment, in words or facial expressions, especially to a young adult who is new to the family, might be resented. If there is to be a formal wedding, the mothers may have definite ideas that she thinks need implementing. But watch out. Wedding customs change from decade to decade, and the engaged couple feels that this is their celebration, not their parents'! Thus this first lesson is to keep quiet.

This is a major challenge for every devoted mother who guided her children many times a day: "Don't talk with your mouth full." "Wear your shoes outside." "Stop hitting your brother." "Say please." "Wash your hands." As children grew up, mothers provided a running commentary on activities, habits, and demeanor. By late adolescence, more distance (emotionally and physically) between mother and child meant that comments abated somewhat, and were sometimes ignored, but old habits do not stop. Nor should they; adolescents suffer if their parents seem to have given up trying to guide them.

However, danger threatens if that old habit erupts when an adult child's romance seems headed toward commitment. Negative comments about lovers may boomerang by solidifying an uncertain attraction and then later harming a grandparent relationship, echoing for years.

My friend—let's call her Debbie—flew three thousand miles to dine in Seattle with her twenty-two-year-old son at a four-star restaurant, to celebrate his first serious job after college. He shared some important news: "Sue and I are going to be married." "That's too bad," Debbie responded.

She immediately regretted her words. She had good reasons for her opinion: Her son was young, and Sue was his first serious girlfriend. Months earlier, Debbie had decided that since Sue was raised in another region of the United States, spoke with an unfamiliar accent, and grew up practicing another religion, she was not right for her boy. Moreover, Sue's parents were divorced. That increased the risk of divorce, which would harm any future grandchildren. Added to all that, this boy was her firstborn; she did not want to lose him. That's why she blurted out "That's too bad."

He reacted like a man in love: with anger. To prove his love, he told Sue what his mother said. She also reacted like someone in love: she disliked Debbie.

My friend is in good company. Most parents believe that no one is quite right for their child. As with a telescope, this reaction is magnified when the mate's background—ethnic, religious, regional, economic—produces unfamiliar values, customs, and habits. Disparities between parents and their child's chosen mate are almost inevitable in the United States, a nation of immigrants (some recent, some arriving centuries ago) joining Native Americans from five hundred or so tribes. In the U.S. Census, the number of biracial children is increasing faster than any other group.

Even when outsiders think that a couple shares the same background, partners differ in many ways. Researchers who have studied thousands of couples contend that *every* marriage is "a cross-cultural experience . . . [the new couple creates] rituals of connection, the shared life goals, and shared philosophies of life."[1]

Those shared philosophies almost never mirror those of the future grandparents. The current trend of postponing marriage allows young people to meet thousands of potential partners whose childhoods were unlike their own. That benefits the nation but does not please the parents, who observe "rituals of connection" unlike those they instilled.

I know one woman who was taken aback when her grown daughter changed her wardrobe to please her new husband. In this case, the new clothes were looser, less revealing. The opposite may occur; daughters may don a bikini or stiletto heels. My own mother was upset that I got my ears pierced soon after my wedding; she thought my husband was a bad influence. (I thought he liberated me.) Many brides and grooms change religions, or at least denominations, so both can worship together. That troubles their parents.

New partners who alter childhood patterns to adapt to their mates may strengthen their relationship. Distressed elders need to remember that every couple needs a strong partnership to support any future grandchildren, because sleepless nights, childhood illnesses, and adolescent rebellion will shake the parental bond. If the older mother remembers the goal, she will realize that any criticism—in facial movements, body positions, and words—is best unexpressed.

National diversity may be why North Americans value passionate love and personal choice when it comes to choosing a mate. In many other cultures, the parents (not the unmarried young adult) choose mates, often relatives from the same caste and region. A 2016 report finds that 64 percent of brides in India met the groom for the first time on their wedding day.[2] Love is thought to develop gradually, after the wedding.

In some cultures, in-laws are expected to be involved in a new couple's life. Not in North America. Indeed, American young adults rarely consult their parents about intimate partners, and they discount ethnic and religious differences that their parents think important. Engaged couples announce, not ask. Comments are unwelcome.

One mother wrote of the "challenges of mothering an adult son who does not always understand or appreciate the efforts I've made."[3] She wrote:

> *Last Thanksgiving, my son told me he eloped. I went to bed for a day and a night . . . napping, crying, watching television, or drinking red wine. . . . Why had I been treated with such disrespect? . . . Everyone thought we were so close; I thought so too. How could he marry a person I'd only met for a few hours?*

Notice that she focused on what she had done for her son, on her past actions, not on his current wishes. That son and his mother now discuss only neutral topics—not politics, not romance, not religion—to avoid arguments. Sad.

Mothers of new couples do not realize how their actions and words can be interpreted. For instance, if a mother bakes a special cake for her son's birthday, as she has done since he was a boy, isn't it wonderful that she still expresses her love? Not necessarily! It could imply that his new bride does not properly celebrate her husband or that she is an inferior cook. It could signify that the mother wishes he were still her little boy. Or if a mother comments that the newlyweds are gaining or losing weight, is she saying that marriage is harming their health? That is not what she meant, but it might be taken that way. Comments that seem neutral may sound hostile to a daughter- or son-in-law.

What if a mother discovers serious problems (a new mate gambles compulsively or uses drugs or is unfaithful)? What to do? Announce the problem, confront the spouse, and rescue her grown child? No. Talk is not helpful. Neither forgive and enable (don't pay off the debt) nor condemn and punish (don't call the police). I imagine that some mothers are horrified by this advice, but remember that the child is an adult. Years ago, the mother taught them how to defend themselves: now the mother's job is to listen, expressing support, not solutions.

Comments intended to fix someone else's marriage may make things worse, particularly if the fixer is the mother-in-law. One mother was upset that her child was getting divorced after years of marriage.

Years ago, she had advised against that marriage and early on told her daughter to divorce. But she said it was now too late, advising her daughter to stay married for the children's sake. That daughter felt rejected, concluding that she could never please her mother.

If adult children complain about their partner, mothers need to hear, not join, the criticism. This does not mean dismissing the complaint or ignoring a crisis. If a problem seems serious, instead of trying to fix it, the mother might suggest where her child might get help, perhaps from a marriage counselor, a clergyperson, or a self-help group.

Over the years, most women have learned from their life experience with friends that intimate relationships are best worked out between the two people directly involved. Some couples move past addiction, infidelity, and other troubles and then spend happy decades in a great marriage. Others separate over problems that seem to be minor. That learning applies to one's own children as well. Comments from mothers-in-law do not help.

Another set of comments also must be kept quiet: those about having a baby. Friends the same age as the would-be grandmother proclaim that having a grandchild is the best thing that ever happened to them. But almost no new couple says that parenthood is the best thing that ever happened to their relationship. No wonder many new couples avoid conception, while many potential grandmothers try to be patient.

Impatience is dangerous. The mother of a young man was diagnosed with fatal cancer. She told him she hoped to see him married and a father before she died. Out of love for her, he married his girlfriend, who quickly became pregnant. The woman died before the birth. Soon after that, the couple split up. I asked, "How is the grandchild?" "Not good" was the answer.[4]

As a young woman in the 1970s, I bristled at any suggestion that girls are born to be mothers. So did most of my closest female friends, some of whom are now happy and child free. The research finds that most of my contemporaries who have chosen to avoid becoming mothers are content with their choice; they say that their worst problem is the attitudes and comments of other people.[5]

Given my past convictions as well as the data on parenthood, I tried not to pressure my children, even when none of the four had pregnancy plans when they were older than I was when I gave birth. I accepted that they did not want children, and I tried to hide my emotional, unexpected, and powerful wish for a grandchild. I failed. When Elissa told me that she and her husband got a puppy, I blurted out, "Oh no. Now you will not have a baby."

I blamed myself for not being a grandmother by age fifty, as all my foremothers were. What had I done wrong? Did my children see me stressed by motherhood, not joyous? That thought was unwanted, unnerving, unexpected. I needed to process it, using my academic expertise.

In former times, when grown children were married by age twenty and gave birth in the next year or two, that signified success. Older women were proud and satisfied with their past child rearing because their children affirmed it by having babies. Even today, some grandmothers brag about how many grandchildren they have, as if high numbers signify mega-success.

To counter my fear that my childless daughters meant failed motherhood on my part, I reviewed statistics. Millions of healthy and happy adults, raised well, are having more sex but fewer, later babies.

- Most (58 percent) high school seniors in the United States have had intercourse,[6] but unlike their grandparents, they avoid pregnancy and birth.
- The average woman worldwide had 5.0 children in 1950; she has 2.5 now.
- In the United States, the fertility rate was 3.3 births per woman in 1950; it is 1.9 in 2015. The only age group with rising birth rates is women over age thirty-five.[7]
- Marriage is often postponed or avoided. In 1960, the average U.S. bride was twenty; now she is twenty-eight (in Western Europe, thirty-one). Many U.S. adults never marry: in 2015, 40 percent of thirty-five- to forty-four-year-olds were not married.

Consequently, grandmotherhood comes later, if at all. In 1980, women became grandmothers, on average, in their forties. Now they are fifty or sixty. Trends in Canada are similar to those in the United States. In 1985, about half of all Canadian women were grandmothers by age fifty, a benchmark not achieved until age sixty in 2011.[8] About 2 percent saw their *first* grandchild when they were over age seventy-five. Many older women have no grandchildren.

Those statistics suggest I am part of history, not a failed mother. But comfort from statistics does not erase feelings; System 2 does not blot out System 1. Despite our emotions, we potential grandmothers must keep our fears quiet, voicing comments to close friends, not to young childless couples.

One way to avoid pressuring young couples is to find other outlets for *generativity*, the psychosocial need that Erik Erikson considered characteristic of adults.[9] Erikson said this psychosocial need is often met by raising children and grandchildren—a comforting thought because my powerful wishes are normal. Erikson also wrote that generativity can be expressed in other ways. Instead of pressuring her children, older women can tutor in schools, assist in hospitals, volunteer in political campaigns, and so on.[10] Specifics change from year to year, and political values vary among older women, as they do for people of every age. Caregiving is often central, however.

For example, a group of grandmothers (called Grannies Respond) took a bus to the U.S./Mexico border to help the immigrant families who were trying to get asylum.[11] Many other women were troubled by policies that separate children from their families and campaigned to reverse that. Yet other older women supported those policies. This is not the place for a political debate. However, across the political spectrum, older women need to become active within their community, especially if they have no grandchildren.

Older women in Canada have connected with grandmothers in South Africa, to their mutual joy. *Grandmother Power: A Global Phenomenon* chronicles that relationship, as well as the activism of many other older women worldwide. That book was written "to inspire grand people to use their wisdom, experience, energy, and power on behalf of grandchildren everywhere."[12] Good advice: older women need to let their children decide when, and whether, to give birth.

LESSON 2: RESPECT THE GATEKEEPERS

Future grandmothers need to do more than becoming involved in global concerns while keeping their comments to themselves. They need to build relationships. That begins early, long before conception.

Margaret Mead wrote about jungles; the current equivalent is gates, sometimes locked, with sentries to keep intruders out. All the research on grandparents emphasizes that the middle generation can open or close the gates that allow access to grandchildren. Some gatekeepers forbid contact, some simply move far away, and some poison the grandmother-grandchild relationship, creating a virtual wall instead of a physical one.

It is difficult to pry open a gate that has been shut. That is why mothers-in-law must strengthen their relationship to the future parents early on, oiling the gate so it swings open easily when the time comes.

In chapter 4, you read about grandparents who sued the grandchildren's parents because they closed a gate that had been wide open. The result of the lawsuits was a gate slammed shut and locked. Lawsuits are extreme, but milder versions are common.

Remember Debbie, who alienated her son's future bride? Two years later, when their first child was born, Sue forbade her mother-in-law to care for him alone. (Debbie was allowed when the parents or the grandfather was present.) The ostensible reason was that Debbie was impulsive and scattered and might harm the precious baby. That deeply hurt my friend, who insisted that her devotion and dedication to her grandson crowded out every other thought when she was with him.

Debbie promised to protect the grandson with her life; she praised her daughter-in-law's many good qualities; she never criticized. Sue did not soften: perhaps she thought Debbie's praise was, at best, insincere and, at worst, sarcastic. The new father sided with his wife, not his heartbroken mother.

As in this case, hostile gatekeepers are more often the son's wife than the daughter's husband, especially if the mother was close to her son. Many young men react to their mother's distress by distancing themselves. That may be wise; if he takes sides, he risks divorce or heartbreak.

Debbie took lesson 1 to heart: after her initial mistake, she did not express her many opinions about everything her son and daughter-in law did, from their medical decisions to where they hung pictures, from when they took vacations to how they cooked beans. All those opinions Debbie expressed only to close friends (like me) who would keep them quiet. Her son and daughter-in-law soon had two more children (the grandmother had opinions about that, but she had learned to keep quiet).

Eventually she tried a new strategy: she praised Sue's devotion to her children and to her professional work. Gradually, Sue relented (the burden of caring for three children helped). Recently, the two older children stayed overnight with Grandma.

This family had a troubled beginning but a happy ending. That is not always true. Things can get worse, not better.

One young bride lived with her husband's parents when he was in the military, stationed far away.[13] His parents thought they were gracious, helping her fit in with her new family. She seemed docile, even appreciative. But she wrote to her husband, "Your parents were horrible to me. Always criticizing and giving me no privacy. . . . They criticized my church, my clothes, everything. When you come back make sure we move far away from them."

He did. Those grandparents do not know their grandchildren. Both adult generations share the blame, but the third generation suffers. The ten-year-old grandchild said, "I've got a lot of relatives but I can't see them because my mother hates their guts."

Were those future grandparents really horrible? No. They assumed, as most people do, that their habits and beliefs were best, and that their son's wife needed to learn how to fit into the family.

In both of these examples, it is the daughter-in-law who closes the gate. Less often, but more devastating, a mother's own daughter rejects her. One excluded grandmother knew that her past relationship with her daughter was troubled. But she also remembered that as a little girl, that daughter happily spent weekends with her grandmother. Remembering that history, the grandmother mistakenly believed that her daughter's fond grandmother memories would transfer, so the daughter would encourage her son to bond with his grandmother. Wrong. That boy stayed with Grandma for a week each summer until he was five. Then the gate slammed shut.

> *My daughter tells me—confesses would be too gentle a word—that my grandson came to me for a week under duress, pushed by her because she needed a break, to spend time with a grandmother she does not in some ways trust or like. She tells me she remembers my parenting as verbally abusive, and wonders if I have changed. I accuse her of making her son a stand-in for old issues between us, of setting me up as a Mean Old Grandma so that she can sweep in as Mommy the Savior. Our past, it seems, is impossible to escape, resolve, or even discuss with civility for long.*[14]

Do you wonder why this example with the five-year-old grandson is presented in the chapter on new couples, not the chapter on early childhood? There are two reasons. The first is that keeping comments to oneself is a lesson that needs to be learned early on because it will affect later gatekeeping. But the second reason is more important: if the early mother-child relationship was "verbally abusive" or worse, the time for repair is before any grandchildren are conceived. This woman thought that old problems were forgotten, but that is rarely true.

Almost always, for reasons inherent in the nature of family life, grandmothers consider their relationship with their grown children closer and warmer than the children do. Developmentalists refer to this as a *generational stake*, meaning that the older generation has a bias toward believing all was good, and the younger generation wants to believe that they improved on their parents' caregiving. As a result, older mothers do not realize when repair is needed, when they must listen and apologize. Instead they defend themselves against criticism and complain that the young do not even have "common courtesy."

Indeed, every generation has a particular perspective on family interaction. Young children idolize their mothers, adolescents disparage them, and young adults—it depends.[15] If older adults expect the politeness they learned in their youth, they may conclude that the younger generation has no manners, unaware that manners are a product of each cohort and change in every decade.

The good news is that family bonds are dynamic, not fixed. Some abusive mother/child relationships improve markedly in adulthood because adult children understand the past pressures on their parents, who ask forgiveness for mistakes they never knew they made. The bad news is that some relationships are stuck in the past: if a mother had a difficult relationship with her children, those children may lock the gate when they are grown.

Accepting responsibility for past lapses takes humility and effort. As with this mother, the first impulse of many people is to be defensive, blaming past failings on others (the spouse, the child, the zeitgeist, the neighborhood) rather than accepting an adult child's perception. The grandmother above who wanted to discuss the past "with civility" may unwittingly keep the old wounds raw. If she cannot express a heartfelt apology, she must keep her civil comments to herself.

Beyond working to repair past problems with their own adult child, mothers also need to build a relationship with their child's partner. Many mothers wonder how to respect a future gatekeeper, a stranger who joins the family. Each connection follows its own path, of course, but psychological research has six suggestions regarding relationship building, especially with a new stranger.

1. Make eye contact often, but carefully. Looks, glances, stares, gazes—all are crucial in human communication, more than in any other species.[16] (That's why human eyes have so much white space.) But cultures differ markedly regarding eye contact. Future grandmothers must notice the visual habits of the new spouse, avoiding staring and yet meeting glances with openness, warmth, and respect.

2. Follow emotional and physical leads. Mirror whatever emotion is expressed: smile or look serious, as the moment requires.

Laughter may be abrasive or welcome. Mirror body position, too—lean forward, stand tall—whatever. If someone backs away, don't move forward.

3. Listen actively. Say "yes, uh-huh, oh my, amen, really, okay, oh no," nod, clap, use facial expressions (pursed lips, eyes wide, eyebrows raised, nose lifted)—whatever signifies attention. Still faces and silence are hostile.

4. Find shared joy. Humor is bonding . . . or alienating. Laughing at oneself is best. Never make fun of a child or an adult, including those not present. Never joke about any ethnic group or religion, including your own.

5. Respect cultural differences. Loud voices, slang, and drama are bonding for some people, alienating for others. Praise can be grating or welcome; smiles can be considered friendly or insincere. Observe carefully, learn pathways and customs before judging or joining.

6. Avoid landmines. Every mother-in-law has beliefs that clash with the new couple, perhaps about religion or politics, or maybe about habits such as when and how to brush teeth or prepare salad. Keep quiet until you know what another person thinks.

None of this means that older women must always be passive, accepting everything with a smile, as grandmothers of old were said to do. That would betray the great strides that women have made. But remember the goal: strong, supportive relationships, so that no one shuts the gate.

LESSON 3: RECOGNIZE LINKED LIVES

Some people assume that modern times reduce family connections. Developmental scientists think the opposite is more accurate.[17] Smaller families mean fewer siblings and cousins but stronger intergenerational links. When mutual affection, frequent contact, and reciprocal help are tallied, the generations are closer than they were fifty years ago. Longer lives, increased nonmarital child bearing, more divorces, cheaper cell phones, faster internet—all this increases intergenerational links.

Family closeness leads to *linked lives*, the idea that each family member's experiences are buffered, extended, or moderated by the others.[18] Suppose someone has a great job, a happy marriage, a healthy newborn. Every relative celebrates. Conversely, each problem reverberates up and down the family line.

The links between the generations are strengthened by modern times, or at least they can be. Here are three examples:

1. Grandmothers who are themselves divorced or widowed are often closer to their children and grandchildren than married grandmothers.
2. Longevity adds years to relationship strengthening.
3. Since many older women have been active employees, they can share more worldly knowledge and economic support than grandmothers once did.

Because of linked lives, family members help each other when trouble strikes. Family businesses often provide work and money for everyone, and, especially when someone has a serious problem (a teenager jailed, an adult fired, cancer diagnosed), family members provide essential support. Each person's life is affected by their family members: people quit jobs, move hundreds of miles, or postpone pregnancies and donate time and money for relatives.

I know personally that family links are activated when one person is in crisis. When I was an infant, my father left to serve in the navy for three years. Two aunts and my maternal grandmother (a widow) came to live with us, and my uncle visited often to play with my brother, who frequently spent the night with my paternal grandparents. According to current research on military families, Dad's deployment added stress for the adults, but the family links were evident.

Understanding intergenerational links requires everyone to appreciate the current situation of other generations. When Debbie's son told his mother he was engaged, she forgot that she was speaking with a young man in love, not a boy who sought his mother's opinion. When a newly married couple wants to be alone, the future grandmother must remember how she felt as a young wife.

Because the grandmother's life is linked with the lives of the younger generation, and vice versa, communication is essential. That requires questions and listening, not assumptions and judgment.

One grandmother complained, "One daughter expects me to come whenever she calls for babysitting even though it disrupts my own plans. It is expected of me because I am the non-working grandmother."[19]

Her complaint is a common one, given the ageism of our culture. Few young adults know that many older adults become busier than ever when they retire.[20] Younger adults may believe the stereotype that older adults are lonely, when actually loneliness is more common among the young.[21] This misperception arises from ageism but is diminished by communication.

In the above example, does this daughter assume that her mother needs something to do, and did the grandmother never mention her plans? The result: resentment in both generations.

Thus, linked lives require intergenerational appreciation, not criticism. This passage is often quoted:

> *The children now love luxury; they have bad manners, contempt for authority; they show disrespect for elders and love chatter in place of exercise. Children are now tyrants, not the servants of their households. They no longer rise when elders enter the room. They contradict their parents, chatter before company, gobble up dainties at the table, cross their legs, and tyrannize their teachers.*

No one knows who first wrote that. It has been attributed to Assyrian cuneiform, Egyptian papyrus, Aristotle, Plato, Socrates, a medieval monk. It is often quoted because it fits two prejudices: (1) that the old complain about the young, and (2) that the young are disrespectful. Attribution to ancient sages suggests that people want to believe that it has always been true.

This idea is relevant to linked lives because each generation perpetuates myths about the other generations, as evident in mother-in-law jokes. As explained in earlier chapters, younger generations are not prepared for grandmothers as they actually are, while elders call *millennials* (a popular name for young adults born between 1980 and 2005) the "me generation," a stereotype that younger generations resist.[22]

Older generations sometimes say, "When I was your age . . ." adding an example of how they were better than the spoiled, selfish, young adults they see now. Meanwhile, younger generations tend to look at older ones and think that they are at best irrelevant and at worst senile.

"When I was your age, I was an adult."

True! Over the past century, a decade or more has been added to the expected age for adulthood, parenthood, grandmotherhood, and even death.
William Haefeli, CartoonCollections.com.

That each generation lauds itself, and mythologizes the past, is easiest to see with a generation that is not one's own. Consider those Americans, now mostly dead, who fought in World War II. They came to believe that they were "the greatest generation . . . who stayed true to their values of personal responsibility, duty, honor, and faith."[23] The evidence is more equivocal. In 1941, young men "volunteered in great numbers for military service but also dodged the draft in great numbers"; 1946 was a peak year not only for marriages but also for divorces; the war effort led to sacrifice, but it also resulted in a thriving black market.[24]

Thus, although everyone wants to believe that their generation is best, memory is selective and each generation has a distinct perspective. Family members need to respect the experience and priorities of people much younger or older. That is the essence of linked lives: each person rises or falls with everyone else, and then families are strong.

• 7 •

The Pregnant Couple

$\mathcal{B}$ethany and I drove to her chosen hospital, forty-three miles from her home. A fibroid tumor, discovered four months earlier after a spontaneous abortion (aka miscarriage), needed to be removed. I acted upbeat. We focused on Google Maps, on finding parking, on anything except impending surgery.

After they wheeled her away, I paced in a well-tended garden, breathing deep and pushing back fear. I then sat in the spacious, sunny, waiting room with free coffee, a huge skylight, and other anxious people. Some read, some dozed, no one talked.

An hour passed. Bethany's surgeon appeared. Smiling, he escorted me to a side room where doctors talk privately about patients. "She is fine. All went well. You can see the tumor."

He proudly handed me a sonogram, pointing to the mass he had removed. I glanced at it, thanking him quickly, and then swallowed. I had something to say. "She thinks she wants to have a baby."

I thought he should be the one to tell her that was impossible. Instead, he said, "I don't see any reason why not."

Many reasons, I thought, including her age (almost forty) and marital status (single). But apparently the condition of her uterus was not one of them. Two years later, Caleb was born, a fount of grand-mother joy, and the reason for lesson 4.

LESSON 4: QUIET FEARS AND ANXIETIES

Many mothers have irrational thoughts regarding their children and their future grandchildren. They want to voice them, or at least to caution their adult children who are pregnant.

Stay mum, for two reasons. The first is that advice may be dated, as mine would have been. Technology has transformed conception and pregnancy.[1] Among the examples:

- Pregnancy can be detected soon after conception, which makes recognition of early miscarriage increasingly common.
- Some newborns have five parents, three biological ones (donor sperm, donor ovum, donor womb) and two non-biological ones—a same-sex or other-sex couple—who have a binding contract with the other three. The couple are the legal parents.
- Many babies begin life in a petri dish in a laboratory (in vitro fertilization [IVF], usually with one sperm injected into an ovum). The single-celled zygote duplicates and is inserted into a uterus. About half of the time, implantation results in a baby, twins, or triplets.
- Other zygotes from the same IVF can be frozen for later insertion, creating siblings conceived at the same time and born years apart.
- Soon after an IVF zygote begins to multiply, one cell can be removed and tested for genetic conditions. If all is well, the mass of other stem cells can be implanted, and a normal fetus can develop.
- Major advances appear every year—mitochondria transplants, fetal surgery, selective abortion—none possible a few decades ago.

Ethics and laws have not caught up. Nor have grandmothers. They cannot know the newest discoveries, nor all the implications. Most of the innovations just listed were considered immoral when today's grandmothers were young; some may still be. A hundred thousand scientists and doctors are developing and implementing extraordinary prenatal measures every day. If a grandmother expresses ignorance or disapproval, she is not building a relationship. Instead, she may be reflecting old misconceptions and assumptions.

Another reason to keep quiet is to avoid stressing the mother, which may harm the fetus. Pregnant women already have irrational fears and fantasies caused by hormones, sleep disruption, cultural myths, and private thoughts. No need to add more. Stress is a teratogen, something that can harm the fetus.

I know about irrational fears. In the middle of my second pregnancy, I awakened from a troubled sleep with the conviction that I had contracted toxoplasmosis (from cat litter; we had two cats), which can damage the fetal brain. I had no symptoms, and my family was on vacation, but I phoned my obstetrician in a panic. He understood pregnancy anxieties, so he scheduled a blood test. I enlisted my husband, my brother, and my sister-in-law to care for my toddler, and I drove hours to the city. Reassurance came the next day; that fetus became Rachel. Grandmothers need to be like my doctor, neither dismissing nor exacerbating anxieties.

What if a daughter or daughter-in-law asks a timeless question? Perhaps "How much weight should I gain?" or "Can I smoke just one cigarette?"

Probably every grandmother wants to answer. Dedication to grandchildren's well-being is wired deep into our brains; we are eager to advise against malnutrition and nicotine. But simple answers become complex.

For example, when a grandmother explains the right amount of weight gain, her answer raises the specter of gaining too much (difficult birth) or gaining too little (starved fetus). If she specifies a number that her doctor told her, that number is almost never the one that current obstetricians recommend. If she tries to be reassuring ("eat as much as you want"), she may be suspected of foolish ignorance.

Anxieties shadow *every* maternal response because every answer is encrusted with barnacles because it comes from her. Trying to scrape away those barnacles, or ignoring them, distorts relationships. Instead, a grandmother can ask the future mother what *she* thinks and what others—the father, a medical professional, her friends—say.

What if the question and answer are straightforward and factual, such as "Will I miscarry if I exercise, carry a heavy box, have sex?" or "Will birth happen on the due date?"

Grandmothers know that the answers are no, no, no, no, but remember the two sets of reasons above—many facts have changed, and emotions awaken anxiety. If the answer is really factual, the future mother has already googled it; if she seeks contrary opinions, the grandmother should not be the source.

What if a question touches on deep emotions and values, such as "Should I abort?" or "Should I give birth at home?"

Questions like these, even more than straightforward ones, require listening, not talking. Grown children know their mother's convictions; usually they share them and want approval. Approval is fine, but why the question? If she knows what her mother thinks, she does not need to ask. If she disagrees, the answer fortifies a barrier, either because the pregnant woman resists the advice or because she follows it resentfully.

Pregnancy raises grandmother fear to a new level. The old worry about infertility morphs into fear of miscarriage, of early labor, of stillbirth, of serious deformity. One outcome of technology confirming pregnancy soon after conception is that we now know that early miscarriage is common, perhaps one pregnancy in every three. If the grandmother's anxiety spreads to the woman, that helps no one—especially not the embryo. Be ready to comfort and reassure, not blame.

None of this means that grandmothers are passive observers. Pregnant women are stressed; grandmothers can listen, affirm, and sympathize. Fears are no help; lesson 5 might be.

LESSON 5: LEARN ABOUT INNOVATIONS

Every grandmother already knows a lot; life teaches. But lest past knowledge undercuts new learning, grandmothers can read medical and practical books, websites, blogs, journals, and so on, seeking unfamiliar perspectives. New facts and viewpoints make us smarter and wiser, added to what we already know. Grandmothers who take lesson 4 to heart know that they are not experts, but some knowledge of fertility, fetal development, and prenatal testing enables them to be supportive, not bewildered or confused.

For instance, the sonogram is now routine. Sonograms were suspect forty years ago; now good obstetric care includes several.

Grandmothers who are allowed to accompany their daughters or daughters-in-law to a sonogram appointment feel more attached to the baby.[2] One grandmother said that seeing the fetus via a sonogram was "an instant shock." She felt her heart would burst when she saw the

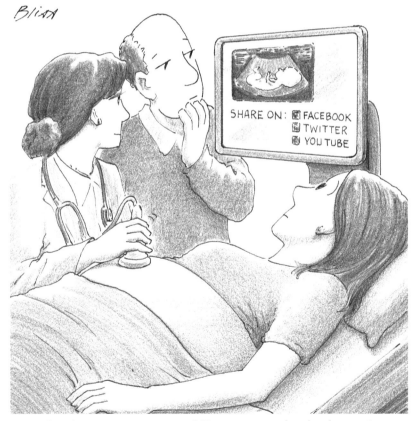

Innovations in pregnancy every year! How can a grandmother keep up?
Harry Bliss, CartoonCollections.com.

blurry outline of her future grandchild.[3] Being invited to see the image of the fetus is an honor, to be earned by not insisting. However, some couples are thrilled with the sonogram and want to share it widely. Again, that is their choice, not the grandmothers'.

One reason to learn about innovations is to rejoice that times have changed; then the future grandmother's joy may spread to the expectant parents. Neonatal mortality has plummeted; maternal mortality is rare. The U.S. maternal death rate is higher than most other developed nations but is still low, about one in five thousand births.[4]

Do not become distracted by isolated cases that illustrate rare problems or innovations. One occurred in 2015, when a sixty-seven-year-old grandmother, Annegret Raunigk, who already had thirteen children, gave birth to surviving quadruplets. Her IVF pregnancy, using donor sperm and donor ova, was illegal in her native Germany, so she traveled to Ukraine for conception, pregnancy, and birth. Annegret caused headlines and outrage, but don't let that diminish the joy: babies are now born to couples who, a few decades ago, would have been childless. In the past twenty years, about a million babies in the United States and five million worldwide began life in a dish, not in a woman.

If that is the way a new grandchild begins life, get ready for emotional ups and downs. The anxiety and frustration attendant to infertility is often compounded during treatment when a couple waits to know whether implantation occurred. If not, despair is likely. If so, anxiety continues throughout the pregnancy. Many couples do not want to tell their parents about infertility treatments; don't pry. Failure is as common as success: an embryo transfer results in a live birth about half of the time (it was a third in 1996). Some couples opt for transfers of several zygotes, which increases the chance of twins but not the chance of a successful pregnancy.[5]

Be careful with sympathy; it is easy to say the wrong thing. Be especially careful with warnings, such as saying that twins are more work. Every couple follows their own path through hope and disappointment; grandmothers need to be good listeners and careful responders.

Much of this applies to every pregnancy, but couples experiencing infertility may be more prone to depression and may need extended patience and understanding.[6] Becoming pregnant isn't as easy as it seemed when unplanned pregnancy was the dominant fear. When hoping to conceive, and in the early weeks of a pregnancy, supportive family and friends are crucial.

A similar set of innovations regards prenatal testing. Fifty years ago, the due date was determined by the beginning of the last menstrual period, minus three months, plus eight days. Pregnancy was not suspected until a woman missed her period and was confirmed at "quickening," when fetal movement was felt, several months after conception.

In about 1960, biologists discovered that pregnancy could be detected earlier. At first, only medical doctors could send a urine specimen to a lab; woman had to see their doctor or wait until quickening to confirm pregnancy. No pregnancy tests were sold at drug stores until 1977; it was feared that women might kill themselves or abort if they privately learned they were pregnant.[7] That idea seems sexist and quaint, but many grandmothers remember it.

Now pregnancy can be detected before the first missed period, and early medical tests (blood, urine, sonogram) routinely discover dozens of genetic and growth problems. A sonogram at the end of the second month reveals multiple pregnancies and estimates the due date better than the last menstrual period. The future mother's health, including immunization history, is assessed, ideally before conception but otherwise in the early weeks.

Early detection of potential problems leads to preventive treatment. For instance, in 2000, maternal HIV was often fatal for a future child. Now prenatal diagnosis, drugs, and a C-section virtually eliminate transmission. Indeed, even paternal HIV can lead to safe conception.[8]

To grasp the enormity of innovations, consider Down syndrome, the result of three, not two, chromosomes at site 21. I cried when I read *Angel Unaware*,[9] Dale Evans Rogers's tribute to her daughter with Down syndrome, born in 1950, dead at age three.

In those years, many women in my cohort refused testing for Down's because they thought that a positive test would imply an abortion. Doctors who opposed abortion sometimes did not mention amniocentesis. Then one older mother of a Down's baby sued her doctor for "wrongful birth" because he did not tell her that a test was available.

Every decade since then, the detection and consequences of Down syndrome have changed. When I was fertile, scientists had discovered that the risk of Down syndrome increased with age. I had my first three children before age thirty-five because I feared Down's. Only when I understood amniocentesis did I become pregnant again. A sonogram guided a thin needle to draw some amniotic fluid at about the fifteenth week of pregnancy. The fluid was cultured, and two weeks later we learned that our fourth child did not have Down's, so we did not need to contemplate abortion nor plan for a special-needs child. Thankfully that child, Sarah, had no other genetic problems; she could not then have been tested for them. and far fewer treatment options were available.

Now, long before fifteen weeks, blood, urine, and sonograms reveal hundreds of possible problems. Elevated levels of certain proteins in the blood and the measurement of the fetal neck—although the fetus itself is less than three inches long—can signal Down's. To confirm the suspicion, chorionic villus sampling at nine weeks has replaced amniocentesis. Further, if a couple fears chromosomal or genetic abnormalities (if one of them carries a gene for a dominant disorder, or both of them carry the gene for a recessive one), they can opt for IVF. Then only zygotes without the harmful genes can be implanted.

Are those innovations wonderful or terrifying? Grandmothers may have strong opinions, as do many other Americans. But the people who decide are the prospective parents: the grandmother's role is to be supportive.

LESSON 6: BUILD RELATIONSHIPS CAREFULLY

Building relationships was stressed in the previous chapter, but new challenges appear during pregnancy. Ghosts of the past and gremlins of the future bedevil future parents.[10] As one group put it, the "transition to motherhood is . . . an important developmental period of psychic transformation and potential reworking of unresolved issues."[11] Emotions are fragile; many couples become intensely private.

This is the time to cement the relationship with the future parents because when the baby is born, that relationship should be solid, with established patterns that allow the new parents to form a supportive family including the grandmother. If that does not happen, birth might lead to loss of contact. For example, one father of a newborn forcefully told his mother, "this is our baby, not yours" and "I never expected grandmothers to be so involved."[12] That young family lived a mile away from Grandma but soon moved to another continent.

Some pregnant couples might welcome the future grandmother to their home, bringing groceries, making a nutritious dinner, and doing the dishes. But others might want to cocoon; they might fear that a visit will lead to criticism of their cooking, cleaning, or eating or simply interfere with their quiet, emotional time. Almost any comment, even innocent or light-hearted ones, such as "where do you keep your olive oil?" or "the color of your couch reminds me of summer," might be misinterpreted. Because of this emotionally precarious time, many couples do not tell the grandparents when pregnancy is first confirmed, nor discuss names they are considering, nor tell about tests until they hear that all is well. Grandmothers need to understand.

This emphasizes again the need to build a strong relationship with the gatekeepers, by respecting the customs and traditions of the new couple. I know a grandmother who criticized her daughter for setting the dinner table with bowls, not plates. (The daughter followed the custom of her husband's family.)

I know another family where the grandmother repeatedly served pork at family gatherings, contrary to the daughter-in-law's Islamic beliefs. The grandmother thought that everyone needed holiday ham, breakfast bacon, and smothered pork chops, all part of her own family heritage. The daughter-in-law wished that she never had to eat at the grandmother's table, but that wish clashed with respect for elders, another strong belief in her culture.

She felt powerless, resentful, and troubled when she was pregnant with a child who might choose a grandmother's diet over the one her faith prescribed. The grandmother should have understood this conflict before the first grandchild was born. That grandmother continues to tempt fate: the daughter-in-law's religious devotion is becoming more important to her every year and may soon overtake her deference to her mother-in-law.

Another example of the need to respect customs is gift giving. Some cultures consider it bad luck for anyone, including the parents, to buy baby clothes, a crib, or anything else before the birth. The historic reason is that many babies died in the first hours. Thus, parents were spared the sorrow of disposing of preparations for a baby who had died.

Newborn fatality rates have severely dropped, but the custom lives on. For example, Poland is one of the nations with that tradition: the newborn death rate was estimated at 110 per thousand births in 1920. It was 18 per thousand in 1970 and 3 per thousand in 2017.[13]

In other cultures, prospective parents expect a baby shower and many gifts, either organized by the future grandmother or by the couple's friends. Again, find out in advance whether this should be done, and by whom.

Most North Americans allow gifts before the birth, but every gift contains a message from the giver and an obligation for the receiver.[14] Some gifts are decidedly unwelcome. Maternity clothes may never be worn, not only because of color and style but also because of fashion trends for pregnant women. If a future grandmother wants to buy maternity clothes, she might purchase a gift certificate or go shopping with her daughter or daughter-in-law—assuming that she can keep her mouth shut.

Buying for a future baby is hazardous. A gift suggests that Grandma knows what babies need, but prospective parents may disagree. For example, baby bottles, blankets, carriages, and cribs are rejected by some new parents; they symbolize a particular way to care for a baby. Stuffed animals and comforters may be seen as a risk for sudden infant death. A baby registry (like a wedding registry, with gifts the parents want) is chosen by some prospective parents, but others reject that idea. If a grandmother wants to buy a gift and there is no registry, ask what the new parents could use. Or provide a gift certificate to a favorite store ("favorite" for the parents, not the grandparents).

Worse are gifts that envision the future, such as a tiny college shirt. Does this imply that the grandparents expect the grandchild to attend their alma mater? I know a woman who was thrilled to find a set of toy cars at a yard sale. She bought them for her unborn grandchild of unknown gender. Her pregnant daughter was furious, asking, "Don't you think we should wait to see if this child even likes cars?"

Because every one is different, relationships differ as well. Some future parents seek new closeness with their mothers and mothers-in-law, others isolate themselves from everyone except each other. Future grandmothers must respect whatever boundaries the couple wants.

An innovation that breaks down some relationship boundaries and also leads to better obstetric outcomes among poor women is group prenatal care.[15] A dozen or so women who are at about the same stage of pregnancy gather for two hours once a month to weigh themselves, take their blood pressure, and led by a midwife, discuss some aspect of pregnancy (such as genetic tests, sleep problems, nutrition). For a few minutes during the session, each woman leaves the group to be examined privately. One woman participant said:

> It made me feel like, more relaxed. It was not just me, and the world's not over. . . . Their stories helped me out with some of the things I was going through. . . . So, it didn't scare me as much. You know how you have the shortness of breath? I just really felt I was the only one going through that. And then when we talked in group, all the other ladies was talking about it.

In this group, women were encouraged to bring guests—their partners, their mothers, whomever. One woman was particularly glad to have her family understand her emotions. She said, "They would come to the group with me. Then they'll understand like why I was acting up. . . . I felt like they understand me more. They started treating me different, not like this big angry person, but as a pregnant person."[16]

Of course, her mother probably already understood why she was acting up. But this woman sought validation for her moods. The fact that she felt better treated after her family came to her prenatal check-up is instructive. Grandmothers should not say "I knew that" but instead "Oh, that is good to know."

Grandmothers also need to attend to the needs of their other adult children, who may be jealous. Brothers and sisters who do not have children might think it unfair that the pregnant one gets extra attention. If the siblings have children, they might feel that the newest grandchild is overshadowing their progeny.

Sibling rivalry is part of human nature, even though grandmothers may not notice it. Ancient stories are filled with brothers fighting: Adam and Eve had two sons, and then Cain killed Abel, for reasons biblical scholars are still trying to figure out. A few chapters later (still in Genesis), Jacob and Esau were twins who engaged not only in rivalry but also in trickery instigated by their mother.

If a future grandchild is not the firstborn, an older sibling might feel ignored. Don't ask, "Isn't it wonderful that you will have a little sister or brother?" Later on, it could be the younger child who feels neglected: Rachel said it was not fair that I knew Bethany sixteen months longer than I knew her. Back to Adam and Eve: they had a third son, Seth, rarely mentioned, and they probably had daughters as well—never mentioned.

Grandmothers must make sure every child and grandchild feels loved and cherished. If this is not the first child of that family, Grandma can take the older children out, treating them as the special people they are. That helps them and the pregnant woman as well.

Taking those older grandchildren to a museum or park is not easy, but good grandmothering is sometimes hard. There are landmines each step of the way, in ancient times as well as now. But good grandmothering is invaluable: a boon for new parents and children as well as older ones. As the next chapters explain, new volatile issues appear once the baby is born.

Birth and the Newborn

"*Jolted*, blindsided by a wallop of loving more intense than any-thing I could remember."[1] Those are the words of Leslie Stahl, the famed television reporter who covered wars, disasters, miracles, and everything else that has awed humanity over the past forty years. What jolted her? Seeing her newborn granddaughter. She joined millions of women, stunned by a late-life emotional explosion as unexpected and overwhelming as the adrenaline that floods the blood stream when a driver almost crashes into another car. Pull to the side, thank God, safe—but why is the body still shaking?

Hormones, unbidden. Brain, hijacked. Emotions, overwhelming. At birth, System 1 may shut out reason: System 2 is desperately needed.[2] This chapter provides that.

LESSON 7: REMEMBER THE OTHER PEOPLE

Birth is thrilling, dazzling, blinding—grandmothers see only the baby. But let System 2 remind every grandmother: birth transforms *everyone*. Evidence is in language: biologists do not call the fetus a baby until it is born; people are not mothers, fathers, sisters, brothers, or grandparents until a birth. A grandmother's obsessions are not hers alone; they echo in another grandmother.

A century ago, two grandmothers per baby was no problem: there were plenty of grandchildren for every mother who lived past age fifty. The only difficulty was buying all the presents and remembering the count; it changed almost every year. My mother's mother had twenty-two grandchildren. Or maybe more (did Uncle Wes give me four cousins, or only three?).

But the demographic revolution now provides many grandmothers and few grandchildren. It is an axiom of economics, psychology, and all the other social sciences: if demand suddenly exceeds supply, fierce competition follows. Chimpanzees fight over bananas,[3] shoppers trample each other to grab Black Friday loss leaders,[4] and nations go to war over oil.[5] Longer lives, fewer births: demand for grandchildren exceeds supply.

A television segment became a viral YouTube video featuring Marcie and Jackie.[6] Moments after their grandson's birth, the mother's mother (Jackie) told the father's mother (Marcie) that she was taking too long photographing the newborn on the delivery room scale. Jackie called Marcie rude; she sing-songed, "Mama's baby, daddy's maybe."

Marcie mumbled, "I can take only but so much," as she went to the hospital corridor to remove her high heels. When Jackie stepped out of the delivery room, Marcie slapped and kneed her (a "tiger knee," an admiring commenter wrote). Jackie, sprawled on the floor, yelled "call 911," demanding that Marcie be put not in but "under the jail." A million people watched this episode, some laughing ("funny as hell"), some complaining (the TV cameramen should not have filmed this), but most were critical of the grandmothers ("selfish," "no class").

Physical fighting by grandmothers is unusual, but jostling for primacy is not. A friend of mine, whose daughter was expecting her first baby, was distressed that the mother-in-law was flying from India a week before the due date in order to be at the birth. My friend said, "My daughter needs to assert herself; she does not need her mother-in-law."

I suggested that she ask the obstetrician to exclude everyone but the father at the delivery. My friend rejected that solution; she herself wanted to be there. Neither grandmother asked the birth mother who she wanted with her.

To make it worse, the tradition in India is for sons to defer to their mothers. Clashing cultures meant both older women assumed that if only one grandmother is allowed at birth, she should be that one. Each expected her own child to defend her.

Birth is a flashpoint, which may begin a rivalry that never ends.

Competition for Most Adored Grandmother seriously heats up when the grandmothers are competing for the same grandchildren, when the mother-in-law of our daughter or son, our grandchildren's other granny, stakes her legitimate claim on their affection. Yes, fond though we may be of this other woman, and glad though we may be that she loves our grandchildren, and resigned though we may be to the fact that our grandchildren love her back, we are hoping our grandchildren love us more. A whole lot more.[7]

Thus, at birth, grandmothers need to lay the foundation for years of peaceful cooperation. Otherwise open conflict might erupt. That is bad for the grandchild, bad for the parents—and one or both competing grandmothers will lose.

Many grandmothers think the other grandmother has an unfair advantage. She was the only grandmother at the birth or she lives closer or she can afford more expensive gifts or she is younger, healthier, retired or—cruelest injustice of all—she is the mother's mother, not the father's. In many cultures, including that of the United States, the data shows that the mother-daughter bond is closer than the mother-son, although, as with every trend, there are exceptions.

This mother-daughter connection may take some grandmothers by surprise. One grandmother felt stunned when her daughter-in-law phoned her own mother, thousands of miles away, to ask about diaper rash. She did not think to ask the son's mother, standing a few feet away.

I have spoken at length to a grandmother who has two grown children, both boys. She is bitter, feeling "abandoned, neglected." She labels the tilt toward daughters the "worst injustice." One of her sons has two children whom she rarely sees, and the other, newly married, was welcomed into his wife's family with a T-shirt that proclaimed "the _____ family." This upset his own mother: "That's not his family, I am his family."

She says that she has lost her sons because neither is coming home for the holidays. One son offered "pre-Christmas," a few days before December 25: she was insulted. The other went with her grandchildren and his wife to the maternal grandmother for Thanksgiving. He said, "Laura [the other grandmother] owns Thanksgiving."

His mother was furious, telling me, "Thanksgiving is an American holiday, nobody owns it."

What is the solution? Start by recognizing that both sides of the family are equally connected to the baby and that the other grandmother may be obsessed, blindsided, or possessive. Instead of resenting that one's child has joined another family, a grandmother can be glad that she has an additional daughter or son. Try to be grateful that the grandchildren have more grandparents, aunts, uncles, cousins, and so on than one grandmother alone can provide.

Remember that new parents may be frightened, vulnerable, and awestruck. They may want to cling to each other or may want reassurance from the grown-ups who comforted them when they were babies. Empathy will stop grandmothers from complaining, intruding, or interfering in that tender moment when their little girl or boy become mother or father. Grandmothers are part of the family; they are not the head.

If only one grandmother is present at birth, she can phone the other, sharing details about the new grandchild and about that grandmother's wonderful child, now a parent. Thanksgiving could include both grandmothers, who divvy up the preparations, each hosting every other year, or a young couple can celebrate at their home, inviting both sets of grandparents. If a grandmother feels excluded, she can diplomatically say how she feels—without accusing anyone or demanding attention.

With careful listening, the grandmothers might care for each other. Sons and daughters, in-law or not, do not want to be cruel to their mothers. But they are riveted on their tiny new child; they may not notice anyone else. The grandmother can do that.

Leslie Stahl writes about the other grandmother, Barbara, who arrived when the baby (Jordan) was one day old: "When she held Jordan, Barbara assumed the grandmother stare, that gaze of soft-eyed enchantment." Leslie found it hard "to share the new center of our life with basically strangers. . . . Handing Jordan over to Barbara was wrenching."

Two years later, when Leslie did some research on grandmothers, she read that the father's mother often feels excluded. She bravely asked Barbara whether "being a grandmother is bittersweet merely because she's the father's mother." The answer: "I do have resentment. Financially, we can't afford to go see them . . . you can do that, and that hurts."[8]

Hearing that, a grandmother might buy plane tickets for the less affluent grandmother. Or at least she might remember to include the other grandmother. When I wrote this, I suddenly realized that I am glad that Asa and Isaac's other grandmother is three thousand miles away. As a result, I am the only grandmother who sees the boys several times each week.

That thought led me to write to their other grandmother, detailing some of the wonderful things the boys do. For example, Asa sometimes is so engrossed in his book that he does not reply to me. She misinterpreted my letter, thinking my joy in their personal quirks was a complaint. That reveals another reason why communication between grandmothers needs to begin at birth: rare missives may be misunderstood.

The new grandmother also needs to remember several other people: the grandfather, the aunts and uncles, the cousins, and the new parents. Some professionals (nurses, doctors) imply that they are the only ones who know how to care for a baby. Grandmothers need to counter that. They must resist the impulse to take charge: no one learns how to parent when someone else says, "No. Let me do it."

Happily, about three hundred hospitals in the United States are certified as *baby friendly*, which requires that everyone encourage mother care, including breastfeeding immediately after birth, especially if the birth was traumatic, if the baby was preterm, or if either mother or baby has special needs.[9]

If the baby is the second born, the parents already know a lot about newborn care, but the grandmother needs to remember the older grandchild. Psychologists write that firstborns are *dethroned* when the second born arrives.[10] That must be an exaggeration: surely no parent treats firstborns like royalty and then pushes them off the throne when a new baby arrives.

But imagine that the love of your life brought home a new partner, much smaller and younger, whose every whimper led to carrying, cuddling, and feeding, all day and night. This new person slept beside your love and was kept nearby all day. You had to sleep elsewhere and were told to be quiet, lest you wake the new arrival. If you were very good, you were allowed to hold the new person on your lap.

Your lover tells you that he loves you now more than ever. Do you believe it? Would you welcome the interloper, staying out of the way by feeding and dressing yourself? Would you admire that tiny creature who cries and never plays or even smiles? Visitors bring baby gifts, coo at how cute the baby is, and might even say "Glad this one is a girl (or boy)." Dethroned?

Once System 2 allows rational thought and empathy, the grandmother role is obvious: reach out to the other grandmother, respect the new parents, and give special attention to older siblings. Birth is a family event; everyone needs grandmothering.

LESSON 8: RECOGNIZE BIRTH AS A PIVOT

Attention to the entire family and giving each couple the privacy they want are crucial lessons, but there is another priority that, for a moment, might conflict: Try to see, hold, and bond with each grandchild within hours after birth. Get on a plane, jump on a bike, cancel a concert, leave work—whatever.

By now grandmothers have learned not to ask about fetal sex, name, or activity if the new parents want privacy. But early connection triggers hormones in adults as well as babies: a stronger connection forms at birth than a few weeks later. If parents hesitate to let you hold the baby, explain that you need contact for your joy and sanity. Don't gush, make sure your hands and clothes are clean, wait patiently, leave quickly if requested—whatever. But know that the first days of life are prime time for human love: a flood of hormones and neurotransmitters make early contact like a bolt of sudden lightening, priming everyone.[11]

That is why, in all of human history, birth is laden with emotion, ritual, and memories; it changes life forever, with hormonal rushes, role changes, and new names. We celebrate birthdays; new parents recount moment-by-moment details of labor; family Bibles and paid statisticians meticulously record every birth; and the United Nations General Assembly states that every newborn has a right to be registered—although in the poorest nations, perhaps as many as one child in four is not.[12] Those newborns are also most likely to die uncounted.

The moments of bonding after birth literally mean survival for a kid—if the kid is actually a kid. Mother goats butt away their own bleating, hungry babies if they do not nuzzle, lick, and smell them soon after birth. From this barnyard fact, in the 1980s, social scientists sanctified mother-infant bonding, finding that mothers who held their newborns immediately after birth were less likely to abuse those children later on.[13]

Unfortunately, that conclusion was amplified and exaggerated, making some mothers feel guilty and keeping some non-mothers away. Yes, immediate contact is crucial for sheep and goats, and yes, grandmothers should try to hold the newborn. But if this does not happen, humans have many other threads to tie the family members together. The birth link is a strong one, but it is not essential.

Newborns who are adopted or born by C-section to an unconscious woman, or whose caregivers arrive days after birth, may be loved as much or more than newborns held immediately by parents who cut the cord. Ideally, however, early contact triggers the love that will sustain the child, the parents, and the grandparents for decades.

Biology combines with thoughts and experiences.[14] Oxytocin, vasopressin, and other hormones flood the birthing mother's brain, but many people who did not give birth—including fathers and grandmothers—also experience bonding hormones. The brain literally restructures itself in reaction to birth and infant care.

As explained in chapter 2, unlike many other mammals, humans welcome *allomothers*—people who are not birth mothers but care for children. This benefits mother and child, of course, but also pulls the allomothers into the intimate circle of care.

Allomothering benefits from early contact with a newborn. Whoever sees and holds the infant is pushed, physiologically as well as psychologically, to connect with that tiny human. One neuroscientist explains, "Seeing infants appears to elicit motivation to care in all adult members of the species, which may have functioned to enhance infant survival throughout human history when many mothers died at childbirth, thus leaving infants to nonparental care."[15]

Traditionally, grandmothers were often the first to welcome a newborn, cleaning, cradling, and feeding (with her own breast milk) before the mother was able to do so. In many cultures, the new arrival is immediately part of the family clan: grandmother care cements multigenerational bonds. In nineteenth-century North America, "granny" was another word for "midwife" because many early midwives were, in fact, grandmothers.

In some African groups, when birth was imminent, mothers returned to their natal home until the baby was several weeks old.[16] In many traditional Japanese and Chinese families, new mothers "do the month," which includes living with their mothers or mothers-in-law, who prepare special foods and care for them and the newborn. All these examples imply that our species has known for centuries that grandmothers should be allomothers from the start.

We do not have solid science confirming the benefits of grandmothers at birth. However, suggestive evidence comes from research on fathers in the United States. In most of the twentieth century, fathers were excluded from births. Now most hospitals expect fathers to be present, mopping foreheads, timing contractions, and holding the newborn. That shift parallels another dramatic shift: fathers have become active caregivers—changing diapers, bathing babies, reading to toddlers, preparing meals for preschoolers.[17] Is there a causal connection? Do men become more involved caregivers if they are present at birth?

Perhaps. We know that birth changes men biologically as well as psychologically: men shift "from mating to parenting . . . link[ing] lower paternal testosterone to increased caregiving."[18] For both parents, hormonal and neurological changes promote caregiving and strengthen the bond between them: typically mothers and fathers feel a rush of love for each other when they share in the birth.

Fathers at birth may affect grandmothers as well. In one study, 241 unmarried women were interviewed six times: when they were 6 months pregnant, at birth, a day or two after birth, and 4, 12, and 24 months after that.[19] The fathers were sorted in two groups: 140 present at birth, 101 not. The researchers controlled for many factors, including marriage plans, infant's sex, mother's education, and father's drug abuse.

Whether a father was at the birth was not necessarily related to his wishes or to his relationship to the mother: some fathers wanted to be at the birth but could not be (because of their jobs, or because the birth was too quick), and some fathers were present but did not plan to be. In the first months of the baby's life, as reported by the mothers, the father's presence at birth made little difference, but at twenty-four months, it did. Those fathers who saw their baby being born did more direct caregiving, paid more bills, were involved in decisions about the child, and talked and played with their toddlers. That affected the paternal grandmothers as well: if their sons had witnessed the birth, those grandmothers were more involved with their grandchildren than if their sons had not.

My advice for grandmothers to hold newborns may trouble those women who gave birth a few decades ago. One set of experts explains, "Today, although many women may want their own mothers' help during labor, most of today's grandmothers are not experienced around birth. The experience of women who gave birth in the 1960s and 1970s may not have been ideal."[20]

"Not have been ideal" is an understatement. Obstetric interventions (including forceps, surgery, episiotomies), general anesthesia that sedated birthing women, being separated from one's baby, who was fed formula by the nurses—all this was routine when grandmothers and great-grandmothers gave birth. A study that asked grandmothers about breastfeeding reveals the contrast.[21] One grandmother said, "Well, my pediatrician told me that I would be stupid to even try to do that if I planned on going back to work . . . it definitely not only was not encouraged, it was severely discouraged." Another said, "That's 35 years ago, and I didn't really get any encouragement to breastfeed or anything. They started feeding both of my children cereal in their bottles before they were ever brought to me . . . probably the third day."

This discussion raises a question: Who should be present at birth? Answers have changed every few decades, from "only grannies" to "only doctors and nurses" to "doctors or nurse-midwives" and now to many possible helpers: midwives, fathers, nurses, grandmothers, and doulas.

We can be glad that grandmothers are more welcome than they were, although, as chapter 1 illustrates, not every hospital understands grandmothers. Their importance for newborns is evident in the question a doctor asks mothers whose newborn is suffering from opioid addiction: "How do we get you here or dad here or grandma here? . . . Because that's what your baby needs."[22] "Here" is a quiet, private room at the hospital, where addicted newborns require less medication and hospitalization than the standard, non-caregiver treatment. To be specific, in standard care, addicted babies are hospitalized an average of twenty-two days. However, when dedicated family members provide calming care, the average stay is only six days. Addicted babies need someone—a father or grandmother is as acceptable as a mother—to ease them into a healthy life.[23]

Three cautionary comments need to be added to the advice for grandmothers to be at the birth if possible.

First, many women do not want their mothers at the actual birth. The reasons are deep, and change is needed, but birth is not the time to effect that change. One doula says that she is sometimes hired because the expectant woman wants to keep her own mother at bay. Grandmas, she adds, "are expected to be wise, helpful, knowledgeable, strong and responsible, until they are suddenly expected to be silent or disappear, and then somehow know when to return."[24]

Leslie Stahl and her husband flew across the country when their daughter, Taylor, began labor. In the hospital,

> *Aaron and I followed her cues and forced ourselves into a state of artificial nonchalance. . . . Just as I was about to let loose my pent-up anxiety with a bellowing, "Where the hell is the goddam doctor?" in he sauntered. . . . [He asked,] "Will your parents stay?" To my disappointment, Taylor said no. So Aaron and I slouched off to the empty waiting room.*[25]

Second, some grandmothers are not helpful. Bethany let me be present; I had attended birthing classes and practiced massage, but, as you read in chapter 3, when her contractions got intense, I was grateful that the doula pounded her back, held her in the shower, and told her when to change position. I lurked, silently crying, in the shadows.

The third cautionary note is that instant adoration eludes some grandmothers, even those present at the birth, as it does some mothers and fathers. Delayed bonding may be related to the circumstances of the pregnancy, to the drugs at birth, to hospital procedures and personnel, or to attitudes either in the culture or in the mother, father, and grandmother. But no matter what the reason, birth is a starting bell: grandmothers need to get ready for the next lessons.

LESSON 9: PREVENT POSTPARTUM DEPRESSION

Once every prospective mother had a simple hope—to survive. Death was looming, not only in poor nations but also in developed ones, for mothers as well as babies. In 1900 in North America, one woman died for every one hundred births, more often with a first birth than with a later one.[26] If she died, her baby almost always died, but if she lived, the baby still often died. Only half of the newborns survived.

My own grandmother, in Minnesota, bore sixteen children. Of the first six, four were dead by age one. She was a woman of strong faith: she thanked God for her own life and for her two surviving children. Some of her childhood friends died in childbirth.

But that situation has changed—first for our ancestors (Grandmother's ten later babies all survived) and now for our descendants. Medical research and technology have transformed birth—with sterilization, anesthesia, monitoring, induction, intravenous drugs, epidurals, episiotomies, Cesareans, and much more. With that, hopes have changed. Prospective mothers write birth plans, expecting minimal pain, moderate medical assistance, and maximum personal control, with music!

Both of those sets of innovations, the medical ones and the personal ones, increase another danger—postpartum depression. The incidence in the United States is now about one in every seven births.[27] This danger does not appear immediately—the incidence of maternal depression rises over the first six weeks; the harm to babies is evident at age one and beyond. However, this topic appears in this chapter because prevention begins at birth.

Contemporary grandmothers are no longer the angels who protected life, as documented from historical records and as reported in chapter 2, but they can be defenders against despair. Indeed, they are ideally suited for that role, unlike fathers, who can be depressed also, or a new mother's friends, who, ignorant of the depths of postpartum depression, may comment that the baby is beautiful and the woman is fortunate. Such comments can increase despair. Grandmothers know at least that moods change over time. They also can provide crucial baby care: infants need talking, smiling, singing, cuddling, and carrying, all of which are difficult for depressed parents to do.

Knowing the causes and sequence makes prevention of postpartum depression possible. Education helps (rates are half as high for women with a college education than women without one),[28] and poverty and prejudice hurt (low-income Latinas have twice the rate of the national average).[29] Married and cohabiting mothers are less likely to develop postpartum depression, but being a single parent (only one grandmother) doubles the risk.[30] All this suggests that knowledge, practical help, financial support, and social connections are prophylactic—and grandmothers can provide each of these.

Postpartum depression is related to depression at other times of life. But rates increase in the weeks after birth, in part because of the discrepancy between the ideal and the actual. Some pain and sleep deprivation are inevitable, few babies are as perfect as the ads depict (real newborns have splotchy skin, misshapen heads, no chins, skinny legs). Another reason for the increase is that the very technology that makes birth easier and safer than it once was also makes it more difficult for other women to help the new mother.

To be specific, new medical procedures are added and old ones abandoned every decade, with each hospital and sometimes each doctor inclined to implement different technology. As a result, a woman's birth experience is unlike those of her friends, sisters, and certainly her mother. That adds stress, especially if parents and grandparents question why particular medical measures were used. Birth almost never follows the birth plan or repeats what the grandmother experienced.

Consider one medical measure in detail: the Cesarean. Before the twentieth century, a Cesarean always meant that death was imminent. Emergency surgery was a last-ditch attempt to save a mother or a baby. Even in midcentury in the United States, when surgery had become safer, only one in twenty births was by C-section. As a girl, I was asked what I would choose: saving the life of a mother or a newborn. That was supposed to encourage moral reasoning; instead, I thought birth was hazardous.

Now, in some nations, Cesareans are less risky than vaginal births. They are quicker, painless, and the newborn looks healthier than babies who have spent hours squeezing through the birth canal. The woman can be conscious because only her lower half is anesthetized. In some circumstances (multiple births, fetal distress, breech position), doctors prefer Cesareans to avoid potential lawsuits and possible complications, especially anoxia (lack of oxygen), which can damage the brain.[31]

Given all those benefits, although birth plans almost never include them, one in every three U.S. births is by Cesarean. The immediate advantages may be dwarfed by later disadvantages: more anesthesia, longer hospital stays, higher medical bills, more pain and moodiness when the drugs wear off, less breastfeeding, less frequent newborn care, more frequent complications in the mother (higher risk of infections) and in the child (including later allergies, asthma, and obesity).

All those factors are physiological, and each increases the rate of postpartum depression. Even more crucial may be the mother's thoughts and memories about her experience: cognition is now recognized as crucial for mood disorders. The evidence finds that cognitive therapy is the most effective long-term treatment for depression. (Anti-depressant drugs are quicker, but effects may not endure.) Thus the mother's anticipation of a happy, uplifting birth may itself become a cause of depression.

That may explain a curious finding: if a mother born in Canada has a Cesarean, she is at higher risk of postpartum depression than a Canadian who had a vaginal birth, but if a mother born elsewhere has a Cesarean in Canada, she is at lower risk.[32] Perhaps Canadian mothers were more likely to have hopeful birth plans that were dashed by surgery, but immigrant mothers, who knew women who suffered because obstetrical surgery was unavailable, were grateful.

Depression may also be affected by the timing of the C-section. If it occurs before a rush of oxytocin starts labor, and if the mother does not breastfeed (perhaps because surgery makes breastfeeding difficult), then oxytocin may be low, and that correlates with postpartum depression. If a C-section occurs after a long labor that does not progress, the mother's birth ideal—short labor, no surgery—is doubly trashed.

For grandmothers, the need to support new parents in the first days and months after birth is obvious, especially if surgery was involved. If one's own son or daughter is low in energy, spends too much time in bed, cries often, eats too little, and rarely goes out, every mother knows she must provide extra care and, if improvement is not apparent, get professional help. The latter may be crucial: depressed new mothers and fathers blame themselves, and they are less likely to seek treatment than depressed people who are not new parents.[33]

It is also crucial for grandmothers to support the father and the baby. Men are taught to hide their feelings, so only the grandmother may realize that the father needs support. Infant brains grow faster than any other part of their bodies in the first year, so the grandmother's attention may be crucial when the mother is depressed.[34]

Do not expect doctors or nurses to diagnose depression. If there are no medical complications, most mothers and newborns are discharged a day or two after birth, too soon to predict the mother's emotional state. Insurance—public or private—does not pay for additional days in the hospital.[35] Many new parents feel euphoric at birth and then overwhelmed a week after coming home.

Fortunately, postpartum depression can be prevented, diagnosed, and treated.[36] A widely used screening measure, the Edinburgh Postnatal Depression scale, asks women to respond to ten statements about how they felt *in the past week.*

1. *I have been able to laugh and see the funny side of things*
     0—As much as I always could
     1—Not quite so much now
     2—Definitely not so much now
     3—Not at all
2. *I have looked forward with enjoyment to things*
     0—As much as I ever did
     1—Rather less than I used to
     2—Definitely less than I used to
     3—Hardly at all
3. *I have blamed myself unnecessarily when things went wrong*
     3—Yes, most of the time
     2—Yes, some of the time
     1—Not very often
     0—No, never

4. *I have been anxious or worried for no good reason*
    0—No, not at all
    1—Hardly ever
    2—Yes, sometimes
    3—Yes, very often

5. *I have felt scared or panicky for no very good reason*
    3—Yes, quite a lot
    2—Yes, sometimes
    1—No, not much
    0—No, not at all

6. *Things have been getting on top of me*
    3—Yes, most of the time I haven't been able to cope at all
    2—Yes, sometimes I haven't been coping as well as usual
    1—No, most of the time I have coped quite well
    0—No, I have been coping as well as ever

7. *I have been so unhappy that I have had difficulty sleeping*
    3—Yes, most of the time
    2—Yes, sometimes
    1—Not very often
    0—No, not at all

8. *I have felt sad or miserable*
    3—Yes, most of the time
    2—Yes, quite often
    1—Not very often
    0—No, not at all

9. *I have been so unhappy that I have been crying*
    3—Yes, most of the time
    2—Yes, quite often
    1—Only occasionally
    0—No, never

10. *The thought of harming myself has occurred to me*
    3—Yes, quite often
    2—Sometimes
    1—Hardly ever
    0—Never

The total score ranges from 0 to 30. Below 9 indicates no problem, 9–12 suggests normal baby blues, above 12 indicates depression. High scores indicate that more intense screening by a trained clinician is needed to discern whether the new mother is truly depressed, anxious, or suicidal. (A 2 or 3 on question 10 is alarming, even if the rest are 0 or 1.)

Grandmother help is needed long before that point.

Any problem in the baby—feeding difficulties, blotchy skin, jaundice, low birth weight, misshapen head, and much more—might trigger feelings of disappointment and self-blame. Both parents also have personal worries—mothers that their shape is still far from normal, and fathers that they are not the providers and helpmates they want to be. All new parents have reasons to be depressed. Grandmothers need to praise and help without making the couple feel inadequate.

One final caution: Although some traditions are wonderful, some are not. This is easier to see in a culture far from standard American. You already read about the Chinese custom of "doing the month," which may benefit mothers and grandmothers. However, in Chinese tradition, mothers were told not to bathe or leave the house for that month.[37] That advice is contrary to what is now known: self-care, cleanliness, and going out are antidotes to depression. Wise Chinese grandmothers now modify the month.[38]

All the lessons of this book can apply at every age, in every culture. Beginning at birth, grandmothers can reduce the stress of parenthood and increase the joy.

· 9 ·

Infants

$\mathcal{I}$s infant care, 24/7, the most stressful work that life entails? Other tasks are harder—ending a love affair, cleaning the basement, walking home on a dusty road after a long, hot day. But they are time limited; it helps to think about an iced drink soon.

Baby care, by contrast, is never finished until babies are able to care for themselves. Infants require hours, days, weeks, months, of repetitive care. One of my students said that she wished she could diaper her baby six times at once and then skip a day. Baby care robs sleep, shreds plans, undermines marriages. According to the Gottmans (famed for research on thousands of romantic partnerships), "for the majority of couples the arrival of the first baby is a catastrophe for their love relationship."[1]

Why catastrophe? Psychologists suspect that dozens of repeated hassles (small, stressful experiences) hurt body and mind more than any single trauma, especially in families.[2] Hassles impair hearts, hormones, and immune systems. For example, washing the dishes is a daily hassle because it entails scrubbing plates and pots again and again, knowing that they will soon be dirty again. That takes a greater toll on well-being than cleaning the basement once a decade. Family life is littered with hassles.[3]

Infants are supreme hassle makers: they need diapering, feeding, cleaning, over and over. Charts of marital satisfaction show a rise in the honeymoon period, a rise during pregnancy and birth, and then a dip during infancy.[4] It does not rebound until adolescence (for the fathers) and early adulthood (for the mothers).

Infant care decreases happiness more for mothers than fathers, especially if the mother is college educated and under age twenty-five. Every new parent sometimes feels troubled by lost sleep, reduced intimacy, interrupted relaxation. Most also feel joy. Grandmothers appreciate both emotions, relieving the former and increasing the latter.

Grandmothers know the stress of infant care; most other people do not. Future parents are particularly unprepared for exhaustion, and instead anticipate the joy. A study of ninth-grade girls, half of whom had a lifelike doll (who cried, needed feeding, and so on) to care for over a weekend, found that four years later, those with the dolls were *more* likely to become pregnant before age twenty than their peers who did not have the doll.[5]

For everyone, tasks that seem simple and fun in fantasy (children enjoy dolls with diapers for a few days) become mind numbing in reality when repeated for months. That realization surprises some lighthearted new parents and plummets others into despair.

Fortunately, there are joys. Fathers as well as mothers enjoy childcare more than they enjoy paid employment, and far more than housework.[6] This is particularly true after age three, but infant care is programmed into the human psyche, preventing parents from dispassionate analysis of the costs of nurturing a baby.

Grandmothers' delight in baby care can make it worse for the parents, who want acknowledgment of the difficulty of the task rather than hearing grandma express the joy of it. That leads directly to the first lesson during infancy.

LESSON 10: NOTICE AND ADMIRE

My exhausted, breastfeeding, baby-caring, daughter said, with a half smile, "It's lucky he is so cute." She sought my admiration for her devotion; she thought he was adorable but also one of the most difficult babies ever. I believed that he was not only cute but also one of the best babies ever. Those reactions are inborn; such perceptions foster species survival. But infant care remains burdensome.

The stress lifts when someone else appreciates the work. Infants can't do that; their brains are too immature. Mothers and fathers can commend each other, but both may be overwhelmed. Grandmothers needed! Appreciation does not mean taking over, or even suggesting—unless with exquisite sensitivity. I lived with Bethany for the first weeks of Caleb's life. She did almost all the baby care, but she said she was glad I was there as a witness. Appreciation came easy: I was genuinely impressed that my daughter, who was once a self-absorbed teenager, had become a dedicated caregiver.

Several paragraphs ago, I wrote "grandmothers know the stress," but that shades the truth. Grandmother *should* know—been there, done that. But memory is selective, as struck me one night long ago.

I was sleeping soundly and peacefully, at 3 a.m., in my bed, a few feet from my fourth baby, Sarah, in her bassinette. Sleep is precious; I need it like a traveler across the Sahara needs water. Sarah whimpered; I listened for her to go back to sleep. She cried. My husband snored. I got up.

A sudden flash—was I insane? This pain was achingly familiar: I had endured three long stretches of it, night after night. What had possessed me to conceive this fourth child? I had celebrated when pregnancy was confirmed. I avoided drugs and alcohol, drank milk, ate liver, swallowed vitamins, kept numerous doctor's appointments, practiced breathing, saw my dentist, sewed maternity clothes—all with great joy for nine months. How had I forgotten it would come to this, rousing from deep sleep at 3 a.m.?

If an experienced mother forgets, no wonder new parents are taken aback.

Have I forgotten again? I wish we had had another child or two, I wish for more grandchildren. In retrospect, joy outweighs the pain. But early days are hard. Grandmothers must refresh their memories; parents need sympathy, admiration, and practical help. Reality clashes with the mirage, and with grandmothers' selective memory.

One new mother thought:

My only problem in life was that I didn't have a baby. On the day I had a baby, I discovered that no, I had other problems. I hadn't any money, I was in debt, the family was fighting about the debt, it was partly my fault . . . and I started to see I wasn't such a good mother as I had thought I would be. I used to think what could be difficult? It's enough for you to love the baby and everything will be fine. This didn't happen because the baby didn't respond. I'm affectionate, I'd come and take her, hug her and the baby didn't like this. She didn't like to be hugged, she didn't like affection.[7]

No one noticed and admired; this new mother became depressed. Her mother lived nearby but stayed away. I wish that grandmother had told her daughter that newborns do not smile in recognition until six weeks; that some hugging is rejected; that infants sometimes cry no matter what. (An average new baby cries two hours and fifteen minutes a day.)[8] Or at least commended her daughter for the hard work she did.

Baby care is like swimming. If you have done it often, you keep afloat when you jump into the water, even if you have not been in a pool for years. But if you toss a non-swimmer into the water, shouting "kick and paddle," they will flail, gasp, swallow water, and sink. Likewise, mothering is not instinctual, but after months of practice, it becomes automatic. My ninety-year-old mother dreamed happily of bathing her first child; that comforted her when a broken hip, combined with childhood polio, kept her in bed.

I had forgotten that I once did not know how to swim or hold a baby. I was sitting with Bethany, who held her firstborn, three-week-old Caleb. He was fussing. "Let me take him." "No, I don't want to give him to you when he is crying."

I was incredulous; who did she think I am? "I have held many crying babies."

Then I remembered. Brain scans confirm that new mothers are neurologically distressed when their baby cries.[9] No wonder Bethany thought crying would distress me. Her brain was on fire. She assumed mine would be, too.

Caleb's cries did not trouble me; I know that infants cry to communicate, seeking comfort or distraction. I also know how to respond. The following dozen suggestions come from my experience interwoven with research (and they may sound familiar to grandmothers):

1. *Feeding.* Breastfed babies may be hungry an hour or two after they have been fed. The solution: nurse again. Formula-fed babies may cry because they are too full. The solution: never entice babies to finish their bottle.
2. *Visual distraction.* Looking distracts infants. Grandmothers can make faces, take the baby to the window, or go outside to watch passing vehicles.
3. *Auditory distraction.* Newborns' most developed sense is hearing; they have been listening for months. That leads to five suggestions:

   - "Sh, sh, sh" is heard prenatally (the mother's gastro-intestinal or cardiovascular systems). Whispering "hush" and "shush" in the baby's ear is comforting.
   - The heartbeat is a familiar rhythm before birth. Newborns may quiet if held with an ear to the caregiver's left chest.
   - Infants are attuned to the human voice; soothing talk helps.
   - Change in tone and rhythm captures attention. That explains music. Babies are not music critics: off-key lullabies are appreciated more than speech.[10]
   - Background white noise—an air-conditioner, a vacuum cleaner, a fan, an audio recording of waves slowly lapping the shore—is soothing.

4. *Swaddling.* Being securely wrapped is reminiscent of the womb.
5. *Rocking.* Movement back and forth, or up and down, may calm a baby. That is why rocking chairs and birth balls are standard nursery equipment. Experiment with speed. Slow may be best.
6. *Traveling.* The motion of strollers, carriages, or cars puts many babies to sleep. Avoid red lights if possible.

7. *Taste.* A drop of water with sugar, ginger, or other ingredients is "gripe water"—not recommended for frequent use, but worth an occasional try.
8. *Sucking.* A small pacifier, designed for tiny mouths—may soothe. So may a finger (very clean, clipped nail).
9. *Massage.* Gentle rubbing of the arms, legs, and so on, is relaxing.
10. *Pressure on the stomach.* My husband sometimes held my infant daughters in the air, his big hand on their tiny bellies, small legs dangling. I said, "Don't drop them." He never did.
11. *Changing positions.* Experienced adults transfer babies from their shoulders, legs, chests, and laps, especially for burping. (Hugging rarely works.)
12. *Reduced stimulation.* Try laying the crying baby in the crib (face up, of course) and walking away. To feel less guilty, set a timer, promising both the baby and yourself that you will return if crying continues for three, five, or ten minutes.

Experienced caregivers have more than these dozen. Noticing and admiring means noticing how the caregiver feels and lifting the burden. A meta-analysis of one hundred studies found that, at every age, social encouragement protects against depression, with "instrumental support" (providing practical help when needed) particularly potent to combat adult depression.[11] I know that hearing your own baby cry is stressful for new parents (part of our human heritage that protects our young). That is why, when Bethany didn't want to give me her crying son, I reached for him. She handed Caleb over, and I took him outside.

I remembered the lessons above. I snuggled crying Caleb into the baby carrier so he was swaddled, close to my heart, and left the house, singing a lullaby with sh-sh-sh after each line. I walked down the block, rhythmically for Caleb, out of earshot for Bethany. He soon fell asleep.

Noticing and admiring sometimes leads to practical help, as it did in this moment, but it never includes criticism. Particulars of infant care vary from mother to mother; the grandchild's mother may have strategies unlike either grandmother's. Some of the twelve suggestions above strike some new mothers as foolish, wrong, or even abusive. Don't insist; this is not the time to argue about baby care. It is time to be sensitive to variations.

A common dispute is whether babies should be offered pacifiers. Doing so has strong advocates and vehement detractors. The simple need to soothe a crying baby escalates online to sudden infant death syndrome (SIDS: pro-pacifier) versus ear infections (language loss: anti-pacifier). Don't argue: Regarding every aspect of infant care, parents consult the internet and their friends—and they rarely ask grandmothers. If they do, the first response might be "What do you think?"

One grandmother writes, "When my daughter's first baby had colic and woke every twenty minutes, I suggested that she be left to cry a little before being picked up. My daughter glared at me, a thousand daggers. 'You would suggest that,' she said and burst into tears herself."[12]

That grandmother wrote, "Silence on certain issues is not just golden; it's essential."

Her suggestion arose from a wish to help her daughter, but the young mother thought it was cold and accusatory. Grandmothers know that sometimes nothing soothes a baby; mothers blame themselves and think that everyone else does, too.

About one baby in five cries more than three hours at a stretch, more than three days a week, in the first three months. That 3-3-3 is the definition of *colic*.[13] The cause might be overstimulation, since inconsolable crying is more common in the late afternoon, when the day's excitement might become too much. Or it might be digestive pain, since colicky babies pull up their legs as they scream.

In any case, colic usually emerges at one week, peaks at about six weeks and disappears by six months. Breastfeeding mothers wonder what they ate—onions, chocolate, broccoli, curry, beans, nuts—almost any food is suspect. Formula-feeding mothers wonder whether the baby is allergic to cow's milk. They fault themselves for not breastfeeding and try formulas made of goat's milk, soy milk, almond milk, and so on. Grandmothers need to undercut this self-blame, lest it turn to "child-blame." One mother of a colicky baby said, "There were moments when, both me and my husband . . . when she was apoplectic and howling so much that I almost got this thought, 'now I'll take a pillow and put it over her face just until she quietens down, until the screaming stops.'"[14]

That baby became a loved, happy four-year-old. But this quote shows why sympathy and respite are crucial. Colic is particularly upsetting if the mother is single and/or young, or has twins, or the colicky baby is her first. But remember my 3 a.m. waking from a sound sleep. I was a married, older, experienced parent when Sarah's cries made me doubt my sanity. I never smothered or shook her (I know about "shaken baby abusive head trauma"). However, I know that love and patience become scarce when babies cry. I try to remember that as a grandmother.

LESSON 11: AVOID ATTACHMENT WARS

Attachment is a strong, reliable bond between an infant and a caregiver. Ideally, every baby becomes securely attached to at least one person, so that every one-year-old explores toys and welcomes new experiences when a familiar, comforting adult is nearby. Insecure attachment (evident in about a third of all babies) is manifested not only by reduced play but also by clinging, hitting, or ignoring the caregiver.

Every psychologist knows that securely attached babies are likely to learn and explore. Some psychologists take this basic understanding further and advocate *attachment parenting*, an ideology that mandates immediate maternal response to babies day and night, with co-sleeping, daytime carrying, frequent and exclusive breastfeeding, and never letting a baby cry.[15]

Other psychologists disagree. Some who are critical of attachment parenting (also called "intensive mothering") promote self-soothing, independence, and individualism. Both perspectives are buttressed by psychological theory: Freud versus Skinner. Those two approaches to baby care are sometimes pitted against each other. It is a mistake for a grandmother to take sides, especially if the baby's mother is on the other side.

Some background provides perspective. Sigmund Freud wrote that mothers are a baby's first "love object." His psychoanalytic theory inspired John Bowlby, who in turn inspired Mary Ainsworth,[16] who studied mothers and infants in Uganda[17] and in Baltimore.[18]

One oft-cited study tracked twenty-six mother-infant pairs.[19] That study noted that when babies cried in their early months, some were ignored, while others were immediately picked up. By age one, those who were picked up cried less than those who were not picked up. Some psychologists concluded that early responsiveness produces happier children and thus that anyone (including many grandmothers) who feared "spoiling" a baby was wrong.

Attachment parenting originally excluded fathers.[20] Then evidence showed that some infants are securely attached to their fathers in addition to, or instead of, their mothers.[21] Other research found that babies can be attached to grandmothers or another caregiver, as long as the caregiver is an important person in the baby's life, responsive to their needs. Ideally, an infant is secure with the mother and with one or two other people.

The contrary ideology arose from behaviorism. John Watson and B. F. Skinner stressed that early experience teaches children how to deal with their emotions. Infants need to learn to comfort themselves, becoming confident individuals, not overly dependent on other people. Therefore, parents should let infants comfort themselves, rather than picking them up as soon as they cry, and let them play alone, so as to develop independence.

Each of these ideologies dominated advice to parents at different times. This is evident in Dr. Benjamin Spock's *Baby and Child Care*, a book that sold more than fifty million copies and was read by almost every North American mother. Spock was famous for respecting a mother's impulses (he wrote, "you know more than you think you know"), but his advice reflected the attachment debate. In the first edition, released in 1946, Spock wrote that babies should sometimes "cry it out," as behaviorists suggest. Then his advice changed: in the third through ninth editions, Spock advocated comforting a crying baby.

The fact that these opposite responses are based in ideology makes advocates on either side more vehement. Advocates on the behaviorism side accuse the attachment parents of spoiling children, who might become adults afraid to leave their mother's side, unable to grow up and form families of their own. Advocates on the psychoanalytic side accuse their opposites of child neglect, suggesting that their children will become adults who endure abuse to get scraps of love and affection, making irrational choices because of unmet needs in infancy.

That advocates of each parenting style are convinced that their way is best was found in a study of Dominican mothers living in Spain.[22] They were critical that wealthy Spaniards endorsed attachment parenting. The Dominicans were poor, with many children, and unable to provide the constant and close attention required by intensive parenting. However, instead of recognizing that attachment parenting was impractical, they thought that Spanish children suffered because they were not allowed to play unsupervised with other children and that Spanish mothers were selfish because they focused all their attention on their own child, neglecting other children.

As in this example, all parents believe their way is best; a grandmother's disagreement is ineffective and stressful.

Like most developmental researchers, I reject both extremes. Evidence worldwide confirms that babies with loving, responsive parents—no matter which ideology they follow—develop well. Best practice for grandmothers is to relieve stress, if possible, rather than to take sides. Indeed, both attachment parenting and behavior training arise from practical circumstances and historical conditions, not rational thought. A grandmother's past experiences may clash with current reality, but reducing parental stress is always good.

Sadly, some attachment advocates exclude grandmothers. For example, in Europe some adoptive parents forbid grandmothers to touch, or even visit, newly adopted children for months so attachment to parents can form.[23] In the United States, the classic book on attachment parenting says that the father's job is to keep grandmothers away and suggests that if she is allowed to babysit, "let grandma know you expect baby's cries to be attended to." That book continues: "Grandparents may be less than enthusiastic or even critical of attachment parenting. Go easy on them. Remember they grew up in a different era. They did the best they could with the advice and information they had."[24]

I react to that comment with fury. It belittles grandparents to say they "did the best they could." Attachment parenting may be ideal or it may not be. It depends. Good mothering comes in various forms; criticisms from grandmothers are rarely helpful, but not because grandmothers are ignorant, foolishly doing their inadequate best.

Even when grandmothers are right, the way to help their grandchildren is by listening and supporting the parents. One grandmother says she has scars on her tongue from having bitten it so often. Another demonstrates "zip the lip" when I ask whether she tells her children how to care for her grandchildren. A mantra often repeated by Australian grandmothers is "open arms and closed mouths,"[25] advice that is hard to follow. Of course, adults have learned never to tell strangers that they are too fat, or advise acquaintances that they should stop smoking, or to tell anyone that their underwear is showing. But when it comes to one's own grandchildren, the impulse to tell the parents what they are doing wrong may overwhelm good sense.

To illustrate this point, consider one common battle of this ideological war: "sleep training." The suggestion from attachment parenting is that infants sleep near their parents, either in the same bed or in a "co-sleeper" beside to the parents' bed. The suggestion arising from the opposite camp is to teach infants to sleep through the night in their cribs. In sleep training, parents are told to eliminate late-night crying by letting the baby cry alone for several minutes.[26] Attachment parents consider that practice cruel; other parents swear by it.

Leslie Stahl tried to do what her daughter wanted, which was to let the baby soothe herself. The two women were talking when Taylor cried in the other room. The mother said to let her cry, this was part of sleep training. The grandmother *thought* she was "totally impassive, nonjudgmental," keeping quiet as she knew she should be. Later, her husband told her that she said, "This is too cruel" and "What a bad idea" and "We never did this and you turned out all right."[27]

Another grandmother was visiting her daughter overnight when cries from her infant grandson awakened her. She tiptoed to his crib, put her hand on him, and murmured comforting words. He went back to sleep. As she left the room, she saw her daughter's shadow in the hall.

The next morning, her daughter excoriated her: "You did a very bad thing last night. We are teaching him to soothe himself; you put us back several months."

The grandmother recounted this incident as an example of her mothering skill and her daughter's neglect. She did not realize she had tiptoed into a pitched battle, joining the troops who opposed her daughter. Opposite sleep strategies within the same family are common—disputes arise between parents and between generations. If this grandmother had known about attachment wars, would she have avoided doing "a very bad thing"?

In both of these examples, the exhausted parents sought sleep training, and the visiting grandmothers wanted to comfort the crying baby. These reactions are opposite to the stereotypes of rigid elders and indulgent parents. That stereotype may have arisen a generation ago: currently the generational clash between *harsh* parenting and *indulgent* parenting (adjectives arising from opposite ideologies) more often finds the grandmothers more permissive. In any case, however, grandmothers need to avoid attachment wars: no child wins when grownups fight.

LESSON 12: DON'T FEED THE BABY, UNLESS . . .

Of course, babies need to be fed. But grandmothers must not feed the baby unless the mother gives explicit instructions. Some pediatricians recommend *exclusive* breastfeeding for the first six months. Since breastfeeding is difficult, especially in the early weeks, mothers need encouragement and a very good breast pump. On occasion, she might pump her milk, bottle it, and let the grandmother feed the baby. That is a bonding time for all three generations, earned by the relationship building that has gone on before.

But, again, be careful. I know one mother who was grateful that her mother-in-law came from abroad to help with newborn care. Because the grandmother was present, her daughter-in-law could nap, shower, shop—all luxuries for new mothers.

The infant was thriving on exclusive breastfeeding—or so his mother thought. Then she discovered an empty bottle of formula. Suspicious, she searched the house and found other empty bottles, in the trash, in the closet, and even a six-pack of full ones under her mother-in-law's bed, bought at the local drug store.

She was horrified, fearing that her baby's health was compromised. Confronted, the grandmother retorted, "I will not let my grandson starve."

The mother told her husband, "Your mother has to leave."

Those two women came from widely divergent cultures, which exacerbated the clash between mother and mother-in-law. But disputes about feeding can arise when a mother and her own mother are from the same community. A New York City career woman moved back to Iowa when she had her first child, working remotely so her mother could take care of the baby. At first all seemed well: the grandfather employed the son-in-law, and the grandmother was thrilled to provide infant care. Two years later, the mother told me, "I fired my mother."

She explained that her mother did not heed her repeated instructions not to give her toddler candy. She hired a caregiver who would follow her feeding advice. Her husband also quit and now works in another company. That family is still in Iowa, now with a second child; they see Grandma on holidays.

Food has always been a pivot for family life and central to grandmother care (note ads touting "Grandma's recipe"). That is why feeding can become a battle between the generations. Don't let it. Begin by understanding that feeding patterns reflect what children need—and those needs have recently metamorphosed. Now the world's major nutritional problem is obesity, a problem that begins in infancy.[28]

Fights about feeding are illustrated by the "milk wars."[29] Combatants choose breast milk or formula, influenced by their culture and cohort. To understand this war, history is needed.

As part of the demographic revolution noted in chapter 1, employment of mothers of young children has increased every decade. At first, breast pumps were crude and inefficient, and no workplace had private pumping areas. Nor was paid maternity leave available. Women who left their jobs to care for their newborns were replaced. So most employed women returned to work soon after giving birth, feeding babies with formula, advertised as ideal for infant nutrition.

In the United States, the nadir of breastfeeding was in 1971, when only 24 percent of U.S. babies were *ever* breastfed, and those were usually newborns of uneducated, unemployed mothers.

I remember those days. My devoted mother formula fed me because she thought that was best, unlike her "ignorant," immigrant mother who breastfed all sixteen babies. As a child of the sixties, I rebelled against established wisdom in many ways, including by breastfeeding my babies. I was fortunate in that my job provided paid sick leave, which I had never used, so I had a few weeks when I could breastfeed my newborn without losing my job. But before my first child was three months old, my pediatrician told me to feed her rice cereal, apple juice, and evaporated milk. No more breastfeeding. By six months, she ate meats, fruits, and vegetables that came from tiny jars. Supermarkets had many shelves of them.

In retrospect, my rebellious generation was strongly influenced by our elders. The few breastfed babies I knew were almost always weaned before their first tooth came in. So were mine. Breastfeeding was private: public breastfeeding was illegal (indecent exposure).

I had heard of a contrary view, touted by seven devout Catholic women. They rejected contraception (they had fifty-six children among them), shunned employment, and advocated breastfeeding. They founded La Leche League (named after a statue of the Madonna). Although I rejected much of their ideology, I read their book *The Womanly Art of Breastfeeding.*[30]

A decade after the first La Leche book appeared, twelve college-educated feminists (some of them professors) founded the Boston Women's Collective. They disputed what doctors (mostly male) said about female hormones, sexuality, conception, birth, menopause, and breastfeeding. In 1971, they published *Our Bodies, Ourselves*, which sold for 75 cents. (Many editions, some for adolescents, some for older women, followed.) I read that book, too, learning that breastfeeding was a symbol of women's liberation.

My cohort was at the vanguard of rapid social change from 1971 to 1981. One observer wrote about that decade:

Over the course of ten short years, it [breastfeeding] had been transformed from an archaic practice that limited women's freedom into an important moral and political activity that protected vulnerable mothers and children against the predatory practices of greedy corporations. It was also a symbol of solidarity in the struggle against world poverty and hunger.[31]

This ideological fervor was fueled by opposition to one particular company (Nestle) that sold infant formula (predating coffee and chocolate) beginning at the end of the nineteenth century. To increase global profits, in the 1960s Nestle hired local women in Africa, dressed them in starched white uniforms, and sent them to birthing mothers, with feeding advice and free formula. By the time the free gift was used up, the women's breast milk had dried up (milk supply depends on frequent sucking). Millions of poor African women bought formula and added non-sterile water, thus increasing both corporate profits and infant deaths.

Those two American groups—the religious women who saw breastfeeding as a womanly art, and the secular women who saw it as symbol of female power—combined to make breastfeeding a moral act. Millions of American women boycotted Nestle and breastfed their babies. I was one of them.

Some of these breastfeeding young women became scientists, documenting over the past three decades that breast milk reduces allergies, increases immunity, and produces healthier children—contrary to the 1950s assumptions. Currently pediatricians (often women, another revolution) advise women to breastfeed *exclusively* (no juice or water) for the first six months. In 2015 in the United States, 81 percent of newborns were breastfed, unlike the 24 percent fifty years ago. More than half of all U.S. babies are still breastfed at six months, as are a sizable minority of one-year-olds.[32] Between 1990 and 2016, every state exempted breastfeeding from laws against indecent exposure.

I considered myself a moral crusader when I breastfed my first two babies. Like many women in my cohort, I was employed full time: I bicycled home midday to nurse. As advice from feminists and doctors changed, I breastfed my later two daughters a few months longer than my first two. It never occurred to me, my pediatrician, or any woman I knew to breastfeed exclusively for six months; yet that is what my daughters did, joining many other women of their cohort.

My experience makes cohort differences salient; my reading makes cultural differences obvious as well. Fewer French babies are breastfed after three months than are English babies. At that age, babies can be enrolled in crèches, which are publicly funded day care centers. That reflects cultural fears: French mothers have "a pervasive worry about mothers being enslaved (esclavage) to their children who could easily become infant kings (l'enfant roi)."[33] No wonder French women stop breastfeeding earlier than their sisters across that tiny channel.

International differences are more dramatic. Most Western babies are weaned by one year, but many children in developing nations are breastfed until age four. In some places, breastfeeding is not allowed until the milk "comes in" about three days after birth;[34] in others, colostrum is thought to be vital for newborns, and thus breastfeeding begins in the delivery room.[35]

As a North American mother, grandmother, and scientist, I am convinced that breast is best, containing essential nutrients for brain and body, developing a protective microbiome. I have read books that convince me that benefits continue, with higher IQs, less obesity, longer lives.[36] I regret weaning my babies before six months.

But history keeps me from being a zealot. Some women have problems with milk supply, some babies have great difficulty latching on, and exclusive breastfeeding may sideline fathers and older children and increase guilt in employed mothers, especially those with little money. Given the heated political climate, grandmothers and mothers need to put down the weapons and remember the goal: thriving babies, happy families, no intergenerational wars.

· *10* ·

Young Children

$\mathcal{C}$urious, playful, emotional, eager to explore—young children are a joy and a handful. From ages two to six, vocabulary increases by several words each day; shrieks of laughter and bursts of tears become regulated; bodies, muscles, and brain maturation enable somersaulting, cartwheeling, bicycling, tree climbing—all dependent on practice, opportunity, and guidance. Obviously, young children have much to learn. Grandmothers can be crucial.

The impulse to help is natural: that's what grandmothers are driven to do. Exuberant, excitable preschoolers need someone to appreciate their magical imagination while keeping them safe. Most grandmothers can meet that challenge: they tend to be more patient, supportive, and perceptive with their grandchildren than they had been with their children, more likely to discuss than to punish.[1] Children need that, especially at this age: they are verbal but not logical, more creative than wise.

Some intergenerational clashes are inevitable. Priorities differ by generation: grandparents want to transmit values, parents want practical assistance, and grandchildren want fun. All three are possible: More lessons needed.

LESSON 13: AVOID ASSUMPTIONS

Do grandmothers know how to care for children? Of course. They did it for years. It is tempting to pass on that hard-won knowledge to younger parents. But parents may consider this advice dated and reject it. A greeting card, designed for daughters-in-law to send to mothers-in-law, reads, "I do not need your advice about how to raise children. I live with one of yours, and he needs a lot of improvement."

It is easy to assume that raising a child has not changed much. Certainly, basic needs have been the same for centuries. But new challenges and customs arise every decade: grandmothers cannot assume that what they did when their children were young is still best.

I thought I knew what to do one morning when I was designated to wake three-year-old Asa and get him breakfasted, dressed, and to nursery school because his parents had to work early. They had told me what to fix for breakfast and laid out his clothes. But they forgot to prepare his lunch. I could have phoned them, but I have packed thousands of school lunches. I assumed that they would thank me for not interrupting their work.

I searched the cupboards and fridge. No juice boxes, baloney, pretzels—my old stand-bys. Just as well, that was too much sugar and salt. I thought of peanut butter and jelly, but I proudly remembered that Asa's school is peanut free. I found cream cheese, a bagel, an apple, a granola bar, and, in the refrigerator door, some bite-sized, wrapped candies. Asa's parents do not give him candy, except as a treat, but I didn't want him to resent me or my lunch; I threw in two of them.

The next day, my daughter told me that Asa was suspicious when he opened his lunch box. He showed the granola bar to his teacher, who read that it contained peanuts and told him not to unwrap it.

That was my first mistake.

Two days later, his mother sent me an email. The subject line: "Did you give these to Asa for lunch?" (with a photo of a bright red and yellow package). Then a four-word message: "They are dog treats."

Insulted, because a glance at the photo showed a dog, I wrote back, "No. I know they are dog treats."

She replied, "Oh, good. He asked me whether they were good for him. I told him they were dog treats. He said he had two of them in his lunch the day you packed the granola bar. He ate one of them but didn't eat the other because it didn't taste good. He must be confused."

That jogged my memory. I reluctantly wrote:

I am sorry, chagrined, and embarrassed. He might not be confused. There were two little things in the door of the refrigerator, not in the box (which I know are dog treats) wrapped up (they didn't say dog treats) and I put them in his lunch. From now on, I will always ask you or Oscar what to put in lunch [remember, I also packed a granola bar with nuts].

She replied:

Okay, well he seems to have survived fine. It's funny because some of our dog treats are healthy enough for human consumption but those are the cheapest kind we have and, if I was going to have Asa eat any of our dog stuff, it would be the last on my list.

I think you shouldn't pack lunch or snacks for Asa. We should do that from now on. It is odd, given how smart and competent you are generally, that this is just a task that seems a struggle for you. It's no big deal for us to make sure we take responsibility for feeding him.

Oscar finds the whole thing hilarious.

My final post on this episode:

My mother told me that I, as an infant, saw some of our dog's deworming pills on the counter and ate them. She said I cried a lot, and my beloved grandmother held me in her arms and rocked me while my mother called the doctor. He laughed, said not to worry, I would be fine.

Yes, I imagine dog treats would be harmless for people, but I wouldn't give him any—even the highest on your list. Since you forgot to pack lunch that day, I thought I was doing you a favor. This does not relate to my competence, but to my ignorance. Mortified, but wiser. Mom.

Wiser, yes. Good intentions and past experience led to false assumptions from all three of us, beginning with me. I assumed that those little things were candy; Asa thought that if I put them in his lunch box, he should eat them; Elissa concluded that I am incompetent at feeding her child. I am glad she asked, forgave, and wrote that she and Oscar would take responsibility.

Was I forever barred from feeding him? Thankfully, no. Since then I have prepared dozens of meals and bought hundreds of snacks. Lesson learned: do not assume that I know best. Now, if Elissa asks me to buy milk, I ask size, brand, fat content, organic or not, cow, soy, or almond. Unlike when I shop for myself, when I buy groceries for that family:

- I bring my reading glasses so I can read small print;
- I check expiration dates;
- I avoid corn syrup; and
- I find food with no added sugar.

One of the flashpoints in many grandmother/parent/grandchild interactions is food, as it is part of grandmothers' evolutionary heritage to make sure that the children eat enough. As grandmothers are well aware, every cohort hears different advice about food. Grandmothers remember that eggs, butter, beef, sugar, nuts, whole milk, pasta, and more have been considered life saving and life shortening. I often consume day-old salad, crusty bread, and browning bananas that my daughters want to put in the compost. My love of leftovers is a family joke, but I have learned not to feed them to my grandchildren.

That granola bar was a small example of a big truth: hundreds of details of current childrearing are unknown to grandmothers. Early on, I suggested taking a taxi ("Mom, no car seat!"); I put diapers on backwards (bewildered by non-sticking tabs); I did not know that teeth brushing is part of a two-year-old's bedtime routine; I mistakenly offered adult toothpaste. I probably made dozens of other mistaken assumptions, still unknown, and thus not written about here. My challenge is not to convince Asa's parents that I am right but to respect their ideas that I think are wrong. If I were convinced that my grand-

Likely customers? Other grandmothers.
Warren Miller, CartoonCollections.com.

children were seriously harmed, and if I then talked to a friend who would restrain me from overstepping, I might say something. But the default is to remember how difficult parenting is, and how diverse good parents are, and be supportive, not critical.

Being supportive rather than corrective is also needed for the children themselves. Young children are great at learning new words (they repeat almost anything, from curses to medical terminology) but impaired in logic. Some simple ideas, such as that the amount of liquid does not change if it is poured into another container (an idea called "conservation"), or that a dead person cannot be awakened, or that their father does not want a toy car for his birthday, are beyond them. These are rightly called the "magic years"; logic comes later.

Some grandmothers understand this concept. One enjoyed asking her young grandson, Harper, about the benign ganglion (a lump of jelly-like fluid) on his wrist.[2]

What do you have there, Harp?

It's my synovial cyst.

She asked him this often; she loved hearing him sound like a physician.

When his mother was pregnant, Harper told Grandma a secret about the lump on his arm:

There's a baby in there, Tata.

Instead of correcting his concept of cysts and fetuses, she said,

Well, can you feature that?

Months later, when Harper first visited his newborn brother, Grandma was waiting for him in the hospital lobby. He ran to her and held up his arm, puzzled:

I still have my baby.

Again, she listened and nodded. A few months later, the cyst reabsorbed. Harper was not at all surprised.

Throughout, Grandma did not assume he could use the same logic that she could. She did not tell him that she was worried about the cyst, that he did not have a baby, or that she was grateful when it disappeared. She listened.

I wish I could write that I no longer make mistaken assumptions about what my grandsons and my daughters need from me. But three years later, I was in my bedroom, reading about grandmothers. I overheard Bethany with five-year-old Caleb and six-year-old Asa.

Now Asa, you can pour this in there.

Caleb, stir it carefully.

No, not like that.

I heard quarreling, rivaling, pushing noises from the boys, and I heard my daughter trying to keep them cooperative and engaged.

My hypocrisy hit me: I was reading about grandmothering when I should be doing it. My assumptions about what I heard led to self-blame; I could not concentrate. I closed my book and walked to the kitchen.

Me: "Do you want to go to the playground with me?"

One grandson: "Yes."

One grandson: "No."

Bethany: "It's fifty-fifty."

Me: "No, three people should vote, not two. I wanted to help you."

Bethany: "We are fine. We are making rice pudding."

Me: "I thought you needed a break."

Bethany: "I am fine."

All three seemed engaged in pudding creation. Both boys were polite, puzzled at my playground offer. Their quarreling was part of being cousins—no problem for either of them. I had assumed that Bethany wished I would intervene, that she was annoyed that I was behind my closed door, that the boys were about to fight. Not, not, and not. I returned to my room, chastened.

Why did I jump from witness to rescue? I misconstrued what I heard. I imagined a problem, assumed I knew the solution, and then acted on it. I need lesson 13 again and again: ask, do not assume.

Chapter 9 reminded grandparents how stressful infant care can be. That stress builds, and it may overflow. Dozens of factors influence anxiety in parents of young children, but stress does not necessarily diminish when toddlers walk, talk, and climb.[3] Ethnic norms, child traits, social conditions, and grandmother involvement all interact to increase or decrease the parents' emotional burden. For example, all the families in one study were poor and urban. Their stress (as measured by answers to various questions such as "Being a parent is much harder than I expected") was as high when their children were three-year-olds as when their children were one-year-olds.[4]

In that study, grandmother involvement affected the mothers in opposite ways, depending on ethnicity. The African American mothers became more stressed if they were living with their mothers but less stressed if not. The opposite was true for Latinas: living with their mothers reduced stress, but living apart from them increased stress as their infants became toddlers. The European American mothers varied: for them there was no general trend.

One conclusion is that grandmother help has advantages and disadvantages. It relieves some financial, emotional, and practical stress, but it can undermine the mother's feelings of competence. This complexity and variation again suggests that parents and grandmother need to communicate about what is helpful and what is not. Assumptions may be wrong.

LESSON 14: ACCEPT BLAME AND MEDIATION

It is not unusual for grandmothers to be unaware of friction in the relationship between themselves and the parents of a grandchild until they explode. The most common time for an explosion is when grandchildren are between ages two and six. Consequently, "do not assume" appears in this chapter, but it begins years earlier. Similarly, mediation is useful whenever the two generations cannot understand each other without help.

One grandmother told another that she had been estranged from her daughter for years but never knew why. The daughter refused to speak with her mother. The grandmother emailed her daughter that she would meet her in a counselor's office. The angry daughter agreed. Each woman thought the counselor would agree with her, but both learned that they were neither the victim nor the culprit. Instead, they shared the problem and had to agree on the solution, which was to set better boundaries and give more respect. That might be obvious, but drawing boundaries is difficult in a culture without guidelines regarding when grandmothers should intervene. The line between expected help and intrusive interference is opaque, changing by cohort, by family, by circumstances. As one scholar wrote, when three generations are involved, "family mediation [is] unique in its complexity and intricacy."[5] No wonder many grandmothers need help.

I can see this in my family. One of my children complained that she does not know how to wear makeup because I never used it when she was a child. Unfair, I said. Another daughter agreed with me. A family dust-up transpired, sister versus sister, with me dumbfounded that my rejection of eye shadow was anything but a noble, personal decision. This illustrates a general problem. There are dozens of maternal behaviors that bother children; yet mothers never know. Some adult children blame their mothers for not providing music lessons, or for providing them but not insisting on practice. Other mothers are blamed for the way they respond to men, or for not practicing ball throwing, or for not guiding the college-admission process. That gives rise to the joke: "If it's not one thing, it's your mother. "

Unfortunately, my profession—psychology—is partly at fault. One clinical psychologist recalls:

> *I became interested in mother blaming when I was working in a clinic where we were evaluating families. I noticed that no matter what was wrong, no matter what the reason for the family's coming to the clinic, it turned out that the mother was always assumed to be responsible for the problem. And if, in the assessment interview, she sat right next to the child, my colleagues would say afterwards, "Did you see how she sat right next to the child? She is smothering and overcontrolling and too close and enmeshed and symbiotically fused with the child." But if she did not sit next to the child she was called cold and rejecting—and, if the child was a boy, castrating.*[6]

Those experiences occurred in about 1980, but some therapists still encourage adults to blame their parents for whatever problems they have. One insightful therapist explains:

> *In some ways, individual psychotherapy is to blame for the distance that some adult children feel from their parents. Part of our success as therapists, at least for those of us who work psychodynamically, comes from our ability to help our clients feel less guilty, shameful, or defective. In so doing, we often look to what they did or didn't get from their parents as a way to help them make sense of their conflicts, increase their feelings of self-awareness, and develop a healthy entitlement to better treatment from others. . . . As a psychologist, I have supported and even encouraged adult children to maintain an estrangement from a parent. . . . I have also supported it when the parents seemed objectively workable but when it was clear that the adult child didn't have*

the psychological wherewithal to develop and maintain an individual identity and be close to the parent at the same time.[7]

Unfortunately, blaming other people and situations for failures while taking personal credit for successes is a reaction so common that social psychologists call it the *fundamental attribution error.* Added to that is *generational solidarity*, the tendency for each age group to sympathize with their peers. That is why children do not snitch on their friends, teenagers laugh together about their clueless parents who, with their own friends, complain about teenagers and grandparents. Likewise, grandmothers tell each other about shoddy treatment from their grandchildren's parents. Do their listeners suggest that the middle generation may have had a reason to act as they did? No, they criticize the middle generation and absolve the grandmothers.

This is apparent in hundreds of internet posts and comments from grandmothers who are offended by their adult sons and daughters.[8] One grandmother posted that she tried to kill herself and then was forbidden to come to her five-year-old granddaughter's birthday party, even though she and that granddaughter had seen each other almost every day during early childhood. The other grandmother was invited, which added to the excluded grandmother's sorrow.

Another grandmother took her grandchildren, without permission, to see an uncle they had never known. The grandchildren's furious parents stopped letting her see the children. On her post to other grandmothers, she said she has apologized many times "every which way," but she still has not seen or held a new grandson, now age three.

In these as well as hundreds of other cases, generational solidarity led other grandmothers nationwide to email encouragement, reassuring the grandmother that she was not at fault. Some cite their own sad stories, and many blame the heartless middle generation. As a grandmother myself, I can cite many scholars who document that excluding grandmothers destroys their physical and psychological health.[9] Someone should bring the generations back together. But I also can imagine that the grandmothers are not as blameless as their internet posts imply.

Fortunately, most psychologists have moved away from mother blame, although many psychologists believe that childhood experiences affect everyone lifelong. Three ideas are widely accepted and suggest that mediation might help:

- Every human makes mistakes. Linked lives means that other family members can understand mistakes and limit the impact of any one family member's error.
- Patterns and personality can improve over the decades of adulthood. Grandparents tend to be more patient, forgiving, and loving of their grandchildren than they were of their children, so their past harshness may be gone.
- Parents and grandparents both want the youngest generation to thrive, happily and successfully. Cooperation, not conflict, makes that possible.

It is not unusual for the middle generation to be stuck on blame, and the older generation to react with self-defense. Neither understands the emotions of the other. Therapists increasingly recognize this: mothers and grandmothers need to do so as well.

Regarding the two banned grandmothers above: How did the parents interpret the situation? Were the suicide attempt and the visit to the uncle isolated events or the last straw of a pattern that had troubled the parents for years, unbeknownst to the grandmothers?

Expressing regret, and apologizing "every which way," as many grandmothers do, can harm a relationship, because "even though apologies can be immensely beneficial, transgressors often do not apologize or do not apologize well."[10] It's crucial not only to acknowledge the mistake but also to listen and learn, gaining a deeper understanding and then verbalizing why the misdeed will not be repeated. Harm comes from perfunctory words—saying "sorry" and expecting forgiveness.

Worse still is a counterattack, especially when the parents' values differ from the grandmothers'; the gap widens when a grandmother says, "I am sorry, but I would not have done that if you hadn't . . ." or "What I did is not as bad as what you or someone else did . . ." or "It's not my fault because I was drinking or upset or stressed . . ." or "You shouldn't be upset because I did what any normal person would do."

Finally, some people never apologize, thinking it won't do any good and that they are not at fault. This is not the time for justification (even if the facts are on your side)—if hurt is felt, an apology is needed.

With the dog treats in the lunch, I did not point out that the problem would not have occurred if they had packed the lunch. Elissa accepted my apology by complimenting me (she called me smart and competent!) and saying that she and Oscar would take responsibility for what Asa eats. The final result is that my apology was accepted, my behavior changed, and I was granted another chance. I now make dinner for that family almost every week, making me and the rest of the family happy.

I am fortunate. The two other grandmothers (suicidal and banned) are suffering, as are more than a million excluded grandmothers. But those most hurt are the grandchildren. Feuding adults need to remember the goal: happy children.

Without a third party, conflict may seem intractable. One of my friends has a married son who is a father. I have met the daughter-in-law's mother; she is far less accomplished, intelligent, and nurturing than my friend. When the daughter-in-law criticizes her mother-in-law, everyone goes to battle stations. My friend mentions the failures of the other grandmother; the loyal daughter-in-law bristles; each husband supports his own wife. Anger and alienation abound, with sad consequences. My friend was not allowed to babysit; her son rejected her.

At least she can see her grandson. Remember *Santi v. Santi* from chapter 4, when Mike and Heather banned his parents completely? The grandparents' wealth fueled the conflict, as did their gift giving, buying treats and presents (first shoes, a visit to Santa Claus) that made their granddaughter love them (or their gifts!) and the parents resent them. A mediator would know that deciding where Taylor would spend Christmas was a flashpoint: holidays are fraught with emotions. The Santi grandmother had not learned lesson 7 (remember the other grandmother).

In that case, the Santi grandparents fanned the flames by hiring a lawyer, a professional who is paid to take the side of the client. The parents hired their own lawyer, again paid to take their side. Instead, compromises would have been apparent if they had jointly hired a mediator or a therapist. Perhaps grandparent holidays could be scheduled on alternate years, or the celebration could include both families, or two celebrations could occur each holiday. (I know a family that eats two Thanksgiving turkeys, with two sets of relatives!)

The benefit of mediation is recognized in other contexts and cultures.

- Before they perform a wedding, many clergy require couples to discuss how they will deal with conflicts.
- Schools schedule parent-teacher conferences when the adults figure out what is best for the child.
- Many therapists specialize in couples counseling or parent-child intervention.
- Australian law mandates mediation if a grandparent sues to have time with their grandchild. Compromise is the goal.

Remember the grandmother in chapter 6 whose grandson came for a week each year until the mother put a stop to that? The grandmother wrote, "My love for my grandson roils what I thought—or wished—has been resolved, forgotten, or forgiven. It stirs up the sediment at the bottom of my relationship with my daughter and clouds the waters."[11]

Happily, relationships shift over time because people learn from life. But memories and assumptions from childhood linger. Everyone has wounds, blind spots, and biases from childhood. That makes communication essential and mediation helpful. Repairing relationships with adult children may prevent the "sediment" in the old parent-child relationships from "clouding the waters."

Feuding adults tend to be defensive and unforgiving, so someone else—a religious leader, a distant relative, or a professional—is needed. Marital and family therapists specialize in family conflict, although multigenerational therapy is not included in their training.[12] That omission itself illustrates a major theme of this book—grandmothers need to be recognized as part of the family.

LESSON 15: DISCIPLINE WITH CARE

Radically different opinions and practices regarding raising young children are especially apparent with discipline. All children misbehave sometimes. They are punished more during early childhood than at any other age. Some parents yell, some never do. Some parents believe they *must* spank their children because everyone in their community does or because they were spanked when they were children. In other nations, physical punishment is against the law, and parents may be arrested and imprisoned for hitting their children.

Parents differ not only in how they punish but also in why. Lying, masturbating, cursing, and stealing—all are common child behaviors and all are punished severely in some families but not at all in others.

Many grandmothers want to discipline a grandchild for doing something that the parents allow. The opposite is also true: parents may forbid something that grandmothers accept. In both cases, grandmothers need to recognize that times have changed and parents are in charge. Grandmothers might write about their ideas or talk to other grandmothers, but not argue with the parents. One grandmother wrote, "As I do not live in an age when rustling black silk skirts billow about me, and I do not carry an ebony stick to strike the floor in sharp rebuke. . . . If a grandmother wants to put her foot down, the only safe place to do it is in a note book."[13]

Cohorts differ in discipline. This may seem so obvious that readers may wonder why punishment is a major topic, lesson 15. But an article titled "Aren't You Glad You Are Not Your Grandmother" was published in *Good Housekeeping* (a widely read magazine) in 1922.[14] A woman was clearing out her dead grandmother's ancestral home, and she found a letter written decades earlier. It described an incident when that woman's father—also long dead—was a boy:

> When the door was left unlocked for a moment, out he ran in his little velvet suit. We did not miss him for a while because we thought he was doing his Latin Prose, and then some wealthy ladies . . . saw him literally in the gutter, groping in the mud for a marble. . . . Horace's father was white with emotion when he heard of it. He brought Horace in, gave him another whipping, and, saying that since he acted like a runaway dog he should be treated like one, he went out, bought a dog-collar and a chain, and chained Horace to the post of his little bed. He was there all the afternoon, crying so you could hear nothing else in all the house. . . . I went many times up to the hall before his door and knelt there stretching out my arms to my darling child, the tears flooding down my cheeks. But, of course, I could not open the door and go in to him, to interfere with his punishment.

The author is grateful that mothers now (in 1922!) know more than did nineteenth-century parents, who believed the "various cruel, hard sayings out of the Old Testament, in which an ancient and primitive people expressed their ignorance of child-life."

This testimony shows that it is mistaken to glorify grandmothers of early times. Contemporary mothers and grandmothers—despite their many disagreements—are able to express their love and care. None of us will spend an afternoon kneeling, tears streaming down our faces, with arms outstretched toward a wailing, chained child behind a closed door.

We have learned some things. Diana Baumrind studied parental styles fifty years ago.[15] She found that parents differed on four dimensions:

1. *Expressions of warmth.* Some parents are very affectionate; others, cold and critical.
2. *Strategies for discipline.* Some parents spank or beat; others use time out; others talk.

3. *Communication.* Some parents listen patiently and respond sympathetically; others demand silence and issue commands.
4. *Expectations for maturity.* Some parents expect responsibility and self-control; others expect children to be selfish and emotional.

On the basis of these, Baumrind identified three parenting styles.

Authoritarian. The authoritarian parent's word is law, not to be questioned. Misconduct brings strict punishment, usually physical. Authoritarian parents have clear rules and high standards. They seem cold, and do not expect children to offer opinions, especially about emotions. (One adult from such a family said that "How do you feel?" had only two possible answers: "Fine" and "Tired.")

Permissive. Permissive parents (also called *indulgent*) make few demands, hiding any impatience they might feel. Discipline is lax because they expect children to be immature ("he's only a child" or "she is not ready for that"). Such parents are nurturing and accepting, listening to imagination, accepting lies, allowing curses—including directed at them.

Authoritative. Authoritative parents set limits, but they are flexible. They encourage maturity, but they listen and forgive (not punish) if their children fall short. They consider themselves guides, not authorities (unlike authoritarian parents) and not friends (unlike permissive parents).

Baumrind's basic categories have been studied in many nations, with thousands of children of many ages.[16] One conclusion is found over and over: children need warmth and guidance. Permissive parenting has too little guidance; children are adrift and unhappy. Authoritarian parenting is too cold; children are fearful, rebellious, and later depressed and violent. Authoritative parenting is usually best; children know what is expected of them and know they are loved.

Those decades of research have also found that specific contexts, issues, and temperaments render universal proscriptions too simplistic. Children sometimes develop well with all three parenting styles, as long as standards are consistent and discipline is loving. Together, the *Good Housekeeping* articles and the revisions of Baumrind's typology suggest some humility about our current disciplinary practices. That makes a grandmother's best option to follow the parents' lead, especially during early childhood.

Culture continues to be crucial. Many Caribbean grandmothers in the United States find that American children are undisciplined. One says, "Back home, you can spank them. You can't do it here in the system they grow here. Back home, you can talk to your kids, here you can't. Most kids here don't show respect, they don't have it. I believe back home is better."[17]

I heard of one father who took his son back to his home country (Ghana), and as soon as they set foot on the tarmac, the father beat the son for everything he had not been punished for in the United States. I believe that father was wrong, in both beating and timing, but the evidence does not support my fear that the boy was permanently harmed. Many forms of discipline produce healthy adults—unless the child feels rejected as well as punished. However, more than fifty nations have banned corporal punishment of children, based on data that links childhood spanking to adult crime and mental illness.[18] Obviously, methods of discipline (and reasons for punishment) differ by ideology.[19] Whichever discipline style is used, parents justify it as the best for the child—and that makes it almost impossible for grandmothers to convince them otherwise, especially when there are cultural as well as cohort differences between the generations.[20] Instead, grandparents need to know when and for what the parents want their child disciplined.

One common stereotype is that grandmothers are too strict. But the opposite may be closer to the truth. Some grandparents think they are allowed to indulge the children. One grandmother boasts that her granddaughters call her home "the House of Yes." If they ask, "Can we bake cookies for breakfast, make a tent in the living room, go and buy some toys?" the answer is—well, you know what the answer is.[21]

I hope those grandchildren did not spend too much time in the House of Yes because Baumrind and many others find that permissive households may slide into neglectful ones, producing children who are selfish and immature.

The researchers who chronicled the complaints of the Caribbean grandmothers wrote, "Grandmothers are notorious spoilers of children, doting on them, feeding them on demand, indulging their impertinence, and allowing them to play while elders work. Children raised by grannies are seen as incapable of coping with hunger and hardship."[22]

Of course, stereotypes are too simplistic: sometimes the grandmothers are the strict ones. One grandmother said she would "rather eat a bucketful of Legos than give into a tantrum in the toy department."[23] When another grandmother slapped her visiting granddaughter for cursing her, the child's mother was horrified, saying she might never trust her with her daughter again. Overreaction? Yes. That daughter and grandmother reconciled, and Grandma moved more than a thousand miles to live near her grandchildren.

Discipline is, universally, an emotional issue, and many parents argue with each other about it. One might say, "You let that child get away with murder," and the other could respond, "You will kill that child if you don't stop." Both exaggerate; the child is not about to kill or be killed. But such arguments escalate if each grandmother sides with her own child. Ideally, mothers and fathers listen to each other and then form a cooperative alliance, with grandmothers as part of the caregiving team.[24] Then children know what is and is not allowed, and they thrive.

From a developmental perspective, the issue is not talk versus spank, allow versus forbid, right versus wrong. It is alliance versus war. One grandmother said, "She's a little bit of a dreamy child, and clumsy. . . . I think they're a bit harsh on her at times. . . . But mostly she's a very happy child and mostly they're very fair, but they're consistent the two of them, so they agree on some rules and that's that, and they stick by each other."[25] This grandmother wisely admires parental consistency and rightly focuses on the outcome, "a very happy child." Grandmothers can offer affection and warmth without subverting the parents or confusing the child.

Should grandmothers ever intervene? Is the current "norm of non-interference" sometimes wrong? Probably. When parents are overwhelmed, they may become severely abusive or neglectful. Then the child needs to be rescued. If that occurs, the intervening grandmother should realize that the problem began much earlier. Prevention, with empathy more than criticism and with respite care and comfort, is needed long before protective services comes knocking. Dozens of adults have told me that their grandmothers were a welcome escape from an unhappy home. That is good for the child, probably good for the grandmother, but also good for the parent—if the grandmother can relieve the burden of child care without antagonizing the parents.

Keep in mind that every adult makes mistakes, as does every child. Almost every adult remembers being disciplined unjustly and/or escaping well-deserved punishment. That seems to be part of growing up, not harmful, not something grandmothers should try to fix—especially if it means fighting about discipline. Remember the goal, and remember lesson 15.

· 11 ·

School Children

*W*ith younger children, grandmothers need to support the parents: no comments, no assumptions, build relationships, avoid wars. Each of these is challenging for women who fought for respect decades ago, when their children were young.

Now a new challenge begins. Grandmothers should still support the parents, who remain gatekeepers. In middle childhood, however, the child's growing intellect allows them to consider the world beyond their immediate family. Children are open to learning about their grandmother's history and values, and grandmothers can develop a direct relationship with them.

Solidify those relationships. This requires active engagement in whatever the grandparents and the children enjoy. That could be baking, reading, fishing, shopping, running—whatever. Two admirable grandmothers illustrate the point.

One grandmother noticed that her nine-year-old grandson studied special effects by reading about them in FX magazines. When she babysat in the evenings, his parents allowed her to watch a movie with him. She wrote:

> *He liked horror movies. But in truth, I would have done almost anything to hold on to his love and the connection between us. So I agreed with his selections, and we watched Freddy Krueger's nighttime slaughters and sometimes Michael Myer's. And when the screen ran red with blood, I would slide from the couch to the floor with my hands over my face. . . .*

And he would explain to me how the moviemakers had created the gore, what the blood really was, the eyeballs, the trailing entrails.

Once we watched a movie of my choice; a modern day romance. When a fairly obvious sex scene came on . . . [he] placed his palm flat across his eyes. . . . I said he didn't enjoy the movie much, did he? He said not really, and we went back to Freddy Krueger.[1]

The second example is my mother, who created a beauty parlor for my daughter, Rachel. In an alcove off her bedroom was what people of her generation called a *vanity*: a small area with a chair, desk, and large mirror. Grandma put a special shawl on the chair and told us to stay away until she and Rachel were ready. Unlike me, but typical of her cohort, my mother had dozens of lipsticks, nail polishes, eye pencils, rouges, perfumes, and curlers. She and Rachel would open, smell, and discuss each item, and then Rachel would choose. Grandma was the artist; Rachel was the beauty; grandfather, father, and I the admirers.

Both grandmothers found ways to build relationships with their grandchildren, developing a strong attachment that continued for decades. That boy who liked horror movies became a gifted sculptor who gave his grandmother one of his large creations, which she proudly displayed on her front porch. That girl who put curlers in her hair left her job in Eastern Europe to be near her grandparents in Minnesota, the only one of their seven grandchildren to live within a thousand miles of them for more than a decade. As they became frail, Rachel visited her grandparents in a nursing home several times a week.

LESSON 16: KEEP THEM SAFE AND SOCIAL

The need to keep children both safe and social creates a dilemma for parents and grandparents. Children learn from experience, so keeping children far from danger may also restrict social learning. But the line between safe and social has moved in the past decades. Mothers and grandmothers may be shocked at the boundary set by the other.

This is most evident when children play together. Children are drawn to peers: adults are inadequate playmates.[2] Few grown-ups are imaginative superheroes, or kings, or princesses; few love kicking a ball for hours; few play jacks all afternoon, or dress up in oversized garments, or laugh at bathroom jokes, or . . . whatever. Other children are companions and co-conspirators; children seek each other out.

One historical example has already been mentioned. Remember the eight-year-old who sneaked out "in his little velvet suit . . . literally in the gutter, groping in the mud for a marble." He was whipped and chained for leaving "his own safe, pious home, out to play in the city with the lowest, dirtiest boys!"[3] The woman who published his story criticized the punishment but failed to praise the boy for choosing marbles with dirty playmates over the solitary study of Latin prose. Physical play (chasing, wrestling, and so on) makes children agile and strong; cognitive play (jokes, ditties) advances memory; social play (games and drama) aids emotional control and cooperative skills.

A current example is Halloween. When I was young, I went trick-or-treating with friends; my parents stayed home to answer the door. Now many parents accompany even their older costumed children and examine each treat, checking for razor blades in apples or, recently, marijuana in a gummy bear. No child has been seriously hurt by Halloween booty, but parents convey distrust of neighbors nonetheless.[4] It would be easier if children stayed home, but a child might sneak out in a ghost sheet, gorilla mask, or velvet suit.

Another contemporary example comes from *screen time*, the name for time spent watching TV, playing electronic games, sending texts, or connecting to the internet on a computer, tablet, or cell phone. Sometimes parents must choose between having a child at a screen at home or outside, out of sight, playing with friends. Most parents choose home, sometimes forbidding social networking sites. Again, parental fears are misplaced: children need to connect with friends.

Psychologists object that screen time undercuts social play and family interaction. That also troubles many grandmothers, who remember when human interaction was more interesting than video games. Excessive screen time also contributes to obesity, attention deficit disorder (ADD), sleep deprivation, and aggression.[5] The American Society of Pediatricians advises no screens at all for children under age two, and less than two hours a day in middle childhood.[6] But few parents or professionals follow that advice. My grandson chipped his tooth; the pediatric dentist had a screen on the ceiling. Asa watched a video, obligingly opening his mouth wide.

The solution, moderation, is not easy to enforce. Some parents limit screen time: allowing no television in the bedroom, blocking certain websites, forbidding screens until homework is done. Kids push back, sneaking cell phones under the blankets or insisting that homework requires the internet. The underlying problem is not only that children are mesmerized by screens but also that parents appreciate what watching provides: quiet and safe children.

I know one grandmother who is appalled that her daughter lets the grandchildren look at their iPads instead of at their grandmother. I know another grandmother who lets her grandchildren watch videos day and night when they visit her. She says, "my house, my rules"—to the dismay of the parents. In both families, I see resentment building and alienation imminent.

Virtually every developmentalist wishes children had less screen time and more social time, through activities such as multiplayer board games that teach math; play that requires turn taking, which teaches cooperation; or sports, drama, band, chorus, and so on, to advance many personal and social skills. They also advocate unscheduled time so that children can play with other children without adult direction. Grandmothers could help make this happen, providing the watchful presence that modern parents think necessary but letting children create their play activities. Grandparents could also instigate more organized interaction, such as sponsoring a scout group or setting up a board game.

Taking grandchildren and their friends to the local park is one way to supervise play, satisfying both the children and their parents. However, that may be complicated, as apparent with my experience.

Background for my trip to the local park comes from my appreciation of one type of social play that scientists have named, described, and praised, called *rough-and-tumble*. It looks dangerous because children chase, wrestle, and fall over one another. This active play develops the prefrontal cortex, helping children regulate emotions, refine social skills, and coordinate their bodies.[7] Counterintuitive, but true: adults who never ran and chased in childhood are less adept at assertion without aggression, at compromise without withdrawal. It teaches how to be social and safe.

Rough-and-tumble thrives among children who are friends, with ample space to chase and freedom to play. It is more common in boys than girls. Some suggest that childhood experience with rough-and-tumble, and with team games organized by children, is the reason men traditionally were more adept than woman at mastering the rough strategies and measured self-promotion of high finance, national politics, and unions/management. Experience with rough-and-tumble may even aid courtship, helping both partners understand when touch is thrilling and when not.

That is speculative, and gender patterns may be changing. But it is not speculative that, decades ago, when almost every child lived near open fields, nearby woods, and empty lots, active outside play was common, unsupervised, and unhampered. Children still chase each other, roughhousing happily if allowed, but adults and smaller spaces make this difficult.

Hoping to allow some social play, I took Asa to a large city park with two other children from his second-grade class, both supervised by their mothers. All three children ran and chased each other, showing the *play face*, the clue that this was fun. I have learned to watch facial expressions. When children are fighting, about to hurt each other, angry scowls signal that intervention may be needed.

On this afternoon, one mother stopped her son from flinging his coat at Asa; the other mother stopped her daughter from kicking him, and Asa himself grabbed the kicker and pushed her down. The kick was a soft, symbolic one, barely making contact, and the ground was a rubberized safety surface, not concrete. I saw friendship and healthy rough-and-tumble; these three friends were laughing, careful not to hurt each other. The two mothers thought I was negligent; I thought they were intrusive.

I tell this incident not to ask readers to take sides. No matter whether our reactions arise from cohort, science, culture, sexism, or something else, caregivers need to appreciate that other caregivers have assumptions about play.

I am about to express my thoughts, which I recognize as biased. My viewpoint is similar to that of many educators of my cohort but at odds with many young parents' beliefs. I hope to illustrate the depth of feeling so grandmothers in particular will respect the attitudes of other caregivers. System 1 may overwhelm System 2 when safety is concerned. Another older woman writes, "Actions that would have been considered paranoid in the '70s—walking third-graders to school, forbidding your kid to play ball in the street, going down the slide with your child in your lap—are now routine."[8]

By choosing the word "paranoid," that author conveyed her conviction that some parents are irrationally fearful. Walking to school, for instance, is usually safe—a child is more likely to be assaulted or kidnapped by a relative at home than by a stranger on the way to school. A few decades ago, children often walked without adults but with other children; going to school was a social occasion. That was true for my four girls.

I imagine readers asking, "What about Etan Patz, who was abducted on his way to school?" His 1979 disappearance began a national campaign that led parents to fear "stranger danger," with President Reagan declaring National Missing Children's Day on the anniversary of Etan's disappearance. However, as one commentator points out, the fact that Etan's name is well known illustrates how rare such cases are. He was in kindergarten when my oldest was in the first grade at the same school; my young children also walked to school, for almost twenty years, without adults.

I can cite statistics. Each year from 1979 to 2017 almost four million six-year-olds lived in the United States.[9] That is 150 million six-year-olds and one lethal abduction by a stranger, a rate of .000000007.

I am not sure of all those zeros—you can calculate the odds yourself. But I am sure that an American six-year-old's chance of obesity, dying from flu, or choking on food is much higher. No parent avoids those risks by keeping their kindergarteners on a strained liquid diet, and half of all parents neglect to get a flu shot for their children. We all rationalize: parents who do not inoculate their children say it's too much trouble to get the flu shot when there is no guarantee that it will work. Added to that, broadcasters highlight the one child in a million who has a bad reaction, not the far greater number who are hospitalized with flu.

A related fear is of public playgrounds. In New York City, most playgrounds have tall fences and signs: "No adults allowed unless accompanied by a child." That forbids older women to sit on playground benches to read the paper, eat lunch, and watch children play unless those children are hers. Some educators fear that numerous safety measures have made playgrounds "very dull play spaces," where children cannot develop social skills or express imagination.[10]

I think the worst part is psychological. Children absorb the underlying message that people are not to be trusted; six- to ten-year-olds can't walk to school, cut vegetables with a knife, dig in dirt to find earthworms, help each other climb trees, learn when to ignore beggars on the street, or figure out how to join a pick-up game in an empty lot. Could this be the part of the reason contemporary children have more depression, higher rates of attention deficit disorder, and, later, fewer marriages and more divorces?

Many readers might dismiss my rant, arguing that parents are rightly protective. They say, "You can't be too safe." But fear may undercut exercise, self-esteem, independent judgment. Everyone has strong views that are influenced as much by their cohort as by any objective facts. My views are the product of my era. Where some see danger, others see learning.

Another grandmother from my cohort was troubled by the overprotection (she thought) from young parents.[11] She asked, "Is it a reaction to how much we took our eyes off our children?"

The answer, a stinging rebuke, was "Yes."

But this should make the lesson clear: logic and math are no match for maternal feelings. Grandmothers—including those who agree and those who disagree with me—need to avoid a generational

"Better safe than sorry, son."

Or is it "nothing ventured, nothing gained"?
Jack Zeigler, CartoonCollections.com.

war. Unless they recognize the concerns of many parents, grandparents may suffer the fate of one woman I know, a widow who doted on her grandchildren:

> *I took my granddaughter and my grandson to a children's play. As we settled in our seats, we chatted with friendly people on both sides of us, who also happened to be grandparents with grandchildren. Once the curtain rose, my granddaughter was mesmerized, but my grandson became bored. He said he had to pee again (I had taken him before the show). I told my granddaughter to come with us, but she said "No." I asked her again, she said she was sure she would be fine without me: I was afraid she would cry if I made her come. So I asked the grandmother next to me to keep an eye on her, and took my grandson to the bathroom. We returned quickly, she didn't seem to notice that we ever left.*

Later I told my son and daughter-in-law. They were livid; saying I could never take the children out again. I told my son I would have done the same for him, when he was little. But he agreed with his wife. The most he grudgingly acknowledged was "Maybe years ago, in your small town in Kentucky, it might have been okay, but not now in Boston."

This grandmother let the girl stay without her and told the parents about it because she was oblivious to current parental fears. Her ignorance led to a horrified mother and closing of the gate. This grandmother's time with her grandchildren was restricted to one hour each week, inside their home, when the parents were present. She was forbidden to bring her new partner, a gentle man who was a grandfather himself. At the end of one visit, she asked for more time because she had not finished reading a book to her grandchildren. "No. Shut the book and leave."

This particular woman now has informally adopted an unrelated family that lives near her. Their grandmothers are in another nation; they welcome her caregiving. They do not share the fears of North American parents.

I pity that restricted grandmother, but I understand the parents. They grew up with photos of missing children on the cartons that poured milk on their Cheerios. Each cohort has fears that seem irrational to people who lived in other times. I did not argue with the two mothers at the playground. I wonder whether they wanted to argue with me.

LESSON 17: PROTECT VICTIMS AND BULLIES

"Sticks and stones can break my bones, but names can never hurt me." My mother taught me that ditty; I sing-songed it to my playmates. But we were repeating a cultural lie: scientists now show that humiliating taunts cause lifetime harm. A broken bone hurts, then heals: words can sting for decades. Neurological research finds that physical pain and social rejection activate similar parts of the brain, each making the other worse.[12]

Every grandchild is aware of bullying. Grandmothers can be crucial in prevention and protection.

A bully was once thought to be a mean, ugly, and alienated boy who pummeled other boys to compensate for his sad life. Bullies were portrayed as lonely and rare; victims were not seriously harmed and "boys will be boys." However, when three bullied boys in Norway killed themselves, a public outcry led the government to fund a national survey. The result shocked that nation: more than one Norwegian child in eight reported that they were bullied. Every school—large and small, public and private, religious or secular—had bullies.[13]

That prompted research in a dozen other nations, with troubling findings.[14] The seemingly high rates of bullying in Norway turned out to be low: in many places a third or more children had been bullied before high school. Bullies were girls as well as boys, and bullying took many forms: physical bullying was more common in the early grades but other forms—verbal, social, and now cyber—increased with age.

The recognition of the social nature of children in middle childhood led to another realization: Bullies are not usually lonely. They have supporters, called *henchmen*. Their classmates fear them; they gain status for bullying, especially in the final years of middle childhood, aged ten and up. As children grow older, not only does social bullying increase, but it also becomes worse. Bullies gain popularity; victims become depressed; bystanders are less likely to intervene.

Words are weapons: victims are called racist epithets and ethnic slurs, children are compared to insects, a child's appearance, clothes, habits, and intelligence are demeaned. Bullies try to render a victim friendless, via shunning, false rumors, embarrassing photos on cell phones, fake social media pages. Girls typically bully verbally and socially, which hurts more than punching and shoving. Children of both sexes are perpetrators and victims of cyber bullying, with a single episode having the power to destroy a fragile ego.[15]

Adults—parents, teachers, and especially grandmothers—are typically ignorant, and that harms children, especially over the long term.

As adults, victims have higher rates of depression, and bullies may become violent, leading to higher rates of failed marriages, imprisonment, and premature death.[16]

Victims are not always chosen because of some oddity—freckles or glasses or skinny legs. Targets may be the only one from an ethnic or religious group, have a disability, be unusually fat or short, be new to a school, or be thought to be gay. However, some such children are accepted, so it is not that trait alone that provokes bullying. A child with none of those characteristics may be bullied. As one boy explained,

> *You can get bullied because you are weak or annoying or because you are different. Kids with big ears get bullied. Dorks get bullied. You can also get bullied because you think too much of yourself and try to show off. Teacher's pet gets bullied. If you say the right answer too many times in class you can get bullied. There are lots of popular groups who bully each other and other groups, but you can get bullied within your group too. If you do not want to get bullied, you have to stay under the radar, but then you might feel sad because no one pays attention to you.*[17]

A graduate student in Arizona spent an entire year as an observer in a fourth-grade class, studying bullying. In the first month, she thought the children were so nice that she might never see any bullying, but as time went on she began to see those fourth graders deliberately hurting each other every day. Teachers often missed it, dismissed it, or misinterpreted it. If they saw it, they often blamed the victim, who was told to ignore an insult or fight back.

When one frequent victim, Michelle, met with a teacher to tell about being bullied, this observer "witnessed her demeanor change over the course of the conversation—from one who is trying to present her perspective, with an eagerness and desire to share her story with another, to one who was submissive and silenced through repeated interruptions by the adult."

In this school, the adults silenced the children, who concluded that they were on their own. This points directly to a role for grandmothers. This observer wrote:

Children need someone to confide in—they need an outlet, as much as any adult does. Unfortunately, when I observed a child discussing some of the issues that were important to him/her with an adult, I often heard advice from the adult rather than real listening. . . . Adults more frequently corrected or explained how the child should behave and change, fix, or control a situation. After such conversations, I often observed the child seemingly to deflate.[18]

Grandmothers can listen and, by doing so, restore self-esteem.

What else can grandmothers do? The best defense against bullying is having a friend; friendship develops naturally between children who spend time together. Can a grandmother facilitate friendship? Yes, she can supervise play dates and playground time. She can take a child and a classmate to a movie, a museum, or a sports event. This is more difficult when the grandmother is custodial, which may be part of the reason that children in skipped-generation families are more likely to be bullied.[19]

Beyond friendship, pride and self-respect buffer the harm of both bullying and victimization. This must be based on what children have actually accomplished: beginning in toddlerhood, honest—not effusive—praise predicts school learning.[20] Accomplishments worthy of notice could be academic, artistic, or athletic—every child can be proud of something they have done, especially if their accomplishment took extra effort. Both bullies and victims need this reinforcement to prevent a vicious attempt to feel superior or a self-defeating conviction that they are inferior. (Erik Erikson's term for the psychosocial crisis of middle childhood was *industry versus inferiority*, reflecting the benefits of accomplishment and the harm of failure.)

The research is strongest on this for African American children, who benefit from *racial socialization*, learning about leaders who overcame prejudice to accomplish great things. But the lessons from that group apply to all children. Every child sometimes feels that their group is inferior, which means that every grandmother needs to describe accomplishments and leaders from their group. Children who are from racial and ethnic minorities or other nations, or with chronic health problems or disabilities, all need reassurance. For instance, every struggling reader needs to know that Hans Christian Andersen and Winston Churchill were both dyslexic, and each man mastered communication skills after a long struggle.

Sometimes a personal story is best. Grandmothers can tell their own history as an outsider, not dwelling on their past experiences but showing that difficulties can be overcome. Be careful with this strategy, however: too much talk with too little listening is dangerous, especially when the talk sounds like bragging or anger, rather than a story of overcoming obstacles.

Were you surprised that lesson 17 advises protection of bullies as well as victims? Both need grandmothering! Children are naturally prosocial (sharing and listening to each other) and naturally antisocial (selfish, mean, unaware of the needs of others).

Every child—bullies and victims alike—needs more empathy. Thus an upset or crying child should not be punished or blamed (that's what bullies do). Grandmothers can model empathy (I see that you are angry, or sad, or afraid) and then help children understand each other (How did that make him feel?). Bullies themselves tend to think they are victims, or at least justified. Listening to them, asking questions, might help them gain insight.

To listen well, use techniques that work in therapy. Active listening involves eye contact, echoing what someone said, nodding, with phrases that encourage more talk (Yes! Oh no! Really? Oh my. Then?).

Psychotherapists use *motivational interviewing* to help addicts quit drugs. The therapist does not give advice but instead waits until the client expresses a useful idea. Via thoughtful listening, the therapist reinforces some statements and ignores others. That method succeeds for grandmothers, too: children often figure out what is best to do if someone listens as they discuss possibilities.

Most childhood problems begin at home in early childhood and get worse or better during middle childhood, depending in part on grandmothers. One example was found in a study of children whose parents were addicted to meth, rendering them neglectful and erratic. In that study, more than half of the children spoke fondly of their grandparents. Those who had good grandparent relationships were less likely to be aggressive in middle childhood, and more likely to have loyal friends, than children of meth-addicted parents who had no reliable grandmothers.[21]

LESSON 18: HELP WITH EDUCATION

A crucial role for grandmothers is to help with the schooling of the grandchildren. Research finds that children with involved and supportive grandmothers learn more in school and are more likely to graduate from high school and even college.

However, in the United States today, this has become contentious because of the current panorama of school choices. Once, "school" meant the nearby institution that every neighbor child attended. No more.

Before wading into school choice, grandmothers need to take a deep breath, relax, and usually keep quiet. Home life affects children's happiness, achievement, and compassion more than school life. Grandmother influence on learning is above and beyond the specifics of school. Despite the array of choice, every school for first- through fifth-grade children is similar in the essentials to all the others: they all have opportunities for friendship, instances of bullying, some excellent and some ineffective teachers, and they all teach reading and math.

No matter which school is chosen, brain development between ages six and ten makes children ideal students. Grandmothers can help, adding to parental support, or compensating if parents are dismissive or uninvolved. That might mean taking children to school if attendance and punctuality is a problem, helping with school trips if supervision is lax, or alerting parents if a particular teacher is destructive. Support the child, supplement the parents, but do not take over.

How well children learn in elementary school depends partly on how prepared they are for kindergarten, and that depends partly on grandmothers who read, play, and talk with them. Once in school,

"Whenever I get a good test grade I show it to my mother. Whenever I get a bad test grade, I show it to my grandma."

Why? Are grandmothers more understanding?

Aaron Bacall, CartoonCollections.com.

grandmothers continue to read, buy notebooks and backpacks, check homework, and attend school events.

Steer clear of controversies. There are "reading wars" (phonics versus whole language), "math wars" (memorization versus concepts), disputes about religion (prayer?), history (nationalism?), and science (evolution?). People fight about school organization and policies: single sex or coed, class size, teachers (ethnicity, sexual orientation, experience), ability grouping, student age, social promotion, discipline, and much more. Each of these affects education, but disputes reflect adult religious, economic, and ethnic backgrounds more than child learning. Grandmothers had best keep quiet, especially if they disagree with the parents.

Added to all that, the United States now has "school wars" with a dizzying array of choices, not only in the three major categories (public, private, and parochial) but also among public schools (charter, magnet, zoned). The very existence of such options varies by state, district, and neighborhood. Added to that is homeschooling, with ten states allowing children to be taught by anyone; other states requiring that home teachers meet certain standards, which vary from state to state; and some states ruling that all children (at age five or six, another controversy) must be enrolled in a school. Overall, in the United States, about 3 percent of children are homeschooled, about 11 percent are in non–public schools, and the rest are in some version of a public school. Tension is evident between national standards (assumed to exist in most nations, not in the United States) and local school variations: many parents buy homes based on school district and zone.[22]

Some schools require uniforms that children hate: ties and white shirts for boys, skirts covering the knees for girls. There are rules about hair, necklaces, chains, bracelets, shoes, T-shirts, hats, head scarves, and more, each upsetting some parents and children. Some religious schools inculcate beliefs that are heresy in other schools; some states allow public funding (vouchers) for religious education that some courts deem illegal. Some private schools let the children decide what to learn; others tightly control the curriculum. Teacher unions are strong in some communities, anathema in others.

School controversies currently erupt in politics: legislators champion policies that were unknown when grandmothers were young. Vouchers, charters, and magnet schools are new, so are hundreds of non-public schools, which means that children attend schools and are taught in ways that grandmothers never imagined. For example, at one time, children were never taught to read until elementary school. That's why young children are called *pre*schoolers, why kindergarten is still not required by law in many places, and why first grade is called *first*. Now teachers expect some six-year-olds to be able to read.

Another example involves homework. Fifty years ago, homework meant chores at home, such as washing dishes, sweeping the floor. No teacher assigned academic work for after school hours until the children were age ten or older. Now many kindergarteners have homework.

Another example of the changes in recent years involves promotion and graduation. It was once assumed that a year of maturation would mean advancing a grade. Now, in the United States, children are tested frequently and must repeat a grade (sometimes third grade, often sixth, almost always twelfth) if they do not meet a certain benchmark. Most kindergarten teachers hope incoming four- and five-year-olds have learned to sit still and pay attention.[23]

Clashes among the adults (parents, teachers, lawmakers, voters) occur regarding all of these aspects of education, and each community argues about different issues. In 2013, Alabama scrapped a difficult test that was required for a high school diploma; in the same year, Pennsylvania instituted such a test. A 2007 law in Texas required fifteen tests before graduation; in 2013, another Texas law reduced that number to four. In 2015, 250,000 parents in New York State refused to have their children take the required state tests. In 2010, the Common Core standards were endorsed by the governors of almost every state; in 2016, rescinding those standards was an issue in national politics.

How does all this information relate to grandmothers? Knowing that controversies and choices ebb and flow, grandmothers need to remember the goal: parents who feel supported and children who feel loved. Weighing in on curriculum, tests, or school choice must be done very carefully, if at all.

What if parents' school choice is contrary to a grandmother's deep convictions? This gets to the heart of the grandmother role. When should she be supportive of the parents, and when should she take a stand against them? Since family life and the child's own personality, ability, and motivation seem more crucial than the specifics of the school, and since the parents are the final arbiters of where the child should be educated, it is wise to avoid a protest.

However, given the complexity, diversity, and controversies about schools, this may be almost impossible. Many adults marry outside their childhood faith, and one parent may want a school with a religious message contrary to the grandmother's convictions. Other families may agree about religion but disagree about school structure, or rigor, or curriculum. But children learn less when the adults argue about their school.

Money adds to the complications. About half of all grandparents pay for some of their grandchildren's education, typically art, sports, or music classes, or preschool or college.[24] Financial pressures on grandparents are increasing because public funds are shrinking. Grandparents can advocate for public school funding, but meanwhile, many parents seek private schools that they cannot afford. The average private school tuition is at least $10,000 a year; some cost four times that. Grandparents may be asked to pay for a school they did not choose.

One grandmother was asked by her newly divorced daughter to pay half of the children's private school tuition (their father paid the other half). She agreed. Her daughter thanked her for helping her grandchildren. She replied, "I am doing it for you, not them." She hated her former son-in-law, was happy about the divorce, and didn't want her daughter to regret it.

Another grandmother was asked to pay for a religious private school for her six-year-old grandchild. She refused. She lectured the young parents about financial planning, as well as about the need for public education in a thriving democracy. The parents did not heed her lecture; they asked the great-grandmother. She also refused. Defiantly, the parents sent their child to their chosen school and asked the grandparents to help them buy a house. They did.

Both of those examples involve private school tuition that created a wedge between parents and grandparents, but complications involve public school as well. Grandparents may disapprove of class assignment, teacher competence, or curriculum (especially math and reading). Because of the many choices now available, and because every family is dedicated to their children, conflicting opinions about school are common. That makes me wonder about a third example: my own.

When Asa was ready for kindergarten, his parents explored options, private and public. I heard about a good school, suggested it, and was told they had rejected that school long ago. Yes, I forgot lesson 1.

That interchange reminded me to keep my opinions to myself when the parents visited several other schools. They consulted an expert, who suggested a public school in another nearby neighborhood. They moved to that school's zone so Asa could walk to school and have neighborhood friends.

Unfortunately, their new address was not verified until midsummer. By then, the school was already full. Asa was on a waiting list. Meanwhile, they learned about another public school, a half-hour subway ride away, that accepted out-of-zone children. They took Asa there on the first day of kindergarten. It was far from ideal, not only in distance but also in physical structure. The building was old, with high ceilings, up/down staircases, scaffolding because the windows needed repair, and a play yard that was closed for renovation.

At the nearby school, some kindergartners did not show up, so for his second day of kindergarten, Asa went there. He cried at lunch because he was supposed to go to the cafeteria, but he didn't know where it was. Meanwhile, Asa's parents visited the distant school, met the principal and the teacher, admired the curriculum, and saw that the class had twenty children with two assistants because it included three students with special needs. The learning environment seemed great, but the commute was daunting.

Then I figured out how to follow lesson 18, to *help with education* without assuming I knew best. I offered to pick up Asa from school and bring him back home every day. Offer accepted: Asa and I ride the subway every afternoon from a school that I never knew existed. His parents thank me, I feel useful, outsiders praise me, but writing this sentence makes me see that I am not selfless: it gives me joy to spend time with him even as I also help with his education. In fact, Asa's school is within walking distance of my house, although a subway ride away from Asa's home. Did I overstep, ignore my own advice, do something no more rational or selfless than the grandmothers I criticize?

These examples return us to the earlier chapters. The ideal balance between involvement and distance keeps shifting. The current norm for grandmothers is non-interference;[25] yet grandmother involvement during middle childhood helps grandchildren in many ways.[26] But families are complicated. Finding the ideal grandmother role becomes even harder as grandchildren become adolescents. But before that chapter, another even more difficult dilemma: what to do when an adult child is divorced.

Divorce and Grandchildren

$\mathscr{D}$ivorce is sometimes portrayed as a family disaster, and sometimes as best for everyone, including parents, grandchildren, and grandparents. Neither is usually true.

In the United States, the *disaster* perspective was often held before 1970 and *best for everyone* was a common view at the end of the twentieth century. Now most research shows that the truth is between these extremes. Longitudinal studies of millions of divorces find that divorce usually—but not always—impairs every generation, at least for months, sometimes for years.[1]

Divorce is now seen as a lengthy process, not a momentary decree. It begins long before the legal actions and may affect all three generations lifelong. Currently, in the United States, an estimated 40 million children are in single-parent families, either because of divorce or because their parents never married.[2] Many more children are in stepfamilies, again faring less well academically, socially, and physically than children living with both biological parents.[3]

On average, grandparents are more likely to be depressed for years after their children have divorced,[4] and formerly divorced adults tend to experience poorer financial, physical, and psychological health than those who have been married or single lifelong.[5] In late adulthood, those who have experienced divorce, either as children or as marriage partners, are more likely to be lonely and less likely to be healthy.[6]

Of course, there are many exceptions to those averages, and grandmothers are sometimes the reason. There are also marked cohort differences. The historical period powerfully affects family formation, unity, and dissolution, which results in varying consequences for the individuals involved. As one pro-marriage source describes it, "while less than 20% of couples who married in 1950 ended up divorced, about 50% of couples who married in 1970 did. And approximately half of the children born to married parents in the 1970s saw their parents part, compared to only about 11% of those born in the 1950s."[7]

That author is happy that divorce rates are not as high as in the 1970s, although other sources find that the impact on children and divorcees was less severe when divorce was more common. The marriage advocate just quoted is not happy that one reason that the divorce rate has fallen is that the marriage rate has fallen. Currently, fewer people are marrying, in part because more are cohabitating. Children are affected when their parents split, no matter what the legal status of the parental relationship, but at least cohabiting couples are less likely to have children than married couples, so more cohabitation means that fewer children experience the separation of their parents.

Many factors, including loss of a job, a difficult child, housing with no privacy, drug addiction, alcoholism, and serious illness, can precipitate divorce. Note that infidelity is not on the list; usually an extra-marital affair is the result, not the cause, of a troubled relationship. Another factor is youth. In the United States, most divorces occur among younger adults who have not been married long and who do not have children. Much as a grandmother wants grandchildren, it is a mistake to pressure newlyweds to have them. Nonetheless, divorce is a possibility for every family with children, which explains why lesson 19 is important.

LESSON 19: STRENGTHEN THE PARTNERSHIP

Romantic partnerships fluctuate along a continuum, like a compass that turns 180 degrees, with one end of the continuum being a loving, cooperative alliance and the other a bitter, destructive battle. The compass can turn back toward 360 degrees (love) or can stay stuck at 180 (war).

This waxing and waning is not always understood by children or young adults. This came to me forcefully when one of my daughters wondered whether she should marry her boyfriend. She considered my thirty-year marriage a happy, enduring one. She asked, "Mom, when did you know that Dad was the man for you, because you would love him forever?"

"About seven years ago," I replied.

She thought I was joking, so she asked my husband. "Dad, Mom said she didn't know that this marriage would last until about seven years ago."

Martin replied, "That's about right."

She immediately told her sisters; they also were taken aback that we wed and raised four children without being certain that our love would endure. Most other grandmothers would not be surprised; they know that relationships are dynamic, dependent on daily interactions and repeated commitments.

Lesson 19, strengthen the partnership, is especially crucial, given that many mothers believe that their child's chosen partner is not as wonderful as their own child, a sleepy opinion that thunders awake if one's child complains that a spouse is so terrible that separation is the only solution.

Avoid that moment if possible, and be quiet if thunder rumbles. Decades of research have led to a robust conclusion: divorce is hard on children and grandchildren. Grandmothers do not have the power to stop divorce, of course, but they need to do what they can to improve the partnership so that both parents are able to care for the children—married if possible, in a cooperative separation if not.

Psychologists write about a *parental alliance*, which is a cooperative relationship between parents to care for the children.[8] That comes more naturally when the parents are married and living together, but it can also transpire when parents are unmarried and apart.[9]

Mutual support and affection is the default among family members, sometimes surprising outsiders, grandparents, and psychologists alike. Human children and their parents develop strong attachments, even when one party behaves badly. Parents dedicate themselves to difficult children and to their child who has done wrong. Mistreated children sometimes want to stay with an abusive parent, and divorcing parents are sometimes amazed when a child chooses to live with the other parent.

Family connections, linked lives, mutual affection—these have sustained people for hundreds of thousands of years. Of course, attachment is not automatic, not inevitable; the ebb and flow of romantic love is one example. The role of grandmothers is to strengthen that natural parental alliance so both parents work together for the grandchild.

Remember lesson 14 in chapter 10, which suggests that grandmothers and their adult children might need a third party to help them understand each other? Mediation is especially useful when divorce is on the horizon for parents. Many jurisdictions require it if children are involved in divorce, but grandmothers might find it for a feuding couple long before the courts become involved.

How else should grandmothers strengthen a relationship? The earlier chapters of this book include many suggestions, beginning with when the mother and father decide to become a couple. There is a natural flow to romantic partnerships: bliss is highest during the honeymoon period, quite high at birth, and then dramatically reduced several months later. It often rises a little during middle childhood and dips again during early adolescence.[10] These are general trends; each couple rides their own rollercoaster. Generally, however, when grown-up children leave home, husbands and wives appreciate each other again. These trends alert grandmothers that major help may be needed early on.

Grandmothers can move their child's partnership several degrees toward the loving side. Money and time are major stresses for new parents; grandmothers might offer childcare for a weekly date night. That may be pivotal because many new parents are so overwhelmed with work, homes, and infant care that they forget their relationship—until it fades and fractures. Trusted babysitting is expensive and anxiety producing. Parents may consider it a needless luxury. However, grandmothers know that private couple time is an investment in the long-term welfare of the grandchild. A *regular* grandmother commitment to babysit, to make dinner, or to take the children out is best: children appreciate routines, and parents feel less beholden if they need not ask.

Grandmothers must remember that the intimate relationship is between the couple, not between the grandmother and the adult child. If a grandmother believes that divorce is tragic, a sign of a failed, broken marriage, producing a depressed and overwhelmed single parent with irreparable harm to children, that is precisely the opinion she needs to keep to herself. She must listen and support the parents and connect with the grandchildren. That is what is needed, not her disapproval.

Fortunately, maturation helps: with age, people are more likely to see the positive aspects of past experiences. Couples can take pride in each other and their children; the grandmothers' perspective can help them do so. Thus, listening to a grown child—out of the hearing of the grandchild—may help that distressed adult avoid sarcasm, defensiveness, and the impulsive, narrow path toward divorce.

Many couples reach the brink of divorce and then reconcile, part of the ebb and flow of marriage. If a grandmother tells a couple to separate or, alternatively, to stay together, at least one gatekeeper will be angry. That risks her seeing the grandchildren either too much or not at all.

LESSON 20: BE A STEADY ANCHOR

Of course, ideally children have two loving parents, supporting them cooperatively throughout life. But although divorce is hard on children, no family problem *always* leads to school failure, criminal behavior, or psychopathology. Children of divorce with caring schools, neighborhoods, and grandparents usually do well. Those other supports become crucial.

Children do *not* need married parents. Instead, each child needs at least one adult who loves and cares for them, always and forever. Some children have many such adults, two parents, two grandmothers, two grandfathers, aunts, uncles, teachers, neighbors. But that abundance is not essential. Especially when divorcing parents are overwhelmed with their own problems, grandmothers may be that one crucial person.

Being overwhelmed with one's own problems is typical after divorce. Newly divorced parents must make financial, emotional, and physical adjustments, especially they have been married for years, which is usually the case when children are involved.

Consider one study that traced the outcome of divorce over twenty-five years. Judith Wallerstein followed 60 families with 131 children who divorced in about 1980.[11] Relatively few had sufficient grandmother help. Blame for that rests not only on the grandmothers but also on the mothers, the fathers, the culture, and the courts. Some mothers tried to move closer to their parents, but judges insisted that they stay in the same jurisdiction—near the father and the judge, distant from the grandmother.

Perhaps because those sixty divorces occurred decades ago, mothers always had custody. Some fathers disappeared. Some mothers became stern gatekeepers, limiting father access, convinced that was best for the children. That kept paternal grandparents away as well. The folly of that decision became evident when the children became adolescents: about a third of them left their mothers to live with their fathers for at least a year.

Although the biological mothers had custody, less than half (46 percent) prioritized their children after the divorce. Some (29 percent) neglected motherhood, focusing on their own employment, education, emotions, and romance.

The researchers write about this group:

As the women turned their attention to rebuilding their lives, the children experienced diminished attention, time, and care. Empty homes awaited them after school and during long weekends. One young woman, who had been 5 years old at the divorce, cried bitterly as she recalled, "Those were the loneliest years of my life. I had no one to talk to and no one to play with." Households, including mealtimes, were often plunged into disorder, as mother's attention shifted from care of the children to her work and social or educational pursuits and the oldest child, often a reluctant and resentful young adolescent, or a 9-year-old, was placed in charge. Not surprisingly, some youngsters enforced discipline by threatening or slapping younger siblings. . . . Typically, after an average of four or more years, most of these mothers regained their balance.[12]

Grandmothers could have filled those empty homes, provided constructive discipline (no slapping), becoming the dedicated caregiver the children needed. Although these mothers "regained their balance," some grandchildren—especially those in early adolescence—never did. Other research at about the same time found that most grandmothers provided immediate help, but three years after the divorce, many resented their daughters' continued dependence. Those who took over for their daughters were also those most likely to pull back.[13]

Some research on child development focuses on one risk or another, such as the risk caused by divorce, by maternal mental illness, or by living in a high-crime neighborhood. Scientists have found dozens of risks, examined one-by-one, that reduce child well-being. For instance, as already mentioned, children of divorce do less well in school and have poorer physical and mental health.

However, the research also uncovered some children, described as *resilient* or even *invulnerable*, who seemed unscathed by a risk that harmed other children. This includes children who experienced divorce.[14] What distinguished resilient children from the rest?[15] Newer analysis suggests that all the risks and protections need to be considered in a bundle; no single risk is determinative. One powerful protection is a strong relationship with a caring adult, who provides stability—the anchor that a grandmother can be.

Apparently, almost every child can withstand one trauma, but "the likelihood of problems increased as the number of risk factors increased."[16] Sadly, risks are not parceled out fairly: every risk makes others more likely. This is apparent with divorce: poverty, chaotic households, family conflict, erratic discipline, and unsupportive neighborhoods often precede and follow divorce. Sometimes divorce leads to remarriage, which may benefit the adults financially as well as emotionally. For children, however, remarriage is one more stress.[17]

Grandmothers, especially when a marital conflict erupts, can be above the fray, the steady family support for the grandchild. Adults may separate, reunite, disengage, reconcile, divorce, remarry—and explain their emotions and conclusions at every stage to the children. But children need stability: they suffer with "churning" (the ups and downs of their parents' relationship).[18] They do not welcome stepparents and stepsiblings, even though many adults, including their parents as well as judges and social workers, consider remarriage to be good for children.[19]

Keep in mind that children naturally are attached to both parents; yet grandmothers are naturally inclined to criticize parents who divorce. They might blame not only their child's partner but also their own child. Forget blaming, and protect the grandchild. That means grandmothers must express respect and harmony, staying "nonpartisan" to help the grandchildren. This is wise, as partisan grandparents risk exclusion.[20]

Exclusion was common for grandmothers whose child was not granted custody after divorce. Remember that a divorce boom occurred in the United States in the 1970s, when laws changed. One aspect of the law did not change, however, and that was the presumption that mothers should care for the children and fathers should pay alimony.

Millions of paternal grandparents lost touch with their grandchildren. As detailed in chapter 4, many of them pressured state legislatures to mandate visitation, and all fifty states enacted laws to that effect. However, as you have also read, the Supreme Court invalidated many of these laws because mothers were assumed to know best. Thus, if a mother had custody, and if she chose to limit or exclude father contact, many paternal grandmothers lost connection with their grandchildren.

Fortunately, this is now changing because courts are often mandating joint physical custody, which results in much more contact between paternal grandparents and grandchildren. Indeed, sometimes the father's mother sees her grandchildren more after divorce than she did before. This custody arrangement is certainly better for grandmothers, and it may be better for parents and children as well. Let me explain.

Joint physical custody requires that two divorcing parents cooperate and coordinate. Children living with each parent part of the time works out best for all involved, especially for the grandparents.[21] Joint custody is now the default judgment in Belgium, Sweden, and Arizona. In those places, judges need to explain why *not* to grant joint custody, instead of explaining why they do.

The possibility of joint custody is another reason why grandmothers should not take sides when a partnership reaches the breaking point: both partners and both grandmothers need to continue to connect with the children. Ideally, they have already established close relationships. In Belgium and Sweden, where the courts now encourage joint physical custody, grandparents on both sides see their grandchildren as much as they did when the couples were married—an ideal arrangement for the children.[22]

This ideal, of course, is difficult for the adults, since everyone has strong feelings about romances that flourished enough to produce children and then faltered. Emotions can turn from love to hate, not only in divorcing parents but also in grandparents. However, if the priority is thriving grandchildren, grandmothers can put aside their emotions about the middle generation.

I know this is not easy. Grandmothers can be angry and feel that they themselves have failed. If they rush to take over, that may imply that the middle generation is hopeless. The grandchildren need reassurance and affection. The danger is that they conclude that their parents hate each other, that their grandparents are angry at their parents, and that they themselves are unwanted. That gives them no safe harbor, no anchor.

Six generalities might help grandmothers protect their grandchildren:

1. Stability is needed, continuity is valued, regularity is reassuring. If a grandmother always visited on a certain day, or always cooked a certain dish, or always read to the child at bedtime, she should continue.

2. Children need friends. Especially when family structure changes, grandmothers can help with school trips, arrange play dates, supervise sleepovers, or whatever is appropriate to encourage peer support.
3. Transitions are disruptive. If children live with their grandparents temporarily, everyone (grandparents, parents, and especially grandchildren) needs to know which routines and values need to change or be maintained and how long three-generation or custodial grandparenting will last.
4. Promises should be kept and disappointment avoided. If a vacation or a visit from Dad or Grandma or a birthday present is promised, it must happen.
5. Overt conflict is frightening. No loud fighting about divorce, childcare, money, or anything else when the children are present.
6. Children want to love and forgive both parents. If a grandmother openly criticizes a parent, children may feel personally attacked.

This rule also applies to criticizing other grandparents. If the grandmother herself is divorced, she must not criticize her former husband—the child's grandfather.

I know a grandmother who was divorced years ago. She wants her grandchildren to sympathize with the difficulties that divorce caused her. When she harps on the faults of her former spouse (now dead), she alienates her sons and grandchildren. One son moved to a distant city; his mother bombarded him with advice about finding an apartment. He hated her for that. Both sons and grandchildren avoid visiting the grandmother; the son's wife makes them.

LESSON 21: STEP INTO THE FAMILY

As you see, grandmothers must help grandchildren when adults divorce. Sometimes the grandchildren are stepgrandchildren, the progeny of a man who divorced his first wife and now is married to another woman, who becomes a stepmother and then a stepgrandmother. Ideally, she develops her own relationship with the children, and the biological grandmother accepts that.

As you remember from chapter 3, one hypothesis for grandmother investment is that selfish genes propel people to care for those who carry their genes. However, every study of non-genetic grandparents finds them more involved with grandchildren than expected.[23] Grandchildren reciprocate. My son-in-law travels two thousand miles every year, bringing my daughter and grandchildren, to visit his stepgrandmother, now virtually blind. She married his biological grandfather when he was young; he says she is the only grandmother he knew.

Women need to work on developing a close relationship with their stepgrandchildren for the same reasons they need to develop a close relationship with their biological grandchildren—all three generations gain.

Is this possible, when no genetic connection is present? Yes. My son-in-law is not an isolated case. Here is another one, reported from the grandmother's perspective.[24] A woman had two sons. One died suddenly at age eighteen; the other, Colin, left home in early adulthood to work a thousand miles away. Three years after his brother's death, Colin fell in love with Andrea, mother of Brandon. As one might expect for a man in love, he did not want to be apart from Andrea for more than a day. And Andrea did not want to be apart from her son.

Consequently, when Colin flew home to celebrate Christmas with his parents, he brought Andrea and Brandon with him. His mother wrote that, when Brandon got off the plane,

> *he rolled straight into my arms. I could not believe it. . . . I had a grandson. . . . Andrea's mother was still alive then, she died a few years later and Brandon didn't see his paternal grandmother much. But we didn't think any of this out; we didn't count up to figure how many grandmothers a boy needed or deserved. In the end, blood counts, but not as much as love.*

This woman and her husband were in mourning for their dead son; they had not had a Christmas tree for three years. But *it wasn't fair, I thought, to ask a child to come for Christmas and not do anything. And so without telling anybody, I tied red ribbons on the branches of the ficus tree in the living room and put wrapped presents beneath its potted trunk, and when we got home from the airport, Brandon's eyes went wide at the sight.*

"Colin said we wouldn't have a tree!" he explained.

"Well, it's not exactly a Christmas tree," I said.

"Yes," he said, "it is."

We stood and looked at it, and everybody knew that if not for Brandon there wouldn't have been ribbons.

A few days later, she had a serious talk with Brandon, explaining that Andrea and Colin might marry, or might break up, but that "I would be his grandmother as long as he wanted me to. . . . And we shook on that. And nothing has changed in the twenty or so years since."

This was a fortunate, lifelong relationship that helped the woman recover from bereavement and that sustained Brandon through school and college. Colin and Andrea married, broke up, and then got back together; the grandmother/Brandon relationship continued to anchor the boy through it all.

Likewise, thousands of other stepgrandmothers develop close connections with their new grandchildren, benefiting everyone. Although stepgrandmothers are similar in many ways to biological grandmothers, they differ as well, as found by that extensive study of 12,959 grandmothers in many European nations.[25] Nine percent of biological grandmothers became daily caregivers, but only 4 percent of stepgrandmothers did. Biological grandmothers also provided more weekly care, but surprisingly, the closer ties of the biological grandmothers disappeared when the researchers tallied how many grandmothers provided no care at all. Fewer stepgrandmothers than biological grandmothers were in that never-caregiving group!

Furthermore, the stepgrandmothers were *less* likely to argue with their stepdaughters about child care. One in every eight biological mothers frequently disagreed with their children about child rearing, but only one in fifteen non-biological grandmothers did. Are the step-

grandmothers less invested in the children, or do some genetic grandmothers have trouble letting go?

As with every human relationship, many factors make it easier or
harder to become close. Stepgrandmothers are more likely to become
close when:

1. a grandchild is young (under five is ideal);
2. the grandchild lives nearby;
3. the stepgrandmother is young (under sixty) and healthy;
4. no biological grandmothers are already active caregivers;
5. the stepgrandmother has no other grandchildren;
6. the stepgrandmother is welcomed by the child's parents;
7. the stepgrandmother joined the family because of death, not
   divorce.

None of these factors determines the relationship (several were not
true for Brandon), but all affect it.

Brandon is not the only one. A study of young adult stepgrandchildren found that about a third of them were distant from their
stepgrandparents but two-thirds were close, with about half surprised
to learn in adolescence that the stepgrandparent was not biological
kin. Although some adults, especially lawyers and genealogists, connect family with genes, children do not, which makes them open
to grandmothers who are not their biological relatives. As one said,
"Seeing my dad get along with her [stepgrandmother] made me
think, 'Oh, okay, well, if Dad can get along with her then it's okay
and, you know, I'll do the same.' Because of that I felt like I could
trust her because we were family."[26]

That child understood what some adults do not. Divorce is an
adult problem; children care about how the family members—grandmothers certainly included in family—cooperate to care for the child.

• 13 •

Adolescents

"*You're* a terrible mother of a teenager!" yelled an angry adolescent. "I'm learning on the job," the mother shot back. "I've never been a mother of a teenager before."

Grandmothers cannot claim that excuse. Their years of experience (the universal benefit of growing old) taught them something. Ideally they have gained wisdom and patience, and teenagers have the imagination and energy of youth. If the two generations combine their strengths, they can enjoy two difficult periods of life, old age and adolescence, when a companion at the other stage provides crucial balance.

There is danger here: each cohort of teenagers enters a world that has never existed before and must reach adulthood amid snares, opportunities, and hazards that their elders never knew. Some grandmothers retreat when the grandchildren are teenagers, fondly remembering the halcyon days when the grandchild could be cradled, or at least sit in a lap. However, grandmothers can be a lifeline during adolescence because decades of experience have woven a guide rope that both parent and child can grab.

LESSON 22: NAVIGATE CHANGING RELATIONSHIPS

Grandparents know that relating to an adolescent is not easy, especially compared to a much smaller, more predictable, and usually compliant child. Parenting a growing person is like "trying to hit a moving target";[1] each time a caregiver thinks she has a bead on her child, that child moves and morphs. The target jumps especially erratically in adolescence. Joy becomes rage, anxiety paralyzes, depression deepens—and then, for no obvious reason, all is well again.[2] Teenagers tell their parents they hate them; a day later they love them. No wonder parents are bewildered.

Because parenting is confusing, grandparenting relationships become more complex. The general strategy—follow the parents' lead—may not be what is needed because parents may veer toward a dead end, or adolescents may resist whatever the parent suggests. The first step is communication. If a grandmother has no intense conversations with her child about her grandchild, and then with the grandchild, something is amiss with the adults, the teenager, or both. In the heat of the moment, teenagers are likely to provoke the parents. A listening grandmother can relieve some pressure to avoid an explosion.

Serious destruction might occur. Drug abuse and risk taking escalate, sometimes with deadly results. The statistics are chilling: violent deaths of fifteen- to nineteen-year-olds are eight times higher than for five- to nine-year-olds, with early adolescents (age ten to fourteen) already showing signs of danger ahead.

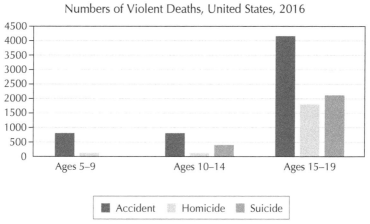

Numbers of Violent Deaths, United States, 2016

Ages 5–9   Ages 10–14   Ages 15–19

Accident   Homicide   Suicide

As you see, teenagers themselves take risks that make them vulnerable to a tragic end. Grandmother protection needed.

Data from *National Vital Statistics Reports* 67, no. 6, July 26, 2018.

Social scientists refer to the "well known age-crime curve," which shows arrests increasing precipitously in mid- to late adolescence in every nation before they decrease.[3] Other hazards—anorexia, bulimia, early sex, deep depression, and more—escalate beginning at age ten until they finally decrease in the mid-twenties.

Grandmothers are desperately needed; their influence is added to that of the parents. For them, mothering a teenager is not new; they can offer perspective, laughter, and often financial support. They can reassure the parents that most teenagers avoid tragedy and eventually appreciate their elders. Lessons that grandmothers needed earlier (notice, admire, keep quiet) may recede when new wisdom and patience are required, or they may be more important than ever.

Experience gives perspective but does not guarantee insight, especially because world politics, technological innovations, and moral shifts have made grandmothering a moving target as well. Teenagers do not naturally respect their parents, or keep their bedrooms neat, or appreciate the luxuries they enjoy, from pop music to interstate travel.

Many grandmothers, recalling past mothering mistakes, try "to master perfection this time around,"[4] as one grandmother expressed it. She drove her three pubescent granddaughters nine hundred miles for a weeklong vacation at a dude ranch, imagining that camping in the luxurious rented van would be a happy adventure for the four of them, as it would have been when she was young.

Instead, beginning at mile one and continuing all week, her granddaughters bickered, quarreled, and complained about the beds, the food, the heat. The AC did not work as well as they wished; they did not agree about which radio station was best; sometimes the music was drowned by static or disappeared with distance and mountains. Never mind that zooming along on an interstate highway, past purple mountains and fields of golden grain, on the way to a dude ranch was a luxury fifty years ago. The destination was not appreciated, either; the girls did not care that, a few decades ago, only the very rich rode horses for fun.

Several days after they arrived at the ranch, this grandmother heard herself shrieking "like a banshee" over a wet towel left too long on the bathroom floor. She then slammed the door to her room, to be alone as she despaired at her abject failure to be the perfect grandmother. Her granddaughters quietly cleaned up the cabin, including the bathroom. The grandmother was upset with herself for the rest of the week.

But a few miles before the van reached home, the granddaughters chorused, "It was the best vacation *ever*," pleading for a repeat next summer. She was shocked and grateful; they, at least, did not expect perfection.

As in this example, grandmothers do not always know what their grandchildren think and need. A joke: *Adolescents like their grandparents because they have a common enemy.* Like most jokes, this contains some truth. Especially when teenagers distance themselves from their parents, they need grandparents. One team of researchers finds that "adolescents perceive grandparents to be more understanding and patient than parents."[5] So far, so good, but watch out.

The human trait *self-serving bias* means that we consider ourselves a little better than other people, whom we view as not quite as smart, compassionate, or honest as we ourselves are. Psychologists are not surprised when grandmothers think they are better caregivers than their own children are, or when they hope that their adolescent grandchildren will recognize and appreciate their merits.

However, rivalry infects everyone. If a grandchild breaks free from mother and clings to grandmother, something is awry. Parents and their children having warm and respectful relationships predicts good grandmother relationships and emotional health for all three generations.

Teenage rebellion ricochets, striking grandparents after hitting parents and then flipping away from both. If a grandchild is encouraged to exclude the middle generation, telling secrets to the grandmother, that might harm all three generations. For example, one grandmother was happy when her teenage grandchild came to live with her but later said, "I had hoped it would be a bonding experience, but I also found, in retrospect, I became the disciplinarian because my daughter wasn't there . . . by the time those 8 months were over, there was a lot of tension and stress between the three of us."[6]

Adolescence brings complexities that require thought, not simple conclusions. Consider two families in which the grandmothers believed they rescued their granddaughters. Did they?

A young adult in divinity school told me the saga of her family. When she was a child, her parents struggled with alcohol and drug addiction, moving from one place to another, usually far from their disapproving parents. In childhood, my informant never knew her grandmother.

Then the middle generation found religion, became saved, quit drugs, prayed loudly and often, moved to a rural community near other believers and also near the metropolis where the grandmother lived. They sent their children (my informant was the oldest of three) to a small, strict, evangelical school, where students were expected to honor their parents and follow school rules. The formerly permissive parents became authoritarian (parenting styles are explained in chapter 10).

Their adolescent daughter hated dogma and restrictions; she quit school. The parents tried to force attendance, but no matter how they entreated, bribed, or punished, the girl refused. The grandmother came to visit, horrified that the teenager was not in school. She announced, "I am taking her," and did so, paying hefty tuition at a selective boarding school in an affluent suburb near her home and furnishing a bedroom in her home for the grandchild on weekends.

That grandchild rarely saw her parents. She attended college in the same city, living with Grandma, in her home. Eventually, that grandmother had trouble walking, and her adult children urged her to enter a senior residence. She retorted, "Stop telling me to move . . . you'll give me a heart attack . . . at least I'm not an alcoholic."

The formerly rebellious grandchild became a devoted caregiver, wheeling her grandma around. When that aging matriarch refused treatment for life-threatening cancer, her grandchild stuck with her, against the entreaties of the middle generation. When she died, the grandchild moved to another city, alienated from all.

The second example comes from a woman whose son wanted to marry right after high school.[7] She told him, "hold off . . . grow wings." (She herself had married young and then divorced.)

Her son postponed the wedding, despite tears from his teenage girlfriend, who was devoutly religious. She believed that teenagers in love should marry before they had sex (or babies).

The wedding occurred a year later. The future grandmother was "immersed" in her career and "frenetic life," living with a man who shared her political passions. She had no time for lessons 2 and 3: "Respect the gatekeepers" and "Recognize linked lives." She rarely saw her son and his wife, even after they had two daughters, Emma and Grace. Her daughter-in-law did not mind; her own mother was an active grandmother, and cohabitation was a sin.

A decade later, when her career was less frenetic and her romance more stable, this grandmother began to connect with her granddaughters: "We ate; we shopped; we played miniature golf; we saw movies and plays; we walked in the park. They talked. I listened. . . . I showed up at one of Emma's swim meets, decked out in her school colors and carrying a little Go Dolphins sign I made. Emma laughed and introduced me to her coach."

Her daughter-in-law did not laugh; she fumed. Her son told her she was undignified and needed to "back off and just be a normal grandmother. . . . You need to keep your political opinions, your religious opinions, all your opinions to yourself. And you need to act your age."

"Act your age" are fighting words. A joke that grandmothers appreciate: "I told my grandmother to act her age. Then she died." Acting your age implies senescent, shrunken old women, docile and passive, wearing flowery, loose-fitting dresses, not decked out in school colors.

Emma asked, "Gramma? How come you don't stay home and make cookies and knit like other grannies?"

"I used to. I knit my way through my divorce, with great heart and lousy technique. I spent a lot of time unraveling my messes and starting over."

Many contemporary grandmothers reject knitting, mending, and baking, and the life they symbolize. They do not "slave over a hot stove" or "work their fingers to the bone," phrases that arose from an earlier time. Modern women put dinner into the microwave; they buy sweaters.

In deference to her son, this grandmother no longer initiated contact with her granddaughters. But Emma often texted, "Gma RUOK? Howz yr day looking?" The grandmother knew that meant "take me to lunch so we can talk." After dutifully telling Em to check with her parents, she drove to the house, saw her hostile daughter-in-law's shadow in the hall, assured Gracie (who greeted her at the door with a bear hug) that she would take her to lunch some other day soon, and spirited Emma away.

At lunch, she tried to "just be a normal grandmother," avoiding politics and religion, changing the subject when Emma complained about her parents. But opinions leaked out, becoming ammunition. After one lunch, her son emailed, "Did you really tell Em that talk radio is geared for monkey-minds?"

She confessed: she did.

Then, for several weeks, no texts. Worried, she phoned. Her son said that Emma had swallowed pills and "*we almost lost her*." Her granddaughter was in a mental ward, refusing to see her mother, unable to phone, asking to see Grandma. The psychiatrist thought a visit might be therapeutic; her son said he and his wife would "not stand in the way." The grandmother visited Emma several times, behind locked doors, in a small room with nothing sharp, nothing hard, nothing breakable, no drapery cords, no electric outlets. She cradled her granddaughter, reassuring her, stroking her hair.

Emma recovered. But back home, silence, no calls, no texts. This grandmother wondered, worried, waited, and then decided that Emma "needs all the love and reassurance she can get." She texted, "Em, RUOK? Howz yr day looking :-). Luv, Gma."

What happened in these two families? Did you notice that the one who rebelled against religion went to divinity school after her grandmother died? Did you wonder why Emma did not text her grandmother? Perhaps her parents confiscated her cell phone, or perhaps Emma herself decided against that relationship? I do not know. This episode came from a wonderful collection of grandmother experiences; the grandmother does not explain.

However, I know some truths: families vary, adolescents are unpredictable, and many interpretations are possible. Both of these grandmothers sacrificed for their granddaughters, both came to the rescue, and neither deserves blame for the drug addiction or teenage marriage. Moreover, it is unethical as well as unwise to judge a family from a distance.

Nonetheless, these family relationships provoke thought. The first child's school refusal and the second child's suicide attempt were preceded by years when the grandmothers had no interactions with the parents or the grandchildren. Every doctor—medical and psychological—finds prevention better than cure. Could the grandmothers have prevented the crisis? Emma's grandmother wrote that she understood her daughter-in-law's anger at her but that she had quit trying to repair that relationship. Mistake? Could the other grandmother have visited her children when their family life was chaotic, establishing family support? Family relationships are lifelong; grandmothers are part of the family, which means that their role begins before grandchildren are born and extends into adulthood.

LESSON 23: RECONSIDER SUICIDE, DRUGS, AND SEX

Time to reassure. Most teenagers, most of the time, respect their elders, and most grandmothers work with parents, not against them. It is true that many teenagers criticize their parents' food, clothes, hair, religion, language, musical preferences, and everything else. Some utter curses, epithets, and slang that shock their grandmothers. Some dye their hair green or shave it all off; some wear jeans waaay below their waists or skirts waaaaay above their knees. Most drink, smoke, inhale, inject, or swallow drugs.[8] Many think about suicide, and some, impulsively, try it.[9] Many become sexually active.

Yes, Erikson's fourth stage, *identity versus role confusion*, is evident.[10] Adolescents struggle to establish who they are religiously, politically, and sexually; the identity crisis sometimes propels them from one set of values and behaviors to another that seems opposite to the first. That search includes words or actions that adults notice, fear, and denounce. Erikson's own children were rebellious adolescents.

But no, the search for identity is not a disaster. Perspective is needed; grandmothers can provide it. Although rates of serious problems are far higher than in childhood, violent deaths are less common now than a century ago.[11] Teenagers are more likely to reach adulthood, alive and thoughtful, than teenagers did when their grandmothers were young.

For example, there is no "epidemic of teen suicide" despite the alarming title of a 2001 book.[12] Completed suicide is rare at any age, (annually less than 1 in 7,000 deaths). Teenage girls rarely kill themselves (although they make more attempts than boys do), so Emma's recovery is expected. In North America, those most likely to quit life are widowers over age eighty-five. Their suicide rate is three times higher than that of teenage boys, who are themselves four times more likely to kill themselves than their female peers.[13] As her prefrontal cortex matures, Emma is likely to wonder what she was thinking when she swallowed those pills.

Although the identity search is common, destructive rebellion is not. Most teenagers hold attitudes similar to their parents', whose attitudes are like their own parents'.[14] If anything, each generation learns from the mistakes of the previous one. Teen pregnancy, school refusal, drug abuse, and delinquency are not the norm, and rates of all are markedly lower than when grandmothers were young. The most dramatic declines are for pregnancy among the youngest adolescents, especially in the ethnic and income groups that had high rates of teen pregnancy a few decades ago. The annual birth rate for girls aged ten to fourteen is one in five thousand, which is one-seventh the 1991 rate.

Today, as decades ago, if both parents attend church regularly or both are college graduates or both avoid cigarettes, alcohol, and other drugs, their teenagers usually follow suit. Grandparents influence parents as well as grandchildren; it is not unusual to have three generations of church goers, dedicated voters, or college graduates. Some of this is

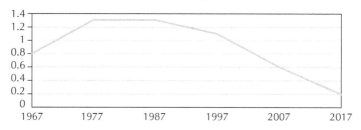

Birth Rate Per 1,000 Women Ages 10–14, United States

Birth Rate Per 1,000 Women Ages 15–19, United States

Some suggest that one reason for this radical decline is that grand-mothers are less able and willing to raise grandchildren. Could that be?
Child Trends, "Teen Births" (2019), retrieved from https://www.child trends.org/indicators/teen-births.

genetic, but some also is the example, and influence, of older generations on younger ones.

Since every young life is like a ship sailing toward the future, an experienced first mate monitors direction, wind, tides, underwater rocks, ice, consulting maps and stars. Adolescents follow their own course, but parents and grandparents guide them, never setting them adrift. Grandmothers remember the dangers of adolescence (they did things that their parents never knew), but they also know that parents should never abandon ship.

Personally, one source of my wisdom comes from my profession, developmental psychology. Other grandmothers might benefit from some of the stars and maps I consult.

One luminary is the cognitive theorist Jean Piaget. He said that after reality-based thinking (concrete operational thought) from ages seven to eleven, the adolescent "thinks beyond the present and forms theories about everything, delighting especially in considerations of that which is not." And "possibility no longer appears merely as an extension of an empirical situation or of action actually performed. Instead, it is reality that is now secondary to possibility."[15]

Consequently, cognitive advances push teenagers to argue forcefully, but not realistically, for sexual freedom and drug acceptance. In such arguments, it is helpful to remember that possibility is stronger than reality. Adults can present their own views without assuming that a child's words reveal actions. Discussion helps the young person make wise decisions; a rigid prohibition might provoke a counter-reaction.

A map through adolescence comes from cognitive-behavior therapy, which most psychologists believe to be the most effect treatment for teenagers with severe anxiety or depression. That requires sympathetic listening, reframing, and suggestions for behavior change. Most adolescents experience emotional distress; they need a sympathetic and wise adult. Ideally, parents fill that role, but a teenage tirade may flood the parents' brain with stress hormones, preventing sympathetic listening. Grandmothers may be less likely to overreact. Adolescence is a pressure cooker; grandparents can release steam.

One group of social scientists found that

> *teenagers viewed grandparents as confidants with whom they could discuss personal issues. Thus, even if teenaged grandchildren do not appear to seek closeness with their grandparents it is important not to underestimate the value they place on them and the comfort they find in having them as an available resource.*[16]

Now consider some details of those maps that can guide the adolescent ship. Much is new regarding sex, drugs, and technology in the past fifty years. Prohibitions, predictions, and practices that were once accepted are gone. Should grandmothers repeat old fears? As a teenager, I thought marijuana was a "gateway drug"; addiction to heroin was on the other side if I dared walk through that gate. My maiden aunt (thankfully not my mother) thought that if she left me alone with a boy, pregnancy would be next.

Those fears came from an earlier era. Instead of repeating such predictions, grandmothers might share insights they gained as they and their friends dealt with rising hormones and social pressures. They know that "stories of the past provide opportunities for teaching about the future."[17]

First, consider sex. Sexual thoughts and desires explode at puberty, as has been true for thousands of years. That is a powerful biological mandate, the reason our species continues to survive. What has changed is better nutrition: puberty begins earlier (around age ten; once, it was fourteen).

Acting on those sexual impulses is determined by the social context. In the United States, with the advent of better birth control and then widespread AIDS, adolescent sexual activity increased in the 1990s and then decreased after 2000. Six factors make adolescent sex unlike that of their grandmothers' youth:

1. more varieties of contraception
2. pregnancy tests available earlier and privately
3. safe and legal abortion
4. mutual consent replacing the double standard
5. date rape recognized as a crime
6. HIV and other sexually transmitted diseases are more common

Consequently, many practices that were unimaginable when grandmothers were teenagers are common today. For example, condoms are sold at supermarkets, available in vending machines, and free in some high schools. Some teenagers ask each other for consent before intercourse. Currently, grandmothers who pontificate about birth control or sexual diseases may seem hopelessly old-fashioned.

Fortunately, no preaching is needed: Adolescents have gotten the message. In the past decades, not only has sexual activity among high school students gone down, but the teen birth rate is also less than a third of what it was.[18] It every nation, marriage is less common, and it occurs later than it did—eight years later in the United States.[19] Intercourse too early, or unwanted, still predicts depression and drug abuse, but at least one study found that chosen sexual activity among older teenagers, when peers are also active, correlates with higher self-esteem.[20]

Because grandchildren sometimes talk with grandparents about sex, and because grandparents are more aware of long-term consequences and less troubled by immediate activity, grandparents may be able to encourage contraception and safe sex. One grandmother did just that and reports happily:

> For her 16th birthday, I talked her mother into getting her on birth control pills, and she called me up and said "thank you, thank you grandma!" because it's just a fact of life and she knows that I was responsible because she knows, we have talked about it before, and I feel good about that, and so does she, she feels really good about it.[21]

Note that this grandmother talked to the mother. If a grandmother got the pill on her own for her granddaughter, that would be a mistake. This scenario is depicted in *Grandma*, a movie in which a grandmother (Elle) tries to get $630 to pay for her granddaughter Sage's abortion. Elle and Sage ask many people, including Sage's lover, several of Elle's friends and admirers, and Elle's ex-husband. After all that, she still needs $500. Finally, Elle asks her daughter (Sage's mother), who angrily pays the full amount. At the end, grandmother and mother are reconciled. The movie would be a dud if Grandma had asked the mother first, but in real life, that is where it should begin.

There is a deeper message here for grandmothers. With experience, a woman learns that lust is not always love, and that everyone needs family. That alone is reason to listen, and then respond, to adolescents and their parents.

One specific that grandmothers may need to understand is same-sex love. I have spoken with several grandmothers who say they would love their grandchildren no matter what, but they worry that their grandchildren are homosexual. Personally, I did not know that homosexuality existed until I was an adult. My mother told me that my older cousin, who had fathered a child with his wife, was getting divorced. "Ray doesn't seem to like women," she said, obliquely. I was bewildered; Ray was always kind to me and my mother. Later, when I was an adult, Ray invited me and my family to dinner with him and his male partner. Watching them, I finally figured it out.

Such ignorance was common when many people were "in the closet." My pastor said that her favorite Sunday school teacher was a man who shared a house with another man, also a devout Lutheran. As an adult, she went to visit them, and only then did it dawn on her that they might be a couple. She asked; they affirmed, adding, "Don't tell."

That has changed. As grandmothers understand the connection between sex and love, they can support their grandchildren, no matter what their sexuality. My local city councilman was captain of his high school football team when he came out as gay. His peers accepted that, but he worried that his grandfather, a blue-collar union member and steadfast Democrat, would reject him.

> *Grandpa, there is something I want to tell you about me.*
> *What is it?*
> *I am gay.*
> *Oh, thank God. I was afraid you were going to tell me you are a Republican.*

Of course, in most families, diverse political views are less contentious than sexual ones. But every kind of divergence between the generations may be easier for grandmothers to accept than for parents. The reason, again, is years of experience. Over their lifetime, grandmothers have witnessed dramatic changes, not only in teen pregnancy and same-sex marriage but also in college attendance, cigarette smoking, social media, racial integration, immigration, political parties, and much more. That makes them better able to hear unexpected adolescent ideas.

Now consider how this relates to another contentious issue between parents and teenagers, drug abuse. I remember the war in Vietnam, the war in Iraq, the war in Afghanistan. Grandmothers have seen radical reversals regarding cigarettes (once a sign of maturity) and marijuana (once a sign of depravity). My husband died of lung cancer partly because when he joined the army, recruits were given free cigarettes. I remember when women smoked to signify "you've come a long way baby." Now cigarettes are nicknamed "cancer sticks" and teenagers know they cause diseases of the heart, brain, senses, and so on. Smoking rates are half what they were. Meanwhile, marijuana, once associated with "reefer madness," is now legal in many U.S. states and all of Canada. Scientists advocate being "clear about risks," unlike the irrational fears of earlier generations.[22]

Having witnessed cultural reversals and revolutions makes grandmothers slower to judge. Meanwhile, many parents are horrified at the possibility of drug abuse, and many adolescents adamantly dismiss parental fears. As one boy said, his mother "does the drugs, alcohol, sex thing. . . . [It is] just like triple threat and I am just like 'God, go away.'"[23]

The sad consequence is that some teenagers hide their own and their friends' drug use from their parents, who may be unaware that their child smokes, drinks, snorts, swallows, or injects toxins until it is too late. Few teenagers imagine that they could become addicts because they believe the *invincibility fable*, the illusion that they are immune to whatever harms ordinary people. Grandmothers who make dire predictions might be ignored, but those who share memories of friends for whom substance abuse diminished their future, hurt their children, or caused their death might have an impact.

The best defense against drug use seems naïve—but massive research found that it works.[24] Grandmothers can take their teenage grandchildren to concerts, plays, and sports events, or join them in volunteering for a local political campaign, park cleanup, or child care center, or strengthen family ties by taking a trip to a relative who lives far away.

Surprisingly, in Iceland, a seventeen-year national campaign to increase exactly those activities found that the number of ninth and tenth graders who were drunk in the prior month was reduced from 30 percent to 4 percent. According to one expert who was not part of the study, Iceland achieved "a sustained drop in adolescent substance use in part through a national policy of expanding access to competing rewards, including recreational and cultural activities, as well as programs that strengthen family and civic ties."[25]

LESSON 24: LEARN TECHNOLOGY

Doing activities with adolescents is an ancient strategy that every grandmother can do, so it is heartening that it is effective. A new strategy is also recommended—learn technology.

In earlier centuries, grandmothers had to see grandchildren face-to-face in order to connect with them. All the research found that close relationships with grandchildren were far more likely if Grandma lived nearby. That probably is still true, but it is no longer essential. Especially as grandchildren grow older and families move, technology might bridge the generation gap, via video conversations, texting, email, and social media.[26] As one developmental psychologist puts it, Skype is "nerd's gift to grandmothers."[27]

With technology, geographical distance need no longer mean emotional distance. For example, in one study, grandparents rated how emotionally connected they were with their adolescent grandchildren. The general trend was more distance as the children aged, but more than a third reported that their relationship steadied or improved over time because of technology.[28]

One grandmother in that study became Facebook friends with her thirteen- and fourteen-year-old granddaughters. She said,

You know, it's so much fun for me, and what I do, I usually keep my mouth shut, they know I'm there and so far they're still comfortable with

it and you know, I never interfere with their relationships with their friends or anything, but it's so fun to see things they do, and I mean if I got on the phone with them and tried to have them tell me some of the things they do, it wouldn't happen.

Another grandmother used Skype—and an astute observation—to bond with her thirteen-year-old granddaughter.

She just put the computer on her bed and I said "oh that looks like a new poster on your wall" and so we kind of did this little virtual tour of her room and it was just like she and I were hanging out, no one else in the house even knew we were talking, her door was shut to her room. I was there on the computer, and it was really cool.

Of course, some adolescents have one Facebook page that relatives can see and another site that is more private. Nonetheless, technology can facilitate a relationship that might die without it. Adolescents routinely send photos and messages to their grandparents via cell phones.[29]

Grandmothers need to be proactive. The oldest generation is far behind the young in technology. A 2018 survey found that 34 percent of those over sixty-five never used the internet, compared to only 2 percent of those eighteen to twenty-nine.[30] Some said they were too old to learn.

"Too old to learn" is an excuse, not a fact. People of every age can learn.

Although the number of older people on social media, with high-speed internet access, and with smart phones is increasing by the thousands every week, many elders are still woefully behind. They may be on Facebook, but few routinely use the special features of social media, smart phones, apps, emoticons, and so on. Some naïvely misuse the tools they have, such as posting photos of their grandchildren, friending a grandchild's friends, or sharing private information. Conventions for forwarding emails, sending links, and so on need to be discussed with grandchildren (who themselves need to understand privacy issues).[31]

Paid experts and classes can teach grandmothers, but many teenage grandchildren know the mechanics (not the implications) of the digital revolution. Ideally, that provides an occasion for grandmother/ grandchild interaction, as each generation teaches the other.

This is not as simple as it might sound. For their part, few grandchildren understand what grandmothers know and do not know. Technology is taken for granted among the young: toddlers routinely use video screens and cell phones, unaware that thirty years ago, few people had computers and that even ten years ago, few had cell phones. My grandson often tells me to text his parents or, when we are lost on city streets, to get directions from "the lady" (on Google). He does not imagine that his requests are challenges for me.

Many grandmothers are suspicious of technology. For example, they worry about sexual predators preying on children. That is "extremely rare."[32] Sexual abuse and sexual harassment are long-standing problems; many women in the MeToo movement cite incidents from decades ago. Technology is merely another venue. Grandmothers have heard that social media use causes depression—another falsehood. In fact, social networks have both beneficial and detrimental effects, depending on how they are used and by whom. That means grandmothers again can be helpful—if they learn how.

Teenagers might conclude that grandmother ignorance means senility, and grandmothers might blame disturbing teenage behavior on the internet, just as grandmothers in earlier generations blamed automobiles, radios, television, and shopping malls for destroying human values. Here the research is reassuring. Although online communication of all types has been accused of promoting isolation, the opposite is more accurate. Almost all emails and texts are sent by people who have met face-to-face; technology strengthens their relationship.[33] Technology is not always a blessing—but neither are cars or malls. Some issues—cyber bullying, privacy, sexting—are new, but the underlying problems are not.

Indeed, proficiency in technology and communication is something that a grandchild and grandmother could attain together. Each can teach the other, both could learn new modes and better practices of intergenerational interaction. Chats could involve several generations separated by great distances; video events could become interactive;

apps could be shared, family history explored. The possibilities for close grandmother-grandchild connections using technology are many.

As explained at the start of this chapter, the combinations of tradition and innovation, grandmother patience and adolescent adventure, can speed teenagers on their way to healthy adulthood and keep grandmothers from lonely isolation. Whether it actually does depends on them.

· *14* ·

Emerging Adults

$\mathcal{T}$his book began with the demographic revolution that transformed grandmothers, creating a chasm between today and tradition. The same revolution transformed everyone else, especially adult grandchildren. Their life is markedly unlike that of earlier generations. They and their grandmothers are in new territory.

LESSON 25: DON'T ADVISE SETTLING DOWN

Some things endure—families and grandmothering among them—yet much has changed. A few decades ago eighteen-year-olds were expected to become adults, which meant finding a steady job (for the men) and finding a husband (for the women). Young adults formed new families, with a baby born a year or two after the wedding. Grandmothers encouraged adult grandchildren to settle down to domestic life, with mate, job, and children. Both of my grandmothers settled down on schedule: they married men who worked hard to support the household, they had their first baby before age twenty, and they never imagined going to college or having a job themselves.

Currently, reduction of teen pregnancy has been a goal for every nation, and all have succeeded to some extent. The median age of first birth is now age thirty in Japan and Spain; every ethnic group in the United States has markedly fewer teen births.[1] So many women are postponing childbirth that the only age group with increasing births is those over age thirty-five, and scholars now wonder whether having a first baby after age thirty is suboptimal![2] Grandmothers no longer urge settling down, lest they be seen as hopelessly out of touch.

A new stage has appeared: *emerging adulthood*.[3] Young adults flourish when they postpone marriage, parenthood, and career as they seek more education, more romances, more temporary jobs. They do not want to be tied down in any way. These trends are international; although age varies, emerging adulthood can begin at fifteen or eighteen and end at twenty-one (Pakistan) or thirty (Germany).[4]

In the past, when grandchildren reached age twenty or so, grandmothers could recycle their caregiving because great-grandchildren were soon born, and the newly married parents wanted advice and help. Now grandmothers must adjust not only to fewer babies but also to fewer queries about baby care. Instead of asking Grandma, new parents consult the internet.

Social norms have shifted, too: paths into adulthood that were sunny and smooth a few decades ago are rough, stormy, or blocked. Sexual diseases, economic recession, college costs, international competition, climate change, political polarization were not part of daily life when grandmothers were young, but every emerging adult must cope with them. Grandchildren in their twenties desperately need understanding, support, and encouragement, but few know that their grandmothers might provide it.

Grandmothers themselves can convince them. A tactical shift that emerged at puberty continues. In early childhood, parents were the terra firma, solid ground, the family foundation. The task for grandmothers was to strengthen that foundation—no comments, no assumptions, no misunderstandings. For contemporary young adults, the challenge is more direct. Grandmothers no longer are moons revolving around earth mothers; they are independent stars, with their own orbit. Ideally, they exert a positive gravitational force instead of twinkling so far away that they disappear.

Is a close relationship possible? Yes. One twenty-six-year-old granddaughter writes:

We hang out, sit and talk, cook and eat together. . . . For the past 5 years, we have had a membership to the theater, and we also go to the cinema together. We talk and laugh about the shows. . . . My grandmother and I always talk about everything; personal, health and social issues, and also family matters. I share with my grandmother my everyday personal issues, tell her about my projects at work, my plans for the future, and share experiences from my work as a waitress. . . . how to decorate my new home, and how my boyfriend and I are getting along. She cares about all of that.[5]

Sadly, this is not the norm. When grandchildren become adults, variation is vast, but close relationships are unusual.[6] Grandmother effort is required, unlike in childhood. Earlier, when an older woman visited her adult child, the grandchildren were underfoot; it was hard not to relate to them. Now the grandchildren live elsewhere or are not home when Grandma comes calling. Yes, grandmothers become independent stars, but they risk becoming invisible, in much the same way that city lights obscure starlight.

About a third of American grandmothers see their most distant grandchild (sometimes their only grandchild) once a year or less.[7] Since distance increases and interaction decreases as grandchildren grow older, most emerging adults do not have a grandmother with whom they "talk about everything" because she "cares about all that."

Thus, although grandmothers have much to offer emerging adults, they rarely give it. Traditionally, grandmothers focus on small grandchildren, but the grown-up ones need the most encouragement. The difficulty is that work, study, and social events create a time famine: emerging adults do not know how to squeeze grandmothers into a life busy with friends and lovers, not to mention the demands of professors and bosses.

Breaking past the barriers of the grandchild's busy life requires creative initiatives. Here are ten suggestions.

1. Text, don't call. Ask a question that triggers a quick answer: if the grandchild cares about politics ("Were you surprised by the

election in France?"); music ("Have you heard the new single by ___?"); sports ("Did you see that amazing catch/kick/goal?"); or personal things ("Did you buy new boots?"). Each of these requires that the grandmother knows what the grandchild cares about, and that she herself is up on that topic. That might mean reading, watching, or listening to media that she would not have done otherwise.

2. Take the grandchildren to lunch at a place of their choice. (They need to eat, and a delicious free meal is a luxury.) Suggest including a friend so you can learn about the grandchild's life without reducing their time socializing with peers.

3. Buy tickets for both of you to a concert, play, movie, basketball game, lecture—whatever your grandchild might enjoy. Again, this might include a friend.

4. Hike, bike, or swim together. (You both need exercise, but say it is for you.)

5. Bring home-cooked food. Cookies, pie, soup—whatever. Depending on your culinary talents, you can cook a traditional dish together.

6. Schedule some private conversation at the next family gathering. For example, ask in advance for ten minutes after Thanksgiving dinner. Listen more than talk: a ratio of four minutes listening to one minute of talking is about right.

7. Be ready to talk about the past, with details and humor, whenever the grandchild asks. Life long ago, or when they or their parents were young might be fascinating. But be careful—notice when memories are repeated or uninteresting.

8. Ask them what you should read about whatever topic concerns them, or find a novel they like, and then discuss it. Listen carefully and genuinely, using active listening (eye contact, repeating their words, adding your sounds and expressions of surprise, appreciation, curiosity).

9. Get involved in some local concern—political, social service, or community, making yourself happier and more interesting. You might take your grandchild with you to knock on doors, or to

feed the hungry, or to plant flowers. Shared action is bonding, and you gain respect as well as become a role model.

10. Buy a present—but make sure it is something wanted and needed.

On this tenth item, research on gift giving finds that givers expect recipients to be happy with their presents, but recipients often resent, never use, and then discard their gifts. One conclusion: "At best, a poorly chosen gift will irritate the recipient, and at worst, it may drive the giver and the recipient apart."[8] I know grandchildren who hate their grandmother's gifts because she never asks what they want. For them, every present implies disapproval: she gives books that they do not read because they contain advice they refuse to follow.

I also know that some grandmothers send gifts that their grand-children never get because the children's mother sends them back, unopened. And I know a grandson who refuses gifts of money because his grandmother tells him to put it in the bank. Gifts can be cannon fodder: be careful not to light a fuse.

Fortunately, one common trait of grandmothers is the wish to understand other people, rather than insisting that their view is the only right one. Grandmothers are less upset when another person is disagreeable. This trait is evident in many studies.[9]

Consider one study in detail. A group of researchers asked 916 older adults to describe a "negative social exchange" (insult, unwanted advice, intrusive comment) they experienced in the past six months.[10] More than a third could not recall a single instance. Those who re-membered something were asked what their goal was in the interac-tion. By far the most common hope was to preserve good will; least common was to change the other person. They usually achieved their goal by compromising, forgiving, or accepting blame.

Overall,

the latter half of life is when we realize that attempting to change the behaviors of others might be counterproductive because doing so might exacerbate conflict . . . interpersonal harmony requires working within the boundaries of relationships and considering the mutual goals that we have with our relationship partners.[11]

LESSON 26: EXPLORE VALUES WITH WORDS AND MONEY

For many grandmothers, transmitting values and cultural heritage is a top priority, one they share with the parents.[12] At the same time, they know that each cohort sees things differently, obviously in regard to sexual interaction but in many other ways as well.[13]

How does this process work? Ideally, grandparents find a balance between expressing their values and understanding the values of their grandchildren. As a springboard, a grandmother and grandchild might rank the following items from one (most important) to ten. This list is adapted from a standard one,[14] originally developed by Shalom Schwartz and used internationally with adults of many ages. It is neither definitive nor diagnostic; there are no wrong answers.

1. **Self-Direction:** wanting autonomy, ignoring others' opinions
2. **Stimulation:** seeking excitement, novelty, adventure
3. **Hedonism:** keeping comfortable, enjoying sensory pleasure
4. **Power:** seeking status, prestige, and dominance
5. **Achievement:** feeling competent, successful
6. **Security:** keeping yourself, your family, and your society safe
7. **Conformity:** respecting social norms, curbing odd impulses
8. **Tradition:** valuing culture and religious beliefs, rituals
9. **Benevolence:** sacrifice for people in your immediate circle
10. **Universalism:** care and protect everyone, all nations

Rank goals, not actions, for these ten, with the most important goal being number 1 and least important, number 10. For example, if someone adamantly seeks independence, that would be ranked number

1, even if they know that they are easily swayed or that other people restrict their autonomy.

After grandmothers and grandchildren individually list these in order, each adds up the rankings of their first five, (a number somewhere between 15 and 40), adds up the second five (again 15 to 40), and compares the two totals with each other. Is one half lower?

People from twenty-nine countries and of all ages have ranked these ten.[15] In every nation, older adults give Security, Conformity, and Tradition lower numbers (indicating more importance) and Stimulation and Hedonism higher numbers, than younger adults do. Local economy and culture affect the other five, although generally, with maturation, Universalism and Benevolence become more important than Self-Direction and Power. Only Achievement seems unaffected by age.

Thus, older people tend to favor the second five, so that half usually has a lower total. The opposite is true for young adults: their top priorities (low scores) tend to be among the first five. True for you? Maybe not.

Individual differences abound, especially when grandchildren reach adulthood. I did this with my family, which led to a lively discussion about what we value and why. Understanding each other is the goal; comparing rankings might open the discussion.

Although there are no wrong answers, aging and experience affect what a person prioritizes. Among the significant experiences are moving to a new culture, gaining advanced education, experiencing religious conversion, raising children, getting married or divorced, losing a loved one, suffering a life-threatening illness, or quitting addictive drugs—all these can reorder priorities, and all are more likely as life goes on.

Maturation matters, not solely because of experience. Brain changes, especially increasing myelination (the formation of the substance covering the fibers in the brain that speeds transmission of impulses, thoughts, and actions), propel quick reactions in adolescents and young adults; they rush into danger with fast cars, new drugs, unprotected sex. Sensory stimulation is thrilling, which is why the young brag about being *smashed* or *wasted*, call good experiences a *blast*, starve themselves or stay up all night, or, the other extreme, eat until their stomachs hurt and boast that they slept past noon.

Older adults are slower and more cautious: their brains include stronger connections from one hemisphere and one lobe (especially the frontal lobe) to another. They do not announce proudly that they did not eat or sleep; they would be ashamed to admit being smashed. The cliché "youth is wasted on the young" means that the energy of youth lacks the wisdom of age. That is one reason grandmothers need to forge close relationships with their grandchildren: together they may combine the best of both.

Of course, grandmothers remember the moral mandates they learned when they were twenty; that memory makes it obvious that values change. In a crossover unimaginable a few decades ago, the average age of first birth in the United States is lower than the average age of first marriage.

If grandmothers understand their adult grandchildren's goals, values, and pleasures, they may be able to avoid destroying the relationship by preaching, scolding, and demeaning. They will not expect that the young will follow the same path into adulthood that they did.

We all tend to believe that our own view is best and then seek reasons to confirm those beliefs. That's *confirmation bias*.[16] Fortunately, with maturation people learn that affection is more valuable than being right and that each cohort has its own context. Grandmothers can listen without assuming that the young are self-centered, sinful, or naïve.

The issue that displays value differences most starkly is money—a cauldron of intergenerational resentment, yet a taboo topic among many families. This may have always been true, as family resources (historically land, housing, food) have often been allocated in ways that seem unfair to the oldest or youngest adults. However, the recent economic recession, added to the demographic revolution, exacerbated resentments because both the oldest and the youngest workers are now pressured by employers who see their profits shrinking. The older ones have seniority and higher salaries: they are pushed to retire, and their

"You'd better ask your grandparents about that, son—my generation is very uncomfortable talking about abstinence."

Or is it the other way around? Each cohort has their own values about sex, climate, religion, and everything else.
Bob Mancoff, CartoonCollections.com.

pensions may be cut. The younger ones are least likely to be hired (a recession affects their employment the most), so they take jobs that are not the ones they imagined. This sets up a classic conflict, with forces in the macro system affecting both generations—each may think the problem originates in the other, not in the economy.[17]

The result may increase the distance between the generations. Adult grandchildren may think that older people are "old farts" or "greedy geezers" with more money than they need, and resent stingy grandmothers who bank substantial funds instead of giving it to their grandchildren. The result of this stereotype is poor mental health in the oldest generation.[18] Some social scientists consider the "slander against older persons" the result of decades of media and political attack.[19]

For their part, grandmothers may consider themselves generous and fear that the grandchildren are ungrateful spendthrifts. Communication is needed because both are wrong. Or both are right.

Consider how it looks from the perspective of the young. Precise numbers vary depending on how income is tallied, but every source finds that the grandmother generation has much more money than the emerging adult one.[20]

The young notice that many people over age sixty have pensions and investment income; many own homes without mortgages; they do not depend on current employment income. Savings abound, both in their habits and in the social fabric. Compared to the average twenty-five-year-old, those in their sixties are less likely to eat out, attend concerts, buy new clothes, or go to the movies—and when they do, they get senior discounts. In the United States, the only age group that has gotten richer in past half century is the elders (except the very old, over age eighty).

Unlike when their grandmothers were in their twenties, young adults are now the poorest generation. The recent recession affected them the most, in part because newly hired employees lost jobs while older workers postponed retirement, keeping jobs that the young wanted. Seniority protected seniors and harmed the young.

What the younger generation may not realize, of course, is that some people over age fifty are terrified that they might run out of money. Many doctor, dentist, and drug costs are not covered by Medicare (which does not start until age sixty-five), and medical expenses are the number one cause of bankruptcy. Those over age sixty-five have, on average, several serious chronic conditions (such as heart disease, high blood pressure, diabetes, and cancer).[21] Many need pills, drops, infusions, hearing aids, dental work, and special diets that are costly but not subsidized. Most older people fear poor health, becoming a burden, living their last years as a charity patient with stale urine, dirty floors, and demented companions in a nursing home. Their savings are their firewall against the terrifying, flesh-eating specter of old age.

Especially in the United States, with most caregiving privately provided and most elders fiercely independent, money worries loom large. Savings are not a luxury; they are psychic life support. Furthermore, most elders already contribute to younger generations.[22] Overall, more money flows down the generational ladder than up, sometimes depleting retirement income.[23]

Now consider the grandmother's view of the profligate habits of the young. Emerging adults:

- hail taxis rather than walking;
- purchase prepared meals rather than cooking;
- drink bottled water rather than tap;
- discard food rather than saving leftovers;
- trash old clothes rather than mending;
- buy unwalkable boots, trendy sunglasses, and torn jeans;
- stand in line to buy expensive tickets to ear-splitting concerts;
- purchase new cell phones when the old ones still work;
- pay high prices for clothes that advertise brands; and
- use charge cards as if debt were natural.

By contrast, many elders abhor debt[24] and feel personally insulted when they see their grandchild waste money. Awareness of social media makes it worse because grandmothers notice that adult grandchildren answer texts immediately and post photos of themselves in exotic, expensive places but "forget" to call Grandma to tell her about the trip.

What grandmothers do not realize is that spending and traveling may be psychic life support for the young. They desperately want, and need, to be recognized as someone who understands the current world and fits into it—and new boots may be a way to do that. Many young adults consider networking, visibility, and appearance a path toward friendship, romance, and employment. That makes purchases that grandparents find foolish—striped socks, a weekend trip, an expensive haircut—necessities.

These two perspectives need to come together, partly for intergenerational peace, but also because both want to secure the future. Consider college education, a value that both appreciate, knowing that over a lifetime, the average college graduate earns a million dollars more than the average of someone who never went to college.[25]

Grandmothers underestimate the price of college. Residential private colleges cost more than $100,000 per year (including tuition, room and board, books, transportation), not counting the money young adults could earn if they were not in college. The least costly for students are for-profit institutions, partly because many students live at home and are encouraged to sign for loans, but they also have the lowest graduation rates, fewest job prospects, and highest debt. The most demanding classes lead to well-paid jobs, but college students resent pressure to take courses they hate.

This situation means that decisions about financing education need a long-term perspective—exactly what grandparents provide and what young adults lack. This is particularly evident in college loans. They entice college enrollment for students who have neither the motivation nor the skills to succeed. More than half fail and quit, with massive debts but no degree (graduation rates for incoming freshman vary by institution: from 10 to 95 percent). One solution is to avoid loans, but students are more likely to quit college for financial reasons than academic ones.[26]

With or without a degree, debt increases depression, insomnia, and anxiety for years. Grandparents can encourage studying and learning, pay expenses, explain investment and debt, and help grandchildren explore the implications of choosing, enrolling, and quitting.

Some American young adults even leave the country (and their relatives) in order to escape paying back their loans. One such woman went to Berlin to escape dunning phone calls about the $50,000 she owes. She says:

> *I have this shame on the part of my parents because I really did not want this for them. When I thought about going to college, this is not what I had in mind. I really thought that they were going to be so proud of me. I was the first child in my family. . . . to graduate college. But . . . we weren't thinking about the debt when we were signing up for school. And sometimes I think living in New York City and going to a private university maybe wasn't the best idea. I could have gone somewhere else. . . .*

I don't have the money to pay for loans. I need to eat and live and not be a slave to this debt. But I'm scared. When I look back, I wonder what I could have done differently.[27]

She wonders what she could have done, but I wonder whether the grandmother was part of the conversation when this young woman and her parents signed for loans. Probably not.

Wealth tends to stay in families, which means that wealthy grandparents usually have wealthy children who become parents who pay for their children's college as well as encourage them to stick it out. But that is not always so. Careful calculations about college expenses finds that grandparents have a direct impact, especially when parents are low income.[28]

Another economic investment that grandparents make is in family formation. Grandmothers may want their grandchildren to marry, but many adult grandchildren are convinced they cannot afford to do so. The marriage rate is much higher for those from wealthy families than from poor ones—partly because parents and grandparents subsidize weddings, houses, and child care. Young adults are less likely to marry if they cannot afford college and cannot find a good job. (This is a recent development; it was not the case two decades ago.)

LESSON 27: TAKE CARE OF HEALTH AND ABILITY

Money is the first of the troubling topics that grandmothers and grandchildren need to discuss, clearing up natural misunderstandings and resentments. Death and disease are also taboo. Grandmothers need to take care of their health for many reasons, not only to be able to care for their grandchildren but also to serve as role models.

With age, all the senses become less acute, diseases more prevalent, mobility is reduced, memory fades, and death approaches. Any one of these can be a major problem. But this is exactly why older adults need to model health care, partly to counteract the youthful tendency to avoid doctors. Every one of these age-related disabilities can be postponed, mitigated, or even reversed. Active grandmothering is quite possible at age seventy and beyond—if health has been protected.

Grandmothers are particularly likely live longer, healthier, and more active lives than grandmothers did traditionally. In the past thirty years, every physical disability has become less frequent, and some have disappeared completely. In fact, in 2017 people aged forty-five to seventy-five were about half as likely to die as they were in 1970, with deaths from heart disease, breast cancer, and motor vehicle accidents dramatically reduced. Of course, those improvements are not automatic: grandmothers need to take action to protect their health, with diet, mammographies, seat belts, and more. Doing so models habits for grandchildren. They also need to protect the health of grandfathers, who, because of opioid overdose deaths, are more likely to die in middle age than was true a decade ago.

The basics of daily care—eating well, exercising, and socializing—are especially beneficial for older adults. Nutritionists, physicians, and physical therapists devote their lives to understanding the specifics; grandmothers need to tap into that expertise, remembering to fight against comfortable inaction. Sadly, although exercise is the best antidote to depression, diabetes, heart disease, and much more, adults exercise less with every passing year. In 2015, almost two-thirds (61 percent) of U.S. women over age sixty-five did not meet the federal guidelines for *either* aerobic or muscle-strengthening exercise. Emerging adults did somewhat better, although 38 percent met neither guideline.[29] Thus grandmothers need to run, swim, lift, push, and so on, both for themselves and for their grandchildren.

Unfortunately, modern conveniences—power steering, remote controls, robotic lawn mowers, wrinkle-free clothes, fast or frozen foods, and much more—encourage less motion. The old joke about grandparents telling children they had to walk miles to school, in the snow, *uphill both ways*, is replaced by grandparents saying they had to get out of their chair and walk across a shag rug to change the TV channel.

Actions and attitudes are passed down from grandmothers, who can protect the health of their adult grandchildren as they protect their own. Unfortunately, ageism leads to passive acceptance of losses. For example, some people connect hearing aids, canes, and walkers with aging, so people choose deafness or immobility to avoid looking old. The result is social isolation; people become the frail elders they didn't want to be.

If, instead, grandmothers demonstrate that every health problem can be prevented, postponed, and/or treated, then they can transmit that attitude to their grandchildren. Simple measures—hand washing, healthy eating, exercising, sleeping—are obvious. Beyond that, two health issues are more common in young adults than people of any other age—STDs (sexually transmitted diseases) and drug addiction.

Both benefit from grandmotherly attention. Every older woman probably knows someone who died of AIDS or who became infertile, so every older woman can tell of a memory that encourages protection, as already mentioned in chapter 13. The benefits of this attention have been confirmed by a study of young adult women: they were more likely to care for their sexual health and less likely to contract an STD if their parents and grandparents had talked with them about sexual practices and encouraged their long-term goals.[30]

Similarly, every grandmother has her own experience with addiction, either personally or as a witness, again noted in chapter 13. It is true that addicts themselves must want to break the habit, but it is also true that those who quit a destructive drug are aided by dozens of helpers. Grandmothers can learn to be effective, avoiding the snares of enabling or rejecting.

In many other ways, strengthening a young adult's health is best done by a grandmother who knows the grandchild's vulnerabilities, fears, and defenses. There is cautionary research on terror management. Some young adults, frightened by the possibility of disease and disability, try to control their fear, ironically, by risking death. They smoke more because they fear cancer, they swim alone in the ocean, race over a wall on a motorcycle, swallow drugs that might kill them, have intercourse with a stranger. Fear can lead to defiance, not caution.[31]

Fear of death is itself a topic that grandmothers might discuss with grandchildren. Older adults are, of course, more likely to die: someone who is eighty-six has one chance in ten of dying in the next year, usually from cancer or heart disease, while someone who is twenty-five has one chance in a thousand, usually from an accident or suicide.

The wisdom of age is an especially potent antidote to foolish risks or deep despair that precede young deaths. Young adults chant, "What do we want? Justice! When do we want it? NOW!" They cheer when a dictator is deposed, a dean resigns, an offensive statue is toppled. Then depression sets in when "justice now" does not materialize.

To counteract that depression, grandmothers need to tell their personal history. Each of us has particular experiences, but we all have witnessed worse times. I can chronicle a hundred years of my family.

1. My grandmother fled persecution, spoke accented English, and could not vote in her beloved new nation, the United States. But suffrage came to women in 1920, and my grandmother lived long enough to vote for many of her descendants, male and female, who were elected to public office.
2. My mother quit her job when she married. She told me that "there was a law that married women could not be employed." There was no such law (at least not in Minnesota at that time), but the social norm was so powerful that my mother thought there was.
3. I was first of my female relatives to graduate from college and was happy that new norms meant I could marry, raise children, and be employed lifelong. When my children were young, one of my male coworkers asked, "Do you have someone to watch them?" I thought of laughing and saying, "No, my toddlers watch themselves," but I was quiet. Neither he nor I was prepared for that retort.
4. My daughters assume that women can be mothers and workers at the same time. My coworkers' question in item 3 would be quickly recognized as sexist, and my daughters would call out anyone who said it.

5. My oldest daughter applied to only three colleges—Yale, Wesleyan, and Haverford—none of which admitted women when I applied.

6. My grandsons assume women are police officers, doctors, lawyers, whatever, and that they might grow up to be nurses or school teachers if they want. I remember when I learned to call firemen *fire fighters*, postmen *mail carriers*, and policemen *police officers*.

These six items are personal examples, but every grandmother has seen incremental social changes that now look like seismic shifts, not only for women but also for African Americans, immigrants, and gay people. Dozens of social norms have shifted, including about coal burning, cigarette smoking, pesticide use, leaded gasoline, composting. Hundreds of health innovations have appeared. Polio is gone; measles and chicken pox are rare; and a personal example: my third daughter, at age fifteen, was diagnosed with cancer (Hodgkin's disease), which was a killer fifty years ago. Her doctors treated her, expecting a long life. That was thirty years ago; she is the mother of Asa and Isaac. All this can reassure impatient grandchildren that social change is possible.

A leading intellectual lists things North Americans take for granted:[32]

- Newborns live for more than eight decades.
- Markets are overflowing with food.
- Clean water appears with a twist of a faucet.
- Waste disappears with a flush.
- Pills erase pain.
- Sons are not drafted and sent to war.
- Daughters walk the streets in safety.
- Critics of the powerful are not jailed or shot.
- The world's knowledge and culture is available in shirt pockets (cell phones).

My adult children let me know that more needs to be done, that progress is not inevitable. For instance, critics of authorities are sometimes sidelined, deported, attacked. But grandmothers can testify that social change can occur now as it has in the past, as a marathon, not a sprint.

This testimony reduces youthful impatience, fury, and depression. Moreover, grandmothers know that aging is not a tragedy. One review concludes:

> *If common stereotypes were true, we could be happy only if we were fit, lean, healthy, attractive, and above all, young. Luckily for those of us who grow older year by year, these stereotypes do not have much empirical support. If anything, the opposite is true: Different components of SWB [subjective well-being] are either stable across the lifespan or improve with age, particularly from midlife into early old age.*[33]

As grandchildren grow older, into adulthood, a year-long longitudinal study found that many still had fairly close relationships with their grandparents.[34] Close intergenerational relationships decreased depression in both generations. The best relationships involved more emotional support (expressing appreciation and encouragement) than functional support (paying for things, providing care).

And so we conclude where we began. Support between the generations has sustained humanity for thousands of years because grandmothers have been vibrant and vital members of the human family. In former times, grandmothers were literally life saving; they provided food and medical knowledge. Now we know that social support from family members is the best antidote to depression.[35] When grandmothers are excluded, the result is tragic, not only for the parents and grandchildren but also for the grandmothers themselves.

However, closer connections are possible, and that can continue when grandchildren reach adulthood. Fractured families and ageist attitudes threaten that connection, but problems are not inevitable. Grandmothers, always, to the rescue.

Into the Future

$\mathscr{G}$randmothering starts with one moment—a birth—and never stops. Likewise, this book begins with sentences and chapters, but older women must then carry the message to all the children, all the parents, all the disconnected, lonely people.

Decades of experience, and fierce dedication to children, make grandmothers today a bridge between the ancient women who dug for tubers and the newborns who will shape the future. That entails an awesome responsibility. We must be a soaring, yet sturdy, bridge, reaching toward the heavens while connecting one place to another, continuing the legacy of our ancestors.

Knowing this makes me grateful to be among the billions of other grandmothers. Thank you, and carry on.

Notes

CHAPTER 1: EXCLUDED AND ON THE FLOOR

1. Doreen Rosenthal and Susan Moore, *New Age Nanas: Being a Grandmother in the 21st Century* (Newport, Australia: Big Sky Publishing, 2012).

2. Roxana Robinson, "Nana," in *Eye of My Heart: 27 Writers Reveal the Hidden Pleasures and Perils of Being a Grandmother*, ed. Barbara Graham (New York: HarperCollins, 2010).

3. New York Hospital on East 68th Street, now New York Presbyterian Hospital/Weill Cornell Medical Center, ranked number 1 in *U.S. News & World Report*.

4. Susan Moore and Doreen Rosenthal, *Grandparenting: Contemporary Perspectives* (New York: Routledge, 2017).

5. Rosenthal and Moore, *New Age Nanas*, 62.

6. The American Community Survey reports that in 2015, 60 percent of U.S. mothers were primary or sole breadwinners for their families, up from 11 percent in 1960.

7. One statistic from the *Chronicle of Higher Education* makes the point: In the United States in 1950, men earned three times more BAs than women. In 2016, men earned a third fewer BAs than women.

8. In 1950, life expectancy for newborn U.S. girls was seventy-two. Now it is eighty-two, with almost all of those years, on average, in good health.

9. The diseases of old age are less incapacitating than they were. Surgery, diet, exercise, drugs, hearing aids, and other innovations allow people to be active for decades after illness.

10. Data from several nations find that better health and more education among current elders results in markedly lower rates of dementia. The reference for the United States is Kenneth M. Langa, Eric B. Larson, Eileen M. Crimmins, Jessica D. Faul, Deborah A. Levine, Mohammed U. Kabeto, and David R. Weir, "A Comparison of the Prevalence of Dementia in the United States in 2000 and 2012," *JAMA Internal Medicine* 177, no. 1 (2017): 51–58.

11. In 1960, the average U.S. woman had 3.23 births; in 2015, the average was 1.88. United Nations—Department of Economic and Social Affairs: Population Division, "World Population Prospects: The 2017 Revision," custom data acquired via website. https://esa.un.org/unpd/wpp/.

12. United Nations, "World Population Prospects."

13. Merril Silverstein and Yooumi Lee, "Race and Ethnic Differences in Grandchild Care and Financial Transfers with Grandfamilies: An Intersectional Resource Approach," in *Grandparenting in the United States*, eds. Madonna Harrington Meyer and Ynesse Abdul-Malak (Amityville, NY: Baywood, 2016). Among African Americans, Latinos, and non-Hispanic whites, percentage providing care for grandchildren: 29, 26, and 27 percent; percentage providing money: 31, 25, and 39 percent.

14. United Nations, "World Population Prospects."

15. The U.S. Centers for Disease Control reports that in 1950, the death rate for men aged forty-five to sixty-five was 3.46 percent; for women, 2.05 percent. In 2016, the rates were 1.6 percent for men and 1.0 percent for women. National Center for Health Statistics, *Health, United States, 2017: With Special Feature on Mortality* (Hyattsville, MD: Centers for Disease Control and Prevention, 2018).

16. United Nations, "World Population Prospects."

17. National Center for Health Statistics, *Health, United States, 2017.*

18. Laura L. Carstensen and Linda P. Fried, "The Meaning of Old Age," in *Global Population Ageing: Peril or Promise?* eds. John Beard, Simon Biggs, David Bloom, Linda Fried, Paul Hogan, Alexandre Kalache, and S. Olshansky (Geneva: World Economic Forum, 2012).

19. United Nations, "World Population Prospects."

20. Defined by the Center for Research on the Epidemiology of Disasters, in Belgium. They have kept track of disasters worldwide for more than forty years.

21. Wolfgang Lutz, Raya Muttarak, and Erich Striessnig, "Universal Education Is Key to Enhanced Climate Adaptation," *Science* 346, no. 6213 (2014):

1061–62; Elaine Enarson and Betty Hearn Morrow, eds., *The Gendered Terrain of Disaster: Through Women's Eyes* (Westport, CT: Praeger, 1998).

22. Patricia A. Crawford and Sharika Bhattacharya, "Grand Images: Exploring Images of Grandparents in Picture Books," *Journal of Research in Childhood Education* 28, no. 1 (2014): 128–44.

23. Harriet Sokmensuer, "Grandma, 63, Accused of Smuggling $500k in Cocaine through Detroit Airport," *People*, October 19, 2016.

24. Andrew Kashner, "Ganny Gotti Begs for Baby," *New York Daily News*, November 26, 2017.

25. Anna North, "Hillary Clinton, Unapologetic Grandma," *New York Times*, July 13, 2015.

26. Based on the first thirty photographs in a search in October 2016.

27. Irene Goldenberg, Mark Stanton, and Herbert Goldenberg, *Family Therapy: An Overview* (United Kingdom: Cengage Learning, 2016), 300.

28. Linn Sandberg, "Being There for My Grandchild—Grandparents' Responses to Their Grandchildren's Exposure to Domestic Violence," *Child & Family Social Work* 21, no. 2 (2016): 136–45.

29. Arthur Kornhaber, *Contemporary Grandparenting* (Thousand Oaks, CA: Sage, 1996), 29.

30. Esther M. Friedman, Sung S. Park, and Emily E. Wiemers, "New Estimates of the Sandwich Generation in the 2013 Panel Study of Income Dynamics," *Gerontologist* 57, no. 2 (2017): 191–96; Luc Arrondel and André Masson, "Altruism, Exchange or Indirect Reciprocity: What Do the Data on Family Transfers Show?" in *Handbook of the Economics of Giving, Altruism and Reciprocity*, eds. Serge-Christophe Kolm and Jean Mercier Ythier (Amsterdam: Elsevier, 2006).

31. Barbara Graham, preface to *Eye of My Heart*: 27 Writers Reveal the Hidden Pleasures and Perils of Being a Grandmother, ed. Barbara Graham (New York: HarperCollins, 2010).

CHAPTER 2: WHY GRANDMOTHERS?

1. Kristen Hawkes, James F. O'Connell, and Nicholas G. Blurton Jones, "Hadza Women's Time Allocation, Offspring Provisioning, and the Evolution

of Long Postmenopausal Life Spans," *Current Anthropology* 38, no. 4 (1997): 551–77. doi:10.1086/204646.

2. George C. Williams, "Pleiotropy, Natural Selection, and the Evolution of Senescence," *Evolution* 11, no. 4 (1957): 398–411. doi:10 .1111/j.1558-5646.1957.tb02911.x.

3. The median group size is twenty-one, the mean thirty, according to Frank W. Marlowe, *The Hadza: Hunter-Gatherers of Tanzania* (Berkeley: University of California Press, 2010).

4. Beverly Peterson Stearns and Stephen C. Stearns, *Watching, from the Edge of Extinction* (New Haven, CT: Yale University Press, 2000).

5. Kristen Hawkes and James E. Coxworth, "Grandmothers and the Evolution of Human Longevity: A Review of Findings and Future Directions," *Evolutionary Anthropology* 22, no. 6 (2013): 294–302. doi:10.1002/evan.21382.

6. Rachel Caspari, "The Evolution of Grandparents," *Scientific American* 305, no. 2 (2011): 44–49. doi:10.1038/scientificamerican0811-44.

7. Jared Diamond, "Unwritten Knowledge," *Nature* 410, no. 6828 (2001): 521. doi:10.1038/35069154.

8. Thomas Hobbes, *Leviathan: Or the Matter, Forme, and Power of a Common-Wealth Ecclesiasticall and Civill*, ed. Ian Shapiro (New Haven, CT: Yale University Press, 2010), 78.

9. Marlowe, *The Hadza*, 161.

10. This is well researched by many biologists. One specific example is Hannah M. Atkins, Cynthia J. Willson, Marnia Silverstein, Matthew Jorgensen, Edison Floyd, Jay R. Kaplan, and Susan E. Appt, "Characterization of Ovarian Aging and Reproductive Senescence in Vervet Monkeys (Chlorocebus aethiops sabaeus)," *Comparative Medicine* 64, no. 1 (2014): 55–62.

11. Lauren J. N. Brent, Daniel W. Franks, Emma A. Foster, Kenneth C. Balcomb, Michael A. Cant, and Darren P. Croft, "Ecological Knowledge, Leadership, and the Evolution of Menopause in Killer Whales," *Current Biology* 25, no. 6 (2015): 746–50. doi:10.1016/j.cub.2015.01.037.

12. E. B. White, *Charlotte's Web* (New York: HarperCollins, 2006), 182.

13. "World's Oldest Dad, 97, Devastated after Wife Leaves Him Following Disappearance of Their Son," *Daily Mail*, October 3, 2013.

14. Yash S. Khandwala, Chiyuan A. Zhang, Ying Lu, and Michael L. Eisenberg, "The Age of Fathers in the USA Is Rising: An Analysis of 168,867,480 Births from 1972 to 2015," *Human Reproduction* 32, no. 10 (2017): 2110–16. doi:10.1093/humrep/dex267.

15. Lisette Stolk et al., "Meta-Analyses Identify 13 Loci Associated with Age at Menopause and Highlight DNA Repair and Immune Pathways," *Nature Genetics* 44, no. 3 (2012): 260–68. doi:10.1038/ng.1051.

16. S. Wu, F. Wu, Y. Ding, J. Hou, J. Bi, and Z. Zhang, "Advanced Parental Age and Autism Risk in Children: A Systematic Review and Meta-Analysis," *Acta Psychiatrica Scandinavica* 135, no. 1 (2017): 29–41. doi:10.1111/acps.12666.

17. Alison Gopnik, *The Gardener and the Carpenter: What the New Science of Child Development Tells Us about the Relationship between Parents and Children* (New York: Farrar, Strauss and Giroux, 2016), 16.

18. David A. Coall and Ralph Hertwig, "Grandparental Investment: Past, Present, and Future," *Behavioral and Brain Sciences* 33, no. 1 (2010): 1–59. doi:10.1017/S0140525X09991105.

19. Eckart Voland, Athanasios Chasiotis, and Wulf Schiefenhövel, eds., *Grandmotherhood: The Evolutionary Significance of the Second Half of Female Life* (New Brunswick, NJ: Rutgers University Press, 2005).

20. Eckart Voland and Jan Beise, "Opposite Effects of Maternal and Paternal Grandmothers on Infant Survival in Historical Krummhörn," *Behavioral Ecology and Sociobiology* 52, no. 6 (2002): 435–43. doi:10.1007/s00265-002-0539-2.

21. Harald A. Euler, "Grandparents and Extended Kin," in *The Oxford Handbook of Evolutionary Family Psychology*, eds. Todd K. Shackelford and Catherine A. Salmon (New York: Oxford University Press, 2011).

22. Nicholas Blurton Jones, Kristen Hawkes, and James F. O'Connell, "Hadza Grandmothers as Helpers: Residence Data," in *Grandmotherhood: The Evolutionary Significance of the Second Half of Female Life*, eds. Eckart Voland, Athanasios Chasiotis, and Wulf Schiefenhövel (New Brunswick, NJ: Rutgers University Press, 2005).

23. Marlowe, *The Hadza*, 161.

24. Jan Beise, "The Helping and the Helpful Grandmother: The Role of Maternal and Paternal Grandmothers in Child Mortality in the Seventeenth and Eighteenth-Century Population of French Settlers in Québec, Canada," in *Grandmotherhood: The Evolutionary Significance of the Second Half of Female Life*, eds. Eckart Voland, Athanasios Chasiotis, and Wulf Schiefenhövel (New Brunswick, NJ: Rutgers University Press, 2005), 160–76.

25. Rebecca Sear, Ruth Mace, and Ian A. McGregor, "Maternal Grandmothers Improve Nutritional Status and Survival of Children in Rural

Gambia," *Proceedings of the Royal Society B: Biological Sciences* 267, no. 1453 (2000): 1641–47. doi:10.1098/rspb.2000.1190.

26. Quoted in Susan Moore and Doreen Rosenthal, *Grandparenting: Contemporary Perspectives* (New York: Routledge, 2017), 40.

27. Antti O. Tanskanen, "The Association between Grandmaternal Investment and Early Years Overweight in the UK," *Evolutionary Psychology* 11, no. 2 (2013). doi:10.1177/147470491301100212.

28. Moore and Rosenthal, *Grandparenting*.

29. Courtney A. Polenick, Steven H. Zarit, Kira S. Birditt, Lauren R. Bangerter, Amber J. Seidel, and Karen L. Fingerman, "Intergenerational Support and Marital Satisfaction: Implications of Beliefs about Helping Aging Parents," *Journal of Marriage and Family* 79, no. 1 (2017): 131–46. doi:10.1111/jomf.12334.

30. Jeremy B. Yorgason and Kathryn B. Gustafson, "Linking Grandparent Involvement with the Development of Prosocial Behavior in Adolescents," in *Prosocial Development: A Multidimensional Approach*, eds. Laura M. Padilla-Walker and Gustavo Carlo (New York: Oxford University Press, 2014).

31. Maaike Jappens and Jan Van Bavel, "Regional Family Norms and Child Care by Grandparents in Europe," *Demographic Research* 27 (2012): 85–120. doi:10.4054/DemRes.2012.27.4.

32. Sandor Schrijner and Jeroen Smits, "Grandmothers and Children's Schooling in Sub-Saharan Africa," *Human Nature* 29, no. 1 (2018): 65–89. doi:10.1007/s12110-017-9306-y.

33. Vern Bengtson and Ariela Lowenstein, eds., *Global Aging and Challenges to Families* (New York: Routledge, 2018), 75.

34. Jappens and Van Bavel, "Regional Family Norms"; Katharina Herlofson and Gunhild O. Hagestad, "Transformations in the Role of Grandparents across Welfare States," in *Contemporary Grandparenting: Changing Family Relationships in Global Contexts*, eds. Sara Arber and Virpi Timonen (Bristol, UK: Polity Press, 2012).

35. Antti Tanskanen, Markus Jokela, Mirkka Danielsbacka, and Anna Rotkirch, "Grandparental Effects on Fertility Vary by Lineage in the United Kingdom," *Human Nature* 25, no. 2 (2014): 269–84. doi:10.1007/s12110-014-9200-9.

36. Nicoletta Balbo and Melinda Mills, "The Effects of Social Capital and Social Pressure on the Intention to Have a Second or Third Child in France, Germany, and Bulgaria, 2004–05," *Population Studies* 65, no. 3 (2011): 335–51. doi:10.1080/00324728.2011.579148.

37. Christopher R. DeCou, Monica C. Skewes, and Ellen D. S. López, "Traditional Living and Cultural Ways as Protective Factors against Suicide: Perceptions of Alaska Native University Students," *International Journal of Circumpolar Health* 72, no. 1 (2013). doi:10.3402/ijch.v72i0.20968.

38. May Chazan, *The Grandmothers' Movement: Solidarity and Survival in the Time of AIDS* (Montreal: McGill-Queen's University Press, 2015).

39. Rita Arditti, *Searching for Life: The Grandmothers of the Plaza de Mayo and the Disappeared Children of Argentina* (Berkeley: University of California Press, 1999).

40. Valerie O'Brien, "The Benefits and Challenges of Kinship Care," *Child Care in Practice* 18, no. 2 (2012): 127–46. doi:10.1080/13575279.2012.657610.

41. David A. Coall and Ralph Hertwig, "Grandparental Investment: Past, Present, and Future," *Behavioral and Brain Sciences* 33, no. 1 (2010): 1–59. doi:10.1017/S0140525X09991105.

42. Lynne M. Casper, Sandra M. Florian, C. Brady Potts, and Peter D. Brandon, "Portrait of American Grandparent Families," in *Grandparenting in the United States*, eds. Madonna Harrington Meyer and Ynesse Abdul-Malak (Amityville, NY: Baywood, 2016), 112.

43. J. D. Vance, *Hillbilly Elegy: A Memoir of a Family and Culture in Crisis* (New York: Harper, 2016).

44. Sonia Sotomayor, *My Beloved World* (New York: Vintage Books, 2014), 20.

45. Teun Geurts and Theo van Tilburg, "Grandparent–Grandchild Relationships," in *International Encyclopedia of the Social & Behavioral Sciences*, 2nd ed., ed. James D. Wright (New York: Elsevier, 2015).

46. Margaret M. Manoogian, Juliana Vandenbroeke, Amy Ringering, Tamina Toray, and Eric Cooley, "Emerging Adults' Experiences of Grandparent Death," *OMEGA* 76, no. 4 (2018): 351–72. doi:10.1177/0030222817693140.

CHAPTER 3: DEEP WITHIN, ON THE FLOOR AGAIN

1. The Apgar is a simple way to assess the health of a newborn by rating five vital signs—color, heart rate, cry, muscle tone, and breathing—as 0, 1, or 2. A perfect score is 10; any number above 6 is good; 9 is very good.

2. Anne Lamott and Sam Lamott, *Some Assembly Required: A Journal of My Son's First Son* (New York: Riverhead, 2012), 40–41.

3. Janet Hall Wigler, "Babies, Boredom and Bliss," in *Chicken Soup for the Soul: Like Mother Like Daughter*, eds. Jack Canfield, Mark Victor Hansen, and Amy Newmark (Cos Cob, CT: Chicken Soup for the Soul, 2008), 279.

4. Ynesse Abdul-Malak, "Health and Grandparenting among 13 Caribbean (and One Latin American) Immigrant Women in the United States," in *Grandparenting in the United States*, eds. Madonna Harrington Meyer and Ynesse Abdul-Malak (Amityville, NY: Baywood, 2016), 68.

5. Molly, quoted in Madonna Harrington Meyer, *Grandmothers at Work* (New York: New York University Press, 2014), 80.

6. Lynne Sharon Schwartz, "Now You See Me, Now You Don't," in *Eye of My Heart: 27 Writers Reveal the Hidden Pleasures and Perils of Being a Grandmother*, ed. Barbara Graham (New York: HarperCollins, 2010), 57.

7. Doreen Rosenthal and Susan Moore, *New Age Nanas: Being a Grandmother in the 21st Century* (Newport, Australia: Big Sky Publishing, 2012), 5.

8. Alison Gopnik, *The Gardener and the Carpenter: What the New Science of Child Development Tells Us about the Relationship between Parents and Children* (New York: Farrar, Strauss and Giroux, 2016).

9. Joni Y. Sasaki and Heejung S. Kim, "Nature, Nurture, and Their Interplay: A Review of Cultural Neuroscience," *Journal of Cross-Cultural Psychology* 48, no. 1 (2017): 4–22. doi:10.1177/0022022116680481; Shinobu Kitayama and Cristina E. Salvador, "Culture Embrained: Going Beyond the Nature-Nurture Dichotomy," *Perspectives on Psychological Science* 12, no. 5 (2017): 841–54. doi:10.1177/1745691617707317.

10. Daniel Kahneman, *Thinking, Fast and Slow* (New York: Farrar, Straus and Giroux, 2011).

11. Jason Pohl, "Mesa Grandma's Accidental Thanksgiving Invitee Welcomed Back for Seconds," *Arizona Republic*, November 25, 2017.

12. Richard Dawkins, *The Selfish Gene* (New York: Oxford University Press, 2006).

13. Juliane Degner and Jonas Dalege, "The Apple Does Not Fall Far from the Tree, or Does It? A Meta-Analysis of Parent–Child Similarity in Intergroup Attitudes," *Psychological Bulletin* 139, no. 6 (2013): 1270–304. doi:10.1037/a0031436.

14. Marjorie Rhodes, "Naïve Theories of Social Groups," *Child Development* 83, no. 6 (2012): 1900–16. doi:10.1111/j.1467-8624.2012.01835.x.

15. Hundreds of scientists could be cited. One source that focuses especially on the genes that all primates share is Robert W. Sussman and

C. Robert Cloninger, eds., *Origins of Altruism and Cooperation* (New York: Springer, 2011).

16. Brad J. Sagarin, Amy L. Martin, Savia A. Coutinho, John E. Edlund, Lily Patel, John J. Skowronski, and Bettina Zengel, "Sex Differences in Jealousy: A Meta-analytic Examination," *Evolutionary Psychology* 33, no. 6, (2012): 595–614. doi.org/10.1016/j.evolhumbehav.2012.02.006.

17. Of course, some men are more caregiving than some women. But, on average, a significant gender difference in child care persists even in nations that have attained gender equality in other arenas, such as housework, employment, and divorce. This is true for grandmothers and grandfathers, even more than mothers and fathers. Harald A. Euler, "Grandparents and Extended Kin," in *The Oxford Handbook of Evolutionary Family Psychology*, eds. Todd K. Shackelford and Catherine A. Salmon (New York: Oxford University Press, 2011).

18. Mirkka Danielsbacka, Antti O. Tanskanen, Markus Jokela, and Anna Rotkirch, "Grandparental Child Care in Europe: Evidence for Preferential Investment in More Certain Kin," *Evolutionary Psychology* 9, no. 1 (2011): 3–24. doi:10.1177/147470491100900102.

19. Culture may influence this situation. In Asia and Africa, some grandparents are more involved with their son's children than their daughter's, as reported in research comparing grandfathers in the Netherlands with those in China. Ralf Kaptijn, Fleur Thomese, Aart Liefbroer, and Merril Silverstein, "Testing Evolutionary Theories of Discriminative Grandparental Investment," *Journal of Biosocial Science* 45, no. 3 (2013): 289–310. doi:10.1017/S0021932012000612.

20. Barbara Dolinska, "Resemblance and Investment in Children," *International Journal of Psychology* 48, no. 3 (2013): 285–90. doi:10.1080/00207 594.2011.645482. Behavioral resemblance and paternal investment: Which features of the chip-off-the-old block count?

21. Megan Reid and Andrew Golub, "Low-Income Black Men's Kin Work: Social Fatherhood in Cohabiting Stepfamilies," *Journal of Family Issues* 39, no. 4 (2018): 960–84. doi:10.1177/0192513X16684892.

22. Rosalinda Cassibba, Gabrielle Coppola, Giovanna Sette, Antonietta Curci, and Alessandro Costantini, "The Transmission of Attachment across Three Generations: A Study in Adulthood," *Developmental Psychology* 53, no. 2 (2017): 396–405. doi:10.1037/dev0000242; Andrew Solomon, *Far from the Tree Parents, Children, and the Search for Identity* (New York: Scribner, 2012).

23. Peter A. Bos, "The Endocrinology of Human Caregiving and Its Intergenerational Transmission," *Development and Psychopathology* 29, no. 3 (2017): 971–99. doi:10.1017/S0954579416000973.

24. Renske Huffmeijer, Marinus H. van Ijzendoorn, and Marian J. Bakermans-Kranenburg, "Ageing and Oxytocin: A Call for Extending Human Oxytocin Research to Ageing Populations—A Mini-Review," *Gerontology* 59, no. 1 (2013): 32–39. doi:10.1159/000341333.

25. Idan Shalev and Richard P. Ebstein, "Frontiers in Oxytocin Science: From Basic to Practice," *Frontiers in Neuroscience* 7, no. 250 (2013). doi:10.3389/fnins.2013.00250; Paul J. Zak, *The Moral Molecule: The Source of Love and Prosperity* (New York: Dutton, 2012).

26. Steven W. Gangestad and Nicholas M. Grebe, "Hormonal Systems, Human Social Bonding, and Affiliation," *Hormones and Behavior* 91 (2017): 122–35. doi:10.1016/j.yhbeh.2016.08.005.

27. Benjamin Jurek and Inga D. Neumann, "The Oxytocin Receptor: From Intracellular Signaling to Behavior," *Physiological Reviews* 98, no. 3 (2018): 1877. doi:10.1152/physrev.00031.2017.

28. Hui Wang, Florian Duclot, Yan Liu, Zuoxin Wang, and Mohamed Kabbaj, "Histone Deacetylase Inhibitors Facilitate Partner Preference Formation in Female Prairie Voles," *Nature Neuroscience* 16, no. 7 (2013): 919–24. doi:10.1038/nn.3420.

29. Alaine C. Keebaugh, Catherine E. Barrett, Jamie L. Laprairie, Jasmine J. Jenkins, and Larry J. Young, "Rnai Knockdown of Oxytocin Receptor in the Nucleus Accumbens Inhibits Social Attachment and Parental Care in Monogamous Female Prairie Voles," *Social Neuroscience* 10, no. 5 (2015): 561–70. doi:10.1080/17470919.2015.1040893; Susan Sullivan, Anna Campbell, Sam B. Hutton, and Ted Ruffman, "What's Good for the Goose Is Not Good for the Gander: Age and Gender Differences in Scanning Emotion Faces," *Journals of Gerontology: Series B* 72, no. 3 (2017): 441–47. doi:10.1093/geronb/gbv033; "Special Issue on: 'Oxytocin in Development and Plasticity,'" *Developmental Neurobiology* 77, no. 2 (2017).

30. Andrew E. Reed and Laura L. Carstensen, "The Theory behind the Age-Related Positivity Effect," *Frontiers in Psychology* 3, no. 339 (2012). doi:10.3389/fpsyg.2012.00339; Phoebe E. Bailey, Gillian Slessor, Matthias Rieger, Peter G. Rendell, Ahmed A. Moustafa, and Ted Ruffman, "Trust and Trustworthiness in Young and Older Adults," *Psychology and Aging* 30, no. 4 (2015): 977–86. doi:10.1037/a0039736; Andrew E. Reed, Larry Chan, and

Joseph A. Mikels, "Meta-Analysis of the Age-Related Positivity Effect: Age Differences in Preferences for Positive over Negative Information," *Psychology and Aging* 29, no. 1 (2014): 1–15. doi:10.1037/a0035194.

31. Roxana Robinson, "Nana," in *Eye of My Heart: 27 Writers Reveal the Hidden Pleasures and Perils of Being a Grandmother*, ed. Barbara Graham (New York: HarperCollins, 2010), 53.

32. Ilanit Gordon, Orna Zagoory-Sharon, James F. Leckman, and Ruth Feldman, "Oxytocin and the Development of Parenting in Humans," *Biological Psychiatry* 68, no. 4 (2010): 377–82. doi:10.1016/j.biopsych.2010.02.005.

33. Natalie C. Ebner, Gabriela M. Maura, Kai Macdonald, Lars Westberg, and Fischer Håkan, "Oxytocin and Socioemotional Aging: Current Knowledge and Future Trends," *Frontiers in Human Neuroscience* 7, no. 487 (2013). doi:10.3389/fnhum.2013.00487.

34. Sonja Hilbrand, David A. Coall, Andrea H. Meyer, Denis Gerstorf, and Ralph Hertwig, "A Prospective Study of Associations among Helping, Health, and Longevity," *Social Science & Medicine* 187 (2017): 109–17. doi:10.1016/j.socscimed.2017.06.035.

35. Kai S. MacDonald, "Sex, Receptors, and Attachment: A Review of Individual Factors Influencing Response to Oxytocin," *Frontiers in Neuroscience* 6, no. 194 (2013). doi:10.3389/fnins.2012.00194.

36. Christina Boeck, Anja Maria Gumpp, Enrico Calzia, Peter Radermacher, Christiane Waller, Alexander Karabatsiakis, and Iris-Tatjana Kolassa, "The Association between Cortisol, Oxytocin, and Immune Cell Mitochondrial Oxygen Consumption in Postpartum Women with Childhood Maltreatment," *Psychoneuroendocrinology* 96 (2018): 69–77. doi:10.1016/j.psyneuen.2018.05.040.

CHAPTER 4: TOO LITTLE GRANDMOTHERING

1. D. W. Winnicott, *The Child, the Family, and the Outside World* (Cambridge, MA: Perseus, 1987); D. W. Winnicott, *The Family and Individual Development* (New York: Routledge, 2006).

2. Arthur Kornhaber, *Contemporary Grandparenting* (Thousand Oaks, CA: Sage, 1996), 175.

3. Ibid., 174.

4. Rachel Dunifon, "The Influence of Grandparents on the Lives of Children and Adolescents," *Child Development Perspectives* 7, no. 1 (2013): 55–60. doi:10.1111/cdep.12016.

5. Giorgio Di Gessa, Karen Glaser, and Anthea Tinker, "The Impact of Caring for Grandchildren on the Health of Grandparents in Europe: A Lifecourse Approach," *Social Science & Medicine* 152 (2016): 166–75. doi:10.1016/j.socscimed.2016.01.041.

6. Bruno Arpino and Valeria Bordone, "Does Grandparenting Pay Off? The Effect of Child Care on Grandparents' Cognitive Functioning," *Journal of Marriage and Family* 76, no. 2 (2014): 337–51. doi:10.1111/jomf.12096.

7. Margaret Sims and Maged Rofail, "Grandparents with Little or No Contact with Grandchildren—Impact on Grandparents," *Journal of Aging Science* 2, no. 1 (2014): 4–5. doi:10.4172/2329-8847.1000117.

8. Katherine A. Fowler, Shane P. D. Jack, Bridget H. Lyons, Carter J. Betz, and Emiko Petrosky, "Surveillance for Violent Deaths—National Violent Death Reporting System, 18 States, 2014," *Morbidity and Mortality Weekly Report* 67, no. 2 (2018): 1–36. doi:10.15585/mmwr.ss6702a1.

9. Ye Luo, Tracey A. Lapierre, Mary Elizabeth Hughes, and Linda J. Waite, "Grandparents Providing Care to Grandchildren: A Population-Based Study of Continuity and Change," *Journal of Family Issues* 33, no. 9 (2012): 1143–67. doi:10.1177/0192513X12438685.

10. The Health and Retirement study, National Institute of Aging, NIA U01AG009740 (a longitudinal U.S. study of 20,000 elders), found that functional limitations (e.g., impaired walking, seeing, hearing) reduced the likelihood of grandmother care, but serious health conditions did not.

11. Janine L. Wiles, Kirsty Wild, Ngaire Kerse, and Ruth E. S. Allen, "Resilience from the Point of View of Older People: 'There's Still Life Beyond a Funny Knee,'" *Social Science & Medicine* 74, no. 3 (2012): 416–24. doi:10.1016/j.socscimed.2011.11.005.

12. "Boston: Massachusetts," Top Retirements, accessed January 2018. https://www.topretirements.com/reviews/Massachusetts/Boston.html.

13. Cheryl L. Lampkin, *Insights and Spending Habits of Modern Grandparents* (Washington, DC: AARP, 2012).

14. Lauren R. Bangerter and Vincent R. Waldron, "Turning Points in Long Distance Grandparent–Grandchild Relationships," *Journal of Aging Studies* 29 (2014): 88–97. doi:10.1016/j.jaging.2014.01.004.

15. Goldie Hawn, *Goldie: A Lotus Grows in the Mud* (New York: Putnam, 2005), 455.

16. Melissa Charles, "The Problem with 'Glamma,'" in *Life: Huffington Post*, May 20, 2016.

17. Lesley Stahl, *Becoming Grandma: The Joys and Science of the New Grand-parenting* (New York: Blue Rider Press, 2016), 54.

18. K. Jill Kiecolt, Rosemary Blieszner, and Jyoti Savla, "Long-Term Influences of Intergenerational Ambivalence on Midlife Parents' Psychological Well-Being," *Journal of Marriage and Family* 73, no. 2 (2011): 369–82. doi:10.1111/j.1741-3737.2010.00812.x; Kurt Luescher and Karl Pillemer, "Intergenerational Ambivalence: A New Approach to the Study of Parent-Child Relations in Later Life," *Journal of Marriage and Family* 60, no. 2 (1998): 413–25. doi:10.2307/353858.

19. M. Keith Chen and Ryne Rohla, "The Effect of Partisanship and Political Advertising on Close Family Ties," *Science* 360, no. 6392 (2018): 1020–24. doi:10.1126/science.aaq1433.

20. Constança Paúl, "Loneliness and Health in Later Life," in *The Oxford Handbook of Clinical Geropsychology*, eds. Nancy A. Pachana and Ken Laidlaw (New York: Oxford University Press, 2014); Conor O'Luanaigh et al., "Loneliness and Vascular Biomarkers: The Dublin Healthy Ageing Study," *International Journal of Geriatric Psychiatry* 27, no. 1 (2012): 83–88. doi:10.1002/gps.2695; Lisa Boss, Duck-Hee Kang, and Sandy Branson, "Loneliness and Cognitive Function in the Older Adult: A Systematic Review," *International Psychogeriatrics* 27, no. 4 (2015): 541–53. doi:10.1017/S1041610214002749.

21. Sims and Rofail, "Grandparents with Little or No Contact with Grandchildren," 3.

22. *Troxel v. Granville*, 99–138 U.S (2000).

23. *Santi v. Santi*, 77/00–0181 14–15 (2001).

24. In the United States, births to unmarried mothers have averaged 40 percent for the past decade. Joyce A. Martin, Brady E. Hamilton, Michelle J. K. Osterman, Anne K. Driscoll, and Patrick Drake, *Births: Final Data for 2016* (Hyattsville, MD: National Center for Health Statistics, January 31, 2018).

25. Precise rates of cohabitation nationwide are hard to ascertain, but a recent study found that, before marriage, 70 percent of couples cohabit—for almost three years, on average. Arielle Kuperberg, "Premarital Cohabitation

and Direct Marriage in the United States: 1956–2015," *Marriage & Family Review* (2018). doi:10.1080/01494929.2018.1518820.

26. In 2016, for 70 percent of children who were victims of maltreatment, the perpetrator was their mother (sometime with the father, sometimes alone). U.S. Department of Health and Human Services, *Child Maltreatment 2016* (Washington, DC: Administration for Children and Families, Administration on Children, Youth and Families, Children's Bureau, February 1, 2018).

27. Lampkin, *Insights and Spending Habits of Modern Grandparents.*

28. Mike Glover, "Court Strikes Grandparent Visitation Law," *Associated Press State & Local Wire*, September 6, 2001, Nexis Uni, LexisNexis.

29. Jeff Atkinson, "Shifts in the Law Regarding the Rights of Third Parties to Seek Visitation and Custody of Children," *Family Law Quarterly* 47, no. 1 (2013): 1–34.

CHAPTER 5: TOO MUCH GRANDMOTHERING

1. Deborah Sampson and Katherine Hertlein, "The Experience of Grandparents Raising Grandchildren," *GrandFamilies* 2, no. 1 (2015): 75–96.

2. System 1 and System 2 are explained in chapter 3, following Daniel Kahneman, *Thinking, Fast and Slow* (New York: Farrar, Straus and Giroux, 2011).

3. Ibid.

4. Renee R. Ellis and Tavia Simmons, *Coresident Grandparents and Their Grandchildren: 2012 Population Characteristics: Current Population Reports* (Washington, DC: US Census Bureau, 2014).

5. Virpi Timonen, introduction to *Grandparenting Practices around the World: Reshaping Family*, ed. Virpi Timonen (Bristol, UK: Policy Press, 2018), 9.

6. Estimate based on Ellis and Simmons, *Coresident Grandparents and Their Grandchildren.*

7. Nancy E. Reichman, Julien O. Teitler, Irwin Garfinkel, and Sara S. McLanahan, "Fragile Families: Sample and Design," *Children and Youth Services Review* 23, no. 4 (2001): 303–26. doi:10.1016/S0190-7409(01)00141-4.

8. The U.S. population is about 13 percent African American, but skipped-generation families headed by a sole grandmother are 42 percent African American. Ellis and Simmons, *Coresident Grandparents and Their Grandchildren.*

9. Sampson and Hertlein, "The Experience of Grandparents Raising Grandchildren."

10. Natasha V. Pilkauskas and Rachel E. Dunifon, "Understanding Grandfamilies: Characteristics of Grandparents, Nonresident Parents, and Children," *Journal of Marriage and Family* 78, no. 3 (2016): 623–33. doi:10.1111/jomf.12291.

11. Charles A. Nelson, Nathan A. Fox, and Charles H. Zeanah, *Romania's Abandoned Children: Deprivation, Brain Development, and the Struggle for Recovery* (Cambridge, MA: Harvard University Press, 2014).

12. Marc Winokur, Amy Holtan, and Keri E. Batchelder, "Kinship Care for the Safety, Permanency, and Well-Being of Children Removed from the Home for Maltreatment," *Cochrane Database of Systematic Reviews* (2014). doi:10.1002/14651858.CD006546.pub3.

13. Deborah M. Whitley, Susan J. Kelley, and Dorian A. Lamis, "Depression, Social Support, and Mental Health: A Longitudinal Mediation Analysis in African American Custodial Grandmothers," *International Journal of Aging* 82, no. 2–3 (2016): 166–87. doi:10.1177/0091415015626550; Dana L. Carthron and Maria Rivera Busam, "The Diabetic Health of African American Grandmothers Raising Their Grandchildren," *Clinical Medicine Insights: Women's Health* 9, no. Suppl. 1 (2016): 41–46. doi:10.4137/CMWH.S34694; Jessica C. Hadfield, "The Health of Grandparents Raising Grandchildren: A Literature Review," *Journal of Gerontological Nursing* 40, no. 4 (2014): 32–42. doi:10.3928/00989134-20140219-01.

14. Feinian Chen, Christine A. Mair, Luoman Bao, and Yang Claire Yang, "Race/Ethnic Differentials in the Health Consequences of Caring for Grandchildren for Grandparents," *Journals of Gerontology: Series B, Psychological Sciences and Social Sciences* 70, no. 5 (2015): 793–803. doi:10.1093/geronb/gbu160.

15. Bert Hayslip, Rebecca J. Glover, and Sarah E. Pollard, "Noncaregiving Grandparent Peers' Perceptions of Custodial Grandparents: Extent of Life Disruption, Needs for Social Support, and Needs for Social and Mental Health Services," in *Grandparenting in the United States*, eds. Madonna Harrington Meyer and Ynesse Abdul-Malak (Amityville, NY: Baywood, 2016).

16. Pilkauskas and Dunifon, "Understanding Grandfamilies."

17. Ellis and Simmons, *Coresident Grandparents and Their Grandchildren*, 14.

18. Sandra J. Bailey, Deborah C. Haynes, and Bethany L. Letiecq, "'How Can You Retire When You Still Got a Kid in School?' Economics

of Raising Grandchildren in Rural Areas," *Marriage & Family Review* 49, no. 8 (2013): 671–93.

19. Elizabeth M. Bertera and Sandra Edmonds Crewe, "Parenthood in the Twenty-First Century: African American Grandparents as Surrogate Parents," *Journal of Human Behavior in the Social Environment* 23, no. 2 (2013): 178–92. doi:10.1080/10911359.2013.747348.

20. Deborah Sampson and Katherine Hertlein, "The Experience of Grandparents Raising Grandchildren," *GrandFamilies* 2, no. 1 (2015): 85.

21. Pilkauskas and Dunifon, "Understanding Grandfamilies," 623–33.

22. Rachel Dunifon, Kimberly Kopko, P. Lindsay Chase-Lansdale, and Lauren Wakschlag, "Multigenerational Relationships in Families with Custodial Grandparents," in *Grandparenting in the United States*, eds. Madonna Harrington Meyer and Ynesse Abdul-Malak (Amityville, NY: Baywood, 2016), 152.

23. Lesley Stahl, *Becoming Grandma: The Joys and Science of the New Grandparenting* (New York: Blue Rider Press, 2016), 102.

24. Dunifon, Kopko, Chase-Lansdale, and Wakschlag, "Multigenerational Relationships in Families with Custodial Grandparents"; Valerie O'Brien, "The Benefits and Challenges of Kinship Care," *Child Care in Practice* 18, no. 2 (2012): 127–46. doi:10.1080/13575279.2012.657610.

25. Marcie Fitzgerald, "Déjà Vu," in *Eye of My Heart: 27 Writers Reveal the Hidden Pleasures and Perils of Being a Grandmother*, ed. Barbara Graham (New York: HarperCollins, 2010), 228.

26. Bert Hayslip, Christine A. Fruhauf, and Megan L. Dolbin-MacNab, "Grandparents Raising Grandchildren: What Have We Learned Over the Past Decade?" *Gerontologist* 59, no. 3 (2017). doi:10.1093/geront/gnx106.

27. Theodora Lam and Brenda S. A. Yeoh, "Parental Migration and Disruptions in Everyday Life: Reactions of Left-Behind Children in Southeast Asia," *Journal of Ethnic and Migration Studies* (published electronically 2019). doi:10.1080/1369183X.2018.1547022; Marina Ariza, "Care Circulation, Absence and Affect in Transnational Mothering," in *Transnational Families, Migration and the Circulation of Care*, eds. Loretta Baldassar and Laura Merla (New York: Routledge, 2013).

28. Ernesto Castañeda and Lesley Buck, "Remittances, Transnational Parenting, and the Children Left Behind: Economic and Psychological Implications," *Latin Americanist* 55, no. 4 (2011): 105. doi:10.1111/j.1557-203X.2011.01136.x.

29. Deborah Fahy Bryceson, "Transnational Families Negotiating Migration and Care Life Cycles across Nation-State Borders," *Journal of Ethnic and Migration Studies* (published electronically 2019). doi:10.1080/1369 183X.2018.1547017; Deborah A. Boehm, *Intimate Migrations: Gender, Family, and Illegality Among Transnational Mexicans* (New York: New York University Press, 2012).

30. Megan L. Dolbin-MacNab and Loriena A. Yancura, "International Perspectives on Grandparents Raising Grandchildren: Contextual Considerations for Advancing Global Discourse," *International Journal of Aging and Human Development* 86, no. 1 (2018): 3–33. doi:10.1177/0091415016689565.

31. Zhen Cong and Merril Silverstein, "Custodial Grandparents and Intergenerational Support in Rural China," in *Experiencing Grandparenthood: An Asian Perspective*, eds. Kalyani K. Mehta and Leng Thang (New York: Springer, 2011); Feinian Chen and Guangya Liu, "The Health Implications of Grandparents Caring for Grandchildren in China," *Journals of Gerontology Series B: Psychological Sciences and Social Sciences* 67B, no. 1 (2012): 99–112. doi:10.1093/geronb/gbr132; Hongwei Xu, "Physical and Mental Health of Chinese Grandparents Caring for Grandchildren and Great-Grandparents," *Social Science & Medicine* (published electronically 2018). doi:10.1016/j.socscimed.2018.05.047.

32. Renee R. Ellis and Tavia Simmons, *Coresident Grandparents and Their Grandchildren: 2012 Population Characteristics: Current Population Reports* (Washington, DC: US Census Bureau, 2014).

33. Data is from American Community Survey, Fact Finder, U.S. Census Bureau. About 6,362,268 grandparents live with their grandchildren, under age 18, as well as with at least one of their grandchildren's parents. About 1,687,175 (27 percent) of them consider themselves or their spouse primarily responsible for their grandchildren.

34. The American Fact Finder for 2015–2019 reports that more than 8 million women over age fifty-four live alone. They are counted as nonfamily households. The census does not ask how many of them are grandmothers, but Rachel Margolis and Bruno Arpino report that 85 percent of those over age sixty-five in the United States are grandparents.

35. According to the American Community Survey (Fact Finder, U.S. Bureau of the Census), 12.3 percent of the households with grandparents and grandchildren had no parents present in 2017. That percent has gone down every year of the past decade: in 2007, it was 15.0 percent.

36. American Fact Finder, 2017.

260   *Notes*

37. Sarah Jones, "The Grandparenting Generation: Why Are So Many Children Being Raised by Their Grandparents?" *New Republic*, January 8, 2018.

38. Madonna Harrington Meyer, *Grandmothers at Work* (New York: New York University Press, 2014), 5–6.

39. Madonna Harrington Meyer, "Grandmother's Financial Contributions and the Impact on Grandmothers," in *Grandparenting in the United States*, eds. Madonna Harrington Meyer and Ynesse Abdul-Malak (Amityville, NY: Baywood, 2016), 49.

40. Meliyanni Johar and Shiko Maruyama, "Intergenerational Cohabitation in Modern Indonesia: Filial Support and Dependence," *Health Economics* 20, no. 1 (2011): 87–104. doi:10.1002/hec.1708.

41. Cong and Silverstein, "Custodial Grandparents and Intergenerational Support in Rural China," 123.

42. Sarah E. Oberlander, Fatma M. Shebl, Laurence S. Magder, and Maureen M. Black, "Adolescent Mothers Leaving Multigenerational Households," *Journal of Clinical Child & Adolescent Psychology* 38 (2009): 62–74. doi:10.1080/15374410802575321.

43. Natasha Pilkauskas, "Breastfeeding Initiation and Duration in Coresident Grandparent, Mother and Infant Households," *Maternal and Child Health Journal* 18, no. 8 (2014): 1955–63. doi:10.1007/s10995-014-1441-z.

44. Maureen M. Black, Mia A. Papas, Jon M. Hussey, Wanda Hunter, Howard Dubowitz, Jonathan B. Kotch, Diana English, and Mary Schneider, "Behavior and Development of Preschool Children Born to Adolescent Mothers: Risk and 3-Generation Households," *Pediatrics* 109, no. 4 (2002): 573–80. doi:10.1542/peds.109.4.573.

45. Jessica L. Levetan and Lauren G. Wild, "The Implications of Maternal Grandmother Coresidence and Involvement for Adolescent Adjustment in South Africa," *International Journal of Psychology* 51, no. 5 (2016): 356–65. doi:10.1002/ijop.12178.

46. Bharati Mukherjee, "Gained in Translation," in *Eye of My Heart: 27 Writers Reveal the Hidden Pleasures and Perils of Being a Grandmother*, ed. Barbara Graham (New York: HarperCollins, 2010), 209.

47. Stacy Chandler, "Three Generations Build a Happy Household under One Roof," *News Observer*, January 24, 2014.

48. Michelle Maroto, "When the Kids Live at Home: Coresidence, Parental Assets, and Economic Insecurity," *Journal of Marriage and Family* 79, no. 4 (2017): 1041–59. doi:10.1111/jomf.12407.

49. Rachel Margolis and Bruno Arpino, "The Demography of Grandparenthood in 16 European Countries and Two North American Countries," in *Grandparenting Practices around the World: Reshaping Family*, ed. Virpi Timonen (Bristol, UK: Policy Press, 2018), 23.

50. Rachel E. Dunifon, Kathleen M. Ziol-Guest, and Kimberly Kopko, "Grandparent Coresidence and Family Well-Being: Implications for Research and Policy," *Annals of the American Academy of Political and Social Science* 654, no. 1 (2014): 110–26. doi:10.1177/0002716214526530; Natasha Pilkauskas and Christina Cross, "Beyond the Nuclear Family: Trends in Children Living in Shared Households," *Demography* 55, no. 6 (2018): 2283–97. doi:10.1007/s13524-018-0719-y.

51. Doreen Rosenthal and Susan Moore, *New Age Nanas: Being a Grandmother in the 21st Century* (Newport, Australia: Big Sky Publishing, 2012), 51.

CHAPTER 6: THE LOVING COUPLE

1. John Gottman and Julie Gottman, "The Natural Principles of Love," *Journal of Family Theory & Review* 9, no. 1 (2017): 7–26. doi:10.1111/jftr.12182.

2. Sonalde Desai and Lester Andrist, "Gender Scripts and Age at Marriage in India," *Demography* 47, no. 3 (2010): 667–87. doi:10.1353/dem.0.0118; Keera Allendorf and Roshan K. Pandian, "The Decline of Arranged Marriage? Marital Change and Continuity in India," *Population and Development Review* 42, no. 3 (2016): 435–64. doi:10.1111/j.1728-4457.2016.00149.x.

3. Ethel Morgan Smith, "Mad Hearts," in *Mothers of Adult Children*, ed. Marguerite Guzman Bouvard (Lanham, MD: Lexington, 2013), 13.

4. This was expressed by a grandmother in the Bronx. When she said "Not good," her face looked so sad that I did not ask for specifics.

5. Nicholas H. Wolfinger, "Want to Avoid Divorce? Wait to Get Married, But Not Too Long," *Institute for Family Studies*, accessed January 28, 2019. https://ifstudies.org/blog/want-to-avoid-divorce-wait-to-get-married-but-not-too-long/; Trish Hafford-Letchfield, Nicky Lambert, Ellouise Long, and Dominique Brady, "Going Solo: Findings from a Survey of Women Aging without a Partner and Who Do Not Have Children," *Journal of Women & Aging* 29, no. 4 (2017): 321–33. doi:10.1080/08952841.2016.1187544.

6. Laura Kann et al., *Youth Risk Behavior Surveillance—United States, 2017* (Atlanta: Centers for Disease Control and Prevention, June 15, 2018), 67.

7. Joyce A. Martin, Brady E. Hamilton, and Michelle J. K. Osterman, *Births in the United States, 2015* (Hyattsville, MD: National Center for Health Statistics, September 2016).

8. Rachel Margolis, "The Changing Demography of Grandparenthood," *Journal of Marriage and Family* 78, no. 3 (2016): 610–22. doi:10.1111/jomf.12286.

9. Erik H. Erikson, *Childhood and Society*, 2nd ed. (New York: Norton, 1993).

10. Tara L. Gruenewald, Elizabeth K. Tanner, Linda P. Fried, Michelle C. Carlson, Qian-Li Xue, Jeanine M. Parisi, George W. Rebok, Lisa M. Yarnell, and Teresa E. Seeman, "The Baltimore Experience Corps Trial: Enhancing Generativity via Intergenerational Activity Engagement in Later Life," *Journals of Gerontology Series B: Psychological Sciences and Social Sciences* 71, no. 4 (2016): 661–70. doi:10.1093/geronb/gbv005; Ernest Gonzales, Christina Matz-Costa, and Nancy Morrow-Howell, "Increasing Opportunities for the Productive Engagement of Older Adults: A Response to Population Aging," *Gerontologist* 55, no. 2 (2015): 252–61. doi:10.1093/geront/gnu176.

11. Grannies Respond (also known as Abuelas Responden) was described in the November 2018 issue of *Aging Today* (published by the American Society of Aging). That issue included several articles focused on international concerns and "global inspiration."

12. Paola Gianturco, *Grandmother Power: A Global Phenomenon* (New York: PowerHouse, 2012).

13. Arthur Kornhaber, *Contemporary Grandparenting* (Thousand Oaks, CA: Sage, 1996), 170.

14. Jill Nelson, "Sitting Here in Limbo," in *Eye of My Heart: 27 Writers Reveal the Hidden Pleasures and Perils of Being a Grandmother*, ed. Barbara Graham (New York: HarperCollins, 2010), 101–2.

15. Karen L. Fingerman, Yen-Pi Cheng, Lauren Tighe, Kira S. Birditt, and Steve Zarit, "Relationships between Young Adults and Their Parents," in *Early Adulthood in Family Context*, eds. Alan Booth, Susan L. Brown, Nancy S. Landale, Wendy D. Manning and Susan M. McHale, National Symposium on Family Issues (New York: Springer, 2012).

16. Tobias Grossmann, "The Eyes as Windows into Other Minds: An Integrative Perspective," *Perspectives on Psychological Science* 12, no. 1 (2017): 107–21. doi:10.1177/1745691616654457.

17. Teresa M. Cooney and Pearl A. Dykstra, "Theories and Their Empirical Support in the Study of Intergenerational Family Relationships in Adulthood," in *Handbook of Family Theories: A Content-Based Approach*, eds. Mark A. Fine and Frank D. Fincham (New York: Routledge, 2012).

18. Richard A. Settersten, "Relationships in Time and the Life Course: The Significance of Linked Lives," *Research in Human Development* 12, no. 3/4 (2015): 217–23. doi:10.1080/15427609.2015.1071944.

19. Susan Moore and Doreen Rosenthal, *Grandparenting: Contemporary Perspectives* (New York: Routledge, 2017), 54.

20. Liat Kulik, "The Impact of Multiple Roles on the Well-Being of Older Women: Strain or Enrichment?" in *Women and Aging: An International, Intersectional Power Perspective*, eds. Varda Muhlbauer, Joan C. Chrisler and Florence L. Denmark (New York: Springer, 2015).

21. Manfred E. Beutel et al., "Loneliness in the General Population: Prevalence, Determinants and Relations to Mental Health," *BMC Psychiatry* 17, no. 97 (2017). doi:10.1186/s12888-017-1262-x.

22. Laura M. Padilla-Walker and Larry J. Nelson, eds., *Flourishing in Emerging Adulthood: Positive Development during the Third Decade of Life* (New York: Oxford University Press, 2017).

23. Tom Brokaw, *The Greatest Generation* (New York: Random House, 1998).

24. Kenneth D. Rose, *Myth and the Greatest Generation: A Social History of Americans in World War II* (New York: Routledge, 2008).

CHAPTER 7: THE PREGNANT COUPLE

1. Kim Bergman, *Your Future Family: The Essential Guide to Assisted Reproduction (Everything You Need to Know about Surrogacy, Egg Donation, and Sperm Donation)* (Newburyport, MA: Conari Press, 2019); F. Gary Cunningham,

Kenneth Leveno, Steven Bloom, Catherine Spong, Jodi Dashe, Barbara Hoffman, and Brian Casey, *Williams Obstetrics*, 25th ed. (New York: McGraw-Hill, 2018).

2. Tammy S. Harpel and Kari Gentry Barras, "The Impact of Ultrasound on Prenatal Attachment among Disembodied and Embodied Knowers," *Journal of Family Issues* 39, no. 6 (2018): 1523–44. doi:10.1177/0192513X17710774.

3. Tammy S. Harpel and Jodie Hertzog, "'I Thought My Heart Would Burst': The Role of Ultrasound Technology on Expectant Grandmotherhood," *Journal of Family Issues* 31, no. 2 (2010): 257–74. doi:10.1177/0192513 X09348491.

4. Amy St. Pierre, Julie Zaharatos, David Goodman, and William M. Callaghan, "Challenges and Opportunities in Identifying, Reviewing, and Preventing Maternal Deaths," *Obstetrics & Gynecology* 131, no. 1 (2018): 138–42.

5. Åsa Magnusson, Ulla-Britt Wennerholm, Karin Källén, Max Petzold, Ann Thurin-Kjellberg, and Christina Bergh, "The Association between the Number of Oocytes Retrieved for IVF, Perinatal Outcome and Obstetric Complications," *Human Reproduction* 33, no. 10 (2018): 1939–47. doi:10.1093/humrep/dey266.

6. Adam Lewis, Dawei Liu, Scott Stuart, and Ginny Ryan, "Less Depressed or Less Forthcoming? Self-Report of Depression Symptoms in Women Preparing for In Vitro Fertilization," *Archives of Women's Mental Health* 16, no. 2 (2013): 87–92. doi:10.1007/s00737-012-0317-8.

7. Pagan Kennedy, "The Pregnancy Test Scandal," *New York Times*, July 31, 2016. https://nyti.ms/2anoPzO.

8. Jennifer F. Kawwass, Dawn K. Smith, Dmitry M. Kissin, Lisa B. Haddad, Sheree L. Boulet, Saswati Sunderam, and Denise J. Jamieson, "Strategies for Preventing HIV Infection among HIV-Uninfected Women Attempting Conception with HIV-Infected Men—United States," *Morbidity and Mortality Weekly Report* 66, no. 21 (June 2, 2017): 554–57. doi:10.15585/mmwr .mm6621a2.

9. Dale Evans Rogers, *Angel Unaware* (Westwood, NJ: Revell, 1953).

10. Selma Fraiberg, Edna Adelson, and Vivian Shapiro, "Ghosts in the Nursery: A Psychoanalytic Approach to the Problems of Impaired Infant-Mother Relationships," *Journal of the American Academy of Child Psychiatry* 14, no. 3 (1975): 387–421. doi:10.1016/S0002-7138(09)61442-4.

11. Karin Ensink, Nicolas Berthelot, Odette Bernazzani, Lina Normandin, and Peter Fonagy, "Another Step Closer to Measuring the Ghosts in the

Nursery: Preliminary Validation of the Trauma Reflective Functioning Scale," *Frontiers in Psychology* 5, no. 1471 (2014). doi:10.3389/fpsyg.2014.01471.

12. Barbara Graham, "Eye of My Heart," in *Eye of My Heart: 27 Writers Reveal the Hidden Pleasures and Perils of Being a Grandmother*, ed. Barbara Graham (New York: HarperCollins, 2010), 199.

13. This data is from UNICEF, in March 2018. Other sources differ, but every nation of the world has seen neonatal deaths (first month of life) plummet. About half of those deaths occur in the first day.

14. Jeff Galak, Julian Givi, and Elanor F. Williams, "Why Certain Gifts are Great to Give But Not to Get: A Framework for Understanding Errors in Gift Giving," *Current Directions in Psychological Science* 25, no. 6 (2016): 380–85. doi:10.1177/0963721416656937.

15. Jeannette R. Ickovics, Trace Kershaw, Claire Westdahl, Urania Magriples, Zohar Massey, Heather Reynolds, and Sharon Rising, "Group Prenatal Care and Perinatal Outcomes: A Randomized Controlled Trial," *Obstetrics & Gynecology* 110, no. 2 (2007): 330–39. doi:10.1097/01.AOG .0000275284.24298.23.

16. Gina Novick, Lois S. Sadler, Holly Powell Kennedy, Sally S. Cohen, Nora E. Groce, and Kathleen A. Knafl, "Women's Experience of Group Prenatal Care," *Qualitative Health Research* 21, no. 1 (2010): 97–116. doi:10.1177/1049732310378655.

CHAPTER 8: BIRTH AND THE NEWBORN

1. Lesley Stahl, *Becoming Grandma: The Joys and Science of the New Grandparenting* (New York: Blue Rider Press, 2016), 7.

2. Systems 1 and 2, terms from Daniel Kahneman, *Thinking, Fast and Slow* (New York: Farrar, Straus and Giroux, 2011), are explained on page 40.

3. An oft-cited example comes from primatologists in Tanzania. Chimpanzees don't usually fight over food. In the 1970s, some researchers in East Africa put out a large but limited supply of bananas each morning so they could easily observe their subjects, the nearby chimpanzees. Afterward, the chimps began to sleep near the research station, arriving in "noisy hordes" each morning, fighting for the fruit. When the researchers realized what they had done, they stopped the bounty. The chimps subsequently returned to peaceful food

acquisition. Christopher Ryan and Cacilda Jethá, *Sex at Dawn: The Prehistoric Origins of Modern Sexuality* (New York: Harper, 2010).

4. One man was trampled to death as he tried to stop rampaging shoppers one Black Friday. Robert D. McFadden and Angela Macropoulos, "Wal-Mart Employee Trampled to Death," *New York Times*, November 28, 2008. https://nyti.ms/2kdkvs8.

5. A protest sign when the United States invaded Iran: "If only Iran's main export was broccoli."

6. "Grandmom's Fight in the Hospital," YouTube video, 2:46, from Lifetime's *One Born Every Minute*: "Knockout Delivery," Season 2, Episode 1, posted by K'sJourney, November 29, 2011. https://www.youtube.com/watch?v=Wrz81DxgN14. This same fight is on eight other YouTube videos.

7. Judith Viorst, "The Rivals," in *Eye of My Heart: 27 Writers Reveal the Hidden Pleasures and Perils of Being a Grandmother*, ed. Barbara Graham (New York: HarperCollins, 2010), 180.

8. Stahl, *Becoming Grandma*, 78.

9. Andrea Tran, "Becoming a Baby Friendly Hospital," *MCN* 42, no. 1 (2017): E4–E5. doi:10.1097/NMC.0000000000000317.

10. David Pitcher, ed., *Inside Kinship Care: Understanding Family Dynamics and Providing* (Philadelphia: Jessica Kingsley, 2013).

11. Maria Legerstee, David W. Haley, and Marc H. Bornstein, eds., *The Infant Mind: Origins of the Social Brain* (New York: Guilford, 2013).

12. United Nations Children's Fund, *Every Child's Birth Right: Inequities and Trends in Birth Registration* (New York: UNICEF, 2013).

13. Marshall H. Klaus and John H. Kennell, *Maternal-Infant Bonding: The Impact of Early Separation or Loss on Family Development* (Saint Louis: Mosby, 1976).

14. Abbie E. Goldberg, April M. Moyer, and Lori A. Kinkler, "Lesbian, Gay, and Heterosexual Adoptive Parents' Perceptions of Parental Bonding During Early Parenthood," *Couple and Family Psychology* 2, no. 2 (2013): 146–62. doi:10.1037/a0031834; Robin S. Edelstein, Britney M. Wardecker, William J. Chopik, Amy C. Moors, Emily L. Shipman, and Natalie J. Lin, "Prenatal Hormones in First-Time Expectant Parents: Longitudinal Changes and Within-Couple Correlations," *American Journal of Human Biology* 27, no. 3 (2015): 317–25. doi:10.1002/ajhb.22670; Ruth Feldman and Marian J. Bakermans-Kranenburg, "Oxytocin: A Parenting Hormone," *Current Opinion in Psychology* 15 (2017): 13–18. doi:10.1016/j.copsyc.2017.02.011.

15. Ruth Feldman, "The Adaptive Human Parental Brain: Implications for Children's Social Development," *Trends in Neurosciences* 38, no. 6 (2015): 390. doi:10.1016/j.tins.2015.04.004.

16. Sarah B. Hrdy, *Mothers and Others: The Evolutionary Origins of Mutual Understanding* (Cambridge, MA: Belknap Press of Harvard University Press, 2011); Yan Qun Liu, Marcia Petrini, and Judith A. Maloni, "Doing the Month: Postpartum Practices in Chinese Women," *Nursing and Health Sciences* 17, no. 1 (2015): 5–14. doi:10.1111/nhs.12146.

17. Kenneth J. Gruber, Susan H. Cupito, and Christina F. Dobson, "Impact of Doulas on Healthy Birth Outcomes," *Journal of Perinatal Education* 22, no. 1 (2013): 49–58. doi:10.1891/1058-1243.22.1.49.

18. Feldman, "The Adaptive Human Parental Brain," 393; Martin O'Connell, "Where's Papa? Fathers' Role in Child Care," *Population Trends and Public Policy* 20 (1993); Brian Knop and Karin L. Brewster, "Family Flexibility in Response to Economic Conditions: Fathers' Involvement in Child-Care Tasks," *Journal of Marriage and Family* 78, no. 2 (2016): 283–92. doi:10.1111/jomf.12249.

19. Jennifer L. Bellamy, Matthew Thullen, and Sydney Hans, "Effect of Low-Income Unmarried Fathers' Presence at Birth on Involvement," *Journal of Marriage and Family* 77, no. 3 (2015): 647–61. doi:10.1111/jomf.12193.

20. Marshall H. Klaus, John H. Kennell, and Phyllis H. Klaus, *The Doula Book: How a Trained Labor Companion Can Help You Have a Shorter, Easier, and Healthier Birth* (Boston: Da Capo, 2012).

21. Jane S. Grassley and Valerie Eschiti, "The Value of Listening to Grandmothers' Infant-Feeding Stories," *Journal of Perinatal Education* 20, no. 3 (2011): 134–41. doi:10.1891/1058-1243.20.3.134.

22. Matthew Grossman, quoted in Meghan Rosen, "Shaky Start," *Science News* 191, no. 11 (2017).

23. Matthew R. Grossman, Adam K. Berkwitt, Rachel R. Osborn, Yaqing Xu, Denise A. Esserman, Eugene D. Shapiro, and Matthew J. Bizzarro, "An Initiative to Improve the Quality of Care of Infants with Neonatal Abstinence Syndrome," *Pediatrics* 139, no. 6 (2017). doi:10.1542/peds.2016-3360.

24. Vicky York, "Accepting Love without Perfection: The Roles of Grandmothers and Postpartum Doulas," *Midwifery Today* 99 (2011): 26.

25. Stahl, *Becoming Grandma*, 10.

26. Irvine Loudon, *Death in Childbirth: An International Study of Maternal Care and Maternal Mortality 1800–1950* (New York: Oxford University Press, 1992).

27. Michael W. O'Hara and Jennifer E. McCabe, "Postpartum Depression: Current Status and Future Directions," *Annual Review of Clinical Psychology* 9 (2013): 379–407. doi:10.1146/annurev-clinpsy-050212-185612; Katherine L. Wisner et al., "Onset Timing, Thoughts of Self-harm, and Diagnoses in Postpartum Women with Screen-Positive Depression Findings," *JAMA Psychiatry* 70, no. 5 (2013): 490–98. doi:10.1001/jamapsychiatry.2013.87.

28. Emma L. Barber, Lisbet Lundsberg, Kathleen Belanger, Christian M. Pettker, Edmund F. Funai, and Jessica L. Illuzzi, "Contributing Indications to the Rising Cesarean Delivery Rate," *Obstetrics and Gynecology* 118, no. 1 (2011): 29–38. doi: 10.1097/AOG.0b013e31821e5f65.

29. Jenna L. Gress-Smith, Linda J. Luecken, Kathryn Lemery-Chalfant, and Rose Howe, "Postpartum Depression Prevalence and Impact on Infant Health, Weight, and Sleep in Low-Income and Ethnic Minority Women and Infants," *Maternal and Child Health Journal* 16, no. 4 (2012): 887–93. doi:10.1007/s10995-011-0812-y; Wisner et al., "Onset Timing, Thoughts of Self-harm, and Diagnoses."

30. Ri-hua Xie, Jun Lei, Shuhong Wang, Haiyan Xie, Mark Walker, and Shi Wu Wen, "Cesarean Section and Postpartum Depression in a Cohort of Chinese Women with a High Cesarean Delivery Rate," *Journal of Women's Health* 20, no. 12 (2011): 1881–86. doi:10.1089/jwh.2011.2842.

31. Szu-Nian Yanga, Lih-Jong Shena, Tao Ping, Yu-Chun Wang, and Ching-Wen Chien, "The Delivery Mode and Seasonal Variation Are Associated with the Development of Postpartum Depression," *Journal of Affective Disorders* 132, no. 1/2 (2011): 158–64. doi:10.1016/j.jad.2011.02.009.

32. Wendy Sword, Christine Kurtz Landy, Lehana Thabane, Susan Watt, Paul Krueger, Dan Farine, and Gary Foster, "Is Mode of Delivery Associated with Postpartum Depression at 6 Weeks: A Prospective Cohort Study," *BJOG* 118, no. 8 (2011): 966–77. doi:10.1111/j.1471-0528.2011.02950.x.

33. Oriana Vesga-López, Carlos Blanco, Katherine Keyes, Mark Olfson, Bridget F. Grant, and Deborah S. Hasin, "Psychiatric Disorders in Pregnant and Postpartum Women in the United States," *Archives of General Psychiatry* 65, no. 7 (2008): 805–15. doi:10.1001/archpsyc.65.7.805.

34. Dawn Kingston, Suzanne Tough, and Heather Whitfield, "Postpartum Maternal Psychological Distress and Infant Development: A Systematic Review," *Child Psychiatry & Human Development* 43, no. 5 (2012): 683–714. doi:10.1007/s10578-012-0291-4.

35. Leslie Stahl reports that she wanted the hospital to keep Taylor for an additional day after birth; the hospital said the price would be $3,000. Taylor went home.

36. Cindy-Lee Dennis and Therese Dowswell, "Psychosocial and Psychological Interventions for Preventing Postpartum Depression," *Cochrane Database of Systematic Reviews* 2, no. CD001134 (2013). doi:10.1002/14651858. CD001134.pub3.

37. Lu Tang, Ruijuan Zhu, and Xueying Zhang, "Postpartum Depression and Social Support in China: A Cultural Perspective," *Journal of Health Communication* 21, no. 9 (2016): 1055–61. doi:10.1080/10810730.2016.1204384.

38. Virginia Ironside, "What I Want to Be When I Grow Up," in *Eye of My Heart: 27 Writers Reveal the Hidden Pleasures and Perils of Being a Grandmother*, ed. Barbara Graham (New York: HarperCollins, 2010), 83–84.

CHAPTER 9: INFANTS

1. John Gottman and Julie Gottman, "The Natural Principles of Love," *Journal of Family Theory & Review* 9, no. 1 (2017): 11. doi:10.1111/jftr.12182.

2. Carolyn M. Aldwin, *Stress, Coping, and Development: An Integrative Perspective*, 2nd ed. (New York: Guilford Press, 2007).

3. Yoav Lavee, "Stress Processes in Families and Couples," in *Handbook of Marriage and the Family*, 3rd ed., eds. Gary W. Peterson and Kevin R. Bush (New York: Springer, 2013).

4. Mikko Myrskylä and Rachel Margolis, "Happiness: Before and After the Kids," *Demography* 51, no. 5 (2014): 1843–66. doi:10.1007/s13524-014-0321-x.

5. Sally A. Brinkman, Sarah E. Johnson, James P. Codde, Michael B. Hart, Judith A. Straton, Murthy N. Mittinty, and Sven R. Silburn, "Efficacy of Infant Simulator Programmes to Prevent Teenage Pregnancy: A School-Based Cluster Randomised Controlled Trial in Western Australia," *Lancet* 388, no. 10057 (2016): 2264–71. doi:10.1016/S0140-6736(16)30384-1.

6. Rachel Connelly and Jean Kimmel, "If You're Happy and You Know It: How Do Mothers and Fathers in the US Really Feel about Caring for Their Children?" *Feminist Economics* 21, no. 1 (2015): 1–34. doi:10.1080/13545701.2014.970210.

7. Maureen O'Dougherty, "Becoming a Mother Through Postpartum Depression: Narratives from Brazil," in *Parenting in Global Perspective: Negotiating Ideologies of Kinship, Self and Politics*, eds. Charlotte Faircloth, Diane M. Hoffman, and Linda L. Layne (New York: Routledge, 2013), 190.

8. Dieter Wolke, Ayten Bilgin, and Muthanna Samara, "Systematic Review and Meta-Analysis: Fussing and Crying Durations and Prevalence of Colic in Infants," *Journal of Pediatrics* 185 (2017): 55–61. doi:10.1016/j.jpeds.2017.02.020.

9. James E. Swain, Shao-Hsuan Shaun Ho, and Pilyoung Kim, "Neuroendocrinology of Parental Response to Baby-Cry," *Journal of Neuroendocrinology* 23, no. 11 (2011): 1036–41. doi:10.1111/j.1365-2826.2011.02212.x.

10. Christine Tsang, Simone Falk, and Alexandria Hessel, "Infants Prefer Infant-Directed Song over Speech," *Child Development* 88, no. 4 (2017): 1207–15. doi:10.1111/cdev.12647.

11. Geneviève Gariépy, Helena Honkaniemi, and Amélie Quesnel-Vallée, "Social Support and Protection from Depression: Systematic Review of Current Findings in Western Countries," *British Journal of Psychiatry* 209, no. 4 (2016): 284–93. doi:10.1192/bjp.bp.115.169094.

12. Anne Roiphe, "Grandmothers Should Be Seen and Not Heard," in *Eye of My Heart: 27 Writers Reveal the Hidden Pleasures and Perils of Being a Grandmother*, ed. Barbara Graham (New York: HarperCollins, 2010), 77–78.

13. Jeremy D. Johnson, Katherine Cocker, and Elisabeth Chang, "Infantile Colic: Recognition and Treatment," *American Family Physician* 92, no. 7 (2015): 577–82.

14. Kajsa Landgren and Inger Hallström, "Parents' Experience of Living with a Baby with Infantile Colic—A Phenomenological Hermeneutic Study," *Scandinavian Journal of Caring Sciences* 25, no. 2 (2011): 317–24. doi:10.1111/j.1471-6712.2010.00829.x.

15. William Sears and Martha Sears, *The Attachment Parenting Book: A Commonsense Guide to Understanding and Nurturing Your Baby* (Boston: Little, Brown, 2001).

16. Carol Garhart Mooney, *Theories of Attachment: An Introduction to Bowlby, Ainsworth, Gerber, Brazelton, Kennell, and Klaus* (St. Paul, MN: Redleaf Press, 2010).

17. Mary D. Salter Ainsworth, *Infancy in Uganda: Infant Care and the Growth of Love* (Baltimore: Johns Hopkins Press, 1967).

18. Mary D. Salter Ainsworth, Mary C. Blehar, Everett Waters, and Sally Wall, *Patterns of Attachment: A Psychological Study of the Strange Situation* (New York: Erlbaum, 1978).

19. Silvia M. Bell and Mary D. Salter Ainsworth, "Infant Crying and Maternal Responsiveness," *Child Development* 43 (1972): 1171–90.

20. Jude Cassidy and Phillip R. Shaver, eds., *Handbook of Attachment: Theory, Research, and Clinical Applications*, 3rd ed. (New York: Guilford, 2016).

21. Natasha J. Cabrera and Catherine S. Tamis-LeMonda, eds., *Handbook of Father Involvement: Multidisciplinary Perspectives*, 2nd ed. (New York: Routledge, 2013).

22. Livia Jiménez Sedano, "'Spanish People Don't Know How to Rear Their Children!' Dominican Women's Resistance to Instance Mothers in Madrid," in *Parenting in Global Perspective: Negotiating Ideologies of Kinship, Self and Politics*, eds. Charlotte Faircloth, Diane M. Hoffman, and Linda L. Layne (New York: Routledge, 2013).

23. Katrien De Graeve and Chia Longman, "Intensive Mothering of Ethiopian Adoptive Children in Flanders, Belgium," in *Parenting in Global Perspective: Negotiating Ideologies of Kinship, Self and Politics*, eds. Charlotte Faircloth, Diane M. Hoffman, and Linda L. Layne (New York: Routledge, 2013).

24. Sears and Sears, *The Attachment Parenting Book*, 128.

25. Susan Moore and Doreen Rosenthal, *Grandparenting: Contemporary Perspectives* (New York: Routledge, 2017).

26. Richard Ferber, *Solve Your Child's Sleep Problems* (New York: Touchstone, 2006).

27. Lesley Stahl, *Becoming Grandma: The Joys and Science of the New Grandparenting* (New York: Blue Rider Press, 2016), 50.

28. Many sources recognize overfeeding as a world problem. For instance, "childhood obesity is one of the most serious public health challenges of the 21st century. The problem is global and is steadily affecting many low and middle income countries, particularly in urban settings." Krushnapriya Sahoo, Bishnupriya Sahoo, Ashok Kumar Choudhury, Nighat Yasin Sofi, Raman Kumar, and Ajeet Singh Bhadoria, "Childhood Obesity: Causes and Consequences," *Journal of Family Medicine and Primary Care* 4, no. 2 (2015): 187–88. doi:10.4103/2249-4863.154628.

29. Divya K. Shah, "Is Breast Always Best? A Personal Reflection on the Challenges of Breastfeeding," *Obstetrics & Gynecology* 121, no. 4 (2013): 869–71. doi:10.1097/AOG.0b013e3182878246.

30. Diane Wiessinger, Diana West, and Teresa Pitman, *The Womanly Art of Breastfeeding*, 8th ed. (New York: Ballantine, 2010) (first published in 1958).

31. Courtney Jung, *Lactivism: How Feminists and Fundamentalists, Hippies and Yuppies, and Physicians and Politicians Made Breastfeeding Big Business and Bad Policy* (New York: Basic Books, 2015), 49.

32. Centers for Disease Control and Prevention, *Breastfeeding Report Card—United States, 2016* (Atlanta: Centers for Disease Control and Prevention, August 2016).

33. Charlotte Faircloth, "'Intensive Motherhood' in Comparative Perspective: Feminism, Full-Term Breast Feeding and Attachment Parenting in London and Paris," in *Parenting in Global Perspective: Negotiating Ideologies of Kinship, Self and Politics*, eds. Charlotte Faircloth, Diane M. Hoffman, and Linda L. Layne (New York: Routledge, 2013).

34. Nikki L. Rogers, Jemilla Abdi, Dennis Moore, Sarah Nd'iangui, Linda J. Smith, Andrew J. Carlson, and Dennis Carlson, "Colostrum Avoidance, Prelacteal Feeding and Late Breast-Feeding Initiation in Rural Northern Ethiopia," *Public Health Nutrition* 14, no. 11 (2011): 2029–36. doi:10.1017/S1368980011000073.

35. Meena L. Godhia and Neesah Patel, "Colostrum—Its Composition, Benefits as a Nutraceutical—A Review," *Current Research in Nutrition and Food Science* 1, no. 1 (2013): 37–47. doi:10.12944/CRNFSJ.1.1.04.

36. Karen Wambach and Jan Riordan, *Breastfeeding and Human Lactation*, 5th ed. (Burlington, MA: Jones & Bartlett Publishers, 2014).

CHAPTER 10: YOUNG CHILDREN

1. Anne K. Reitz and Ursula M. Staudinger, "Getting Older, Getting Better? Toward Understanding Positive Personality Development Across Adulthood," in *Personality Development across the Lifespan*, ed. Jule Specht (Cambridge, MA: Academic Press, 2017).

2. Sandra Benitez, "The Owie Tree," in *Eye of My Heart: 27 Writers Reveal the Hidden Pleasures and Perils of Being a Grandmother*, ed. Barbara Graham (New York: HarperCollins, 2010).

3. Kirby Deater-Deckard and Robin Panneton, "Unearthing the Developmental and Intergenerational Dynamics of Stress in Parent and Child Functioning," in *Parental Stress and Early Child Development: Adaptive and Mal-*

adaptive Outcomes, eds. Kirby Deater-Deckard and Robin Panneton (Cham, Switzerland: Springer, 2017).

4. Emily A. Greenfield, "Grandparent Involvement and Parenting Stress among Nonmarried Mothers of Young Children," *Social Service Review* 85, no. 1 (2011): 135–57. doi:10.1086/658395.

5. Amel Ketani, "Family Mediation in England and Wales: A Focus on Children," in *Creative Business and Social Innovations for a Sustainable Future*, eds. Miroslav Mateev and Panikkos Poutziouris (Cham, Switzerland: Springer, 2019).

6. Paula Caplan, "Don't Blame Mother: Then and Now," in *Gender and Women's Studies in Canada: Critical Terrain*, eds. Margaret Helen Hobbs and Carla Rice (Toronto: Women's Press, 2013), 99.

7. Joshua Coleman, "The Many Faces of Parental Estrangement," report for the National Council on Family Relations (2011), 4.

8. Among the many sites of such grandmother comments are sites on AARP and sites on Considerable.com.

9. Virpi Timonen, ed., *Grandparenting Practices around the World: Reshaping Family* (Bristol, UK: Policy Press, 2018).

10. Karina Schumann, "The Psychology of Offering an Apology: Understanding the Barriers to Apologizing and How to Overcome Them," *Current Directions in Psychological Science* 27, no. 2 (2018): 74. doi:10.1177/0963721417741709.

11. Jill Nelson, "Sitting Here in Limbo," in *Eye of My Heart: 27 Writers Reveal the Hidden Pleasures and Perils of Being a Grandmother*, ed. Barbara Graham (New York: HarperCollins, 2010), 102, 106.

12. One of many examples: Irene Goldenberg, Mark Stanton, and Herbert Goldenberg, *Family Therapy: An Overview*, 9th ed. (Boston: Cengage Learning, 2016).

13. Florida Scott-Maxwell, *The Measure of My Days* (New York: Penguin, 1979), 20.

14. Dorothy Canfield Fisher, *What Grandmother Did Not Know* (Boston: Pilgrim Press, 1922), 8, 15.

15. Diana Baumrind, "Current Patterns of Parental Authority," *Developmental Psychology* 4, no. 1, pt. 2 (1971): 1–103. doi:10.1037/h0030372.

16. As one summary explains, Baumrind's work "has had a long-lasting and significant an impact on the field of developmental psychology." Joan E. Grusec, "Socialization and the Role of Power Assertion," *Human Development* 55, no. 2 (2012): 52. doi:10.1159/000337963.

17. Ynesse Abdul-Malak, "Health and Grandparenting among 13 Caribbean (and One Latin American) Immigrant Women in the United States," in *Grandparenting in the United States*, eds. Madonna Harrington Meyer and Ynesse Abdul-Malak (Amityville, NY: Baywood, 2016).

18. Liane Peña Alampay et al., "Severity and Justness Do Not Moderate the Relation between Corporal Punishment and Negative Child Outcomes: A Multicultural and Longitudinal Study," *International Journal of Behavioral Development* 41, no. 4 (2017): 491–502. doi:10.1177/0165025417697852.

19. Robert E. Larzelere, Amanda Sheffield Morris, and Amanda W. Harrist, *Authoritative Parenting: Synthesizing Nurturance and Discipline for Optimal Child Development* (Washington, DC: American Psychological Association, 2013).

20. Jennifer E. Lansford et al., "A Longitudinal Examination of Mothers' and Fathers' Social Information Processing Biases and Harsh Discipline in Nine Countries," *Development and Psychopathology* 26, no. 3 (2014): 561–73. doi:10.1017/S0954579414000236.

21. Mary Pipher, introduction to *Eye of My Heart: 27 Writers Reveal the Hidden Pleasures and Perils of Being a Grandmother*, ed. Barbara Graham (New York: HarperCollins, 2010), 8.

22. Abdul-Malak, "Health and Grandparenting Among 13 Caribbean (and One Latin American) Immigrant Women in the United States."

23. Rona Maynard, "Facebook Grandma," in *Eye of My Heart: 27 Writers Reveal the Hidden Pleasures and Perils of Being a Grandmother*, ed. Barbara Graham (New York: HarperCollins, 2010), 91.

24. Elena Camisasca, Sarah Miragoli, and Paola Di Blasio, "Is the Relationship Between Marital Adjustment and Parenting Stress Mediated or Moderated by Parenting Alliance?" *Europe's Journal of Psychology* 10, no. 2 (2014): 235–54. doi:10.5964/ejop.v10i2.724.

25. Doreen Rosenthal and Susan Moore, *New Age Nanas: Being a Grandmother in the 21st Century* (Newport, Australia: Big Sky Publishing, 2012), 84.

CHAPTER 11: SCHOOL CHILDREN

1. Beverly Lowry, "What Counts," in *Eye of My Heart: 27 Writers Reveal the Hidden Pleasures and Perils of Being a Grandmother*, ed. Barbara Graham (New York: HarperCollins, 2010), 39.

2. Carollee Howes, "Social Play of Children with Adults and Peers," in *The Oxford Handbook of the Development of Play*, eds. Peter Nathan and Anthony D. Pellegrini (New York: Oxford University Press, 2010).

3. Dorothy Canfield Fisher, *What Grandmother Did Not Know* (Boston: Pilgrim Press, 1922), 8, 7.

4. Joseph Frankel, "Halloween Candy Fear: Are Pot Gummies the New Razor Apple?" *Newsweek*, October 27, 2017.

5. Tala H. I. Fakhouri, Jeffery P. Hughes, Debra J. Brody, Brian K. Kit, and Cynthia L. Ogden, "Physical Activity and Screen-Time Viewing among Elementary School-Aged Children in the United States from 2009 to 2010," *JAMA Pediatrics* 167, no. 3 (2013): 223–29. doi:10.1001/2013.jamapediatrics.122; Lauren Hale and Stanford Guan, "Screen Time and Sleep among School-Aged Children and Adolescents: A Systematic Literature Review," *Sleep Medicine Reviews* 21 (2015): 50–58. doi:10.1016/j.smrv.2014.07.007.

6. American Academy of Pediatrics Council on Communications and Media, "Media Use in School-Aged Children and Adolescents," *Pediatrics* 138, no. 5 (2016): e20162592. doi:10.1542/peds.2016-2592.

7. Sergio M. Pellis and Vivien C. Pellis, "Rough-and-Tumble Play: Training and Using the Social Brain," in *The Oxford Handbook of the Development of Play*, eds. Peter Nathan and Anthony D. Pellegrini (New York: Oxford University Press, 2010).

8. Hanna Rosin, "The Overprotected Kid," *Atlantic*, March 19, 2014.

9. The number of babies born in the United States is about four million per year—slightly more in the last decades of the twentieth century, slightly less recently (for example, in 2016, 3.95 million babies were born). Almost all of those babies survive to age six, and a few thousand more young children enter the nation, so four million six-year-olds per year is about right. The 2016 data is from Joyce A. Martin, Brady E. Hamilton, Michelle J. K. Osterman, Anne K. Driscoll, and Patrick Drake, *Births: Final Data for 2016* (Hyattsville, MD: National Center for Health Statistics, January 31, 2018).

10. Susan G. Solomon, "How to Revitalize American Playgrounds," in *The SAGE Handbook of Outdoor Play and Learning*, eds. Tim Waller, Eva Ärlemalm-Hagsér, Ellen Beate Hansen Sandseter, Libby Lee-Hammond, Kristi Lekies and Shirley Wyver (Thousand Oaks, CA: Sage, 2017).

11. Lesley Stahl, *Becoming Grandma: The Joys and Science of the New Grandparenting* (New York: Blue Rider Press, 2016), 52.

12. Naomi I. Eisenberger, "The Pain of Social Disconnection: Examining the Shared Neural Underpinnings of Physical and Social Pain," *Nature Reviews Neuroscience* 13, no. 6 (2012): 421–34. doi:10.1038/nrn3231.

13. Dan Olweus, *Bullying at School: What We Know and What We Can Do* (Malden, MA: Blackwell, 1993).

14. Jaana Juvonen and Sandra Graham, "Bullying in Schools: The Power of Bullies and the Plight of Victims," *Annual Review of Psychology* 65 (2014): 159–85. doi:10.1146/annurev-psych-010213-115030; Christina Salmivalli and Kätlin Peets, "Bullying and Victimization," in *Handbook of Peer Interactions, Relationships, and Groups*, 2nd ed., eds. William M. Bukowski, Brett Laursen, and Kenneth H. Rubin (New York: Guilford, 2018).

15. Marion K. Underwood and Samuel E. Ehrenreich, "The Power and the Pain of Adolescents' Digital Communication: Cyber Victimization and the Perils of Lurking," *American Psychologist* 72, no. 2 (2017): 144–58. doi:10.1037/a0040429.

16. Maria M. Ttofi, David P. Farrington, and Friedrich Lösel, "School Bullying as a Predictor of Violence Later in Life: A Systematic Review and Meta-Analysis of Prospective Longitudinal Studies," *Aggression and Violent Behavior* 17, no. 5 (2012): 405–18. doi:10.1016/j.avb.2012.05.002.

17. Quoted in Nancy G. Guerra, Kirk R. Williams, and Shelly Sadek, "Understanding Bullying and Victimization During Childhood and Adolescence: A Mixed Methods Study," *Child Development* 82, no. 1 (2011): 306. doi:10.1111/j.1467-8624.2010.01556.x.

18. Lisa M. Doskocil, "Where the Bullies Are: A Study of Children's Expressions of Bullying and Compassion in a Fourth Grade Classroom" (master's thesis, Northern Arizona University, 2014). http://www.academia.edu/8896479/Where_The_Bullies_Are_A_Study_of_Childrens_Expressions_of_Bullying_and_Compassion_in_a_Fourth_Grade_Classroom.

19. Oliver W. Edwards, "Bullying among Middle School Children Raised by Grandparents," *GrandFamilies* 2, no. 2 (2015): 66–91.

20. Elizabeth A. Gunderson, Nicole S. Sorhagen, Sarah J. Gripshover, Carol S. Dweck, Susan Goldin-Meadow, and Susan C. Levine, "Parent Praise to Toddlers Predicts Fourth Grade Academic Achievement via Children's Incremental Mindsets," *Developmental Psychology* 54, no. 3 (2018): 397–409. doi:10.1037/dev0000444.

21. Kathryn Sheridan, Wendy L. Haight, and Leah Cleeland, "The Role of Grandparents in Preventing Aggressive and Other Externalizing Behavior

Problems in Children from Rural, Methamphetamine-Involved Families," *Children and Youth Services Review* 33, no. 9 (2011): 1583–91. doi:10.1016/j .childyouth.2011.03.023.

22. In many places in the United States, in 2018, the cost of identical homes, separated by a school zone boundary, differs by $100,000 or more.

23. Daphna Bassok, Scott Latham, and Anna Rorem, "Is Kindergarten the New First Grade?" *AERA Open* 2, no. 1 (2016). doi:10.1177/2332858415616358.

24. Cheryl L. Lampkin, *Insights and Spending Habits of Modern Grandparents* (Washington, DC: AARP, 2012).

25. Virpi Timonen, "Introduction: Widening the Lens on Grandparenting," in *Grandparenting: Practices around the World*, ed. Virpi Timonen (Bristol, UK: Polity Press, 2019).

26. Jeremy B. Yorgason, Laura Padilla-Walker, and Jami Jackson, "Nonresidential Grandparents' Emotional and Financial Involvement in Relation to Early Adolescent Grandchild Outcomes," *Journal of Research on Adolescence* 21, no. 3 (2011): 552–58. doi:10.1111/j.1532-7795.2010.00735.x.

CHAPTER 12: DIVORCE AND GRANDCHILDREN

1. Sanford L. Braver and Michael E. Lamb, "Marital Dissolution," in *Handbook of Marriage and the Family*, 3rd ed., eds. Gary W. Peterson and Kevin R. Bush (Springer: Boston, 2013); Paul R. Amato, "The Consequences of Divorce for Adults and Children," *Journal of Marriage and Family* 62, no. 4 (2000): 1269–87. doi:10.1111/j.1741-3737.2000.01269.x; Thomas Leopold and Matthijs Kalmijn, "Is Divorce More Painful When Couples Have Children? Evidence from Long-Term Panel Data on Multiple Domains of Well-Being," *Demography* 53, no. 6 (2016): 1717–42. doi:10.1007/s13524-016-0518-2.

2. "Forty million" is based on table A-2, United States Census Bureau, which reports 72,199,000 two-parent families and 19,663,000 single parents, about half of them with children under age six. I estimated about 10 percent of those children in two-parent families were stepchildren and that the average single parent had slightly less than two children. That is a conservative number; other scholars might have higher estimate.

3. Kevin Shafer, Todd M. Jensen, and Erin K. Holmes, "Divorce Stress, Stepfamily Stress, and Depression among Emerging Adult Stepchildren,"

Journal of Child and Family Studies 26, no. 3 (2017): 851–62. doi:10.1007/s10826-016-0617-0.

4. Marco Tosi and Marco Albertini, "Does Children's Union Dissolution Hurt Elderly Parents? Linked Lives, Divorce and Mental Health in Europe," *European Journal of Population* (2018). doi:10.1007/s10680-018-9501-5.

5. Matthew E. Dupre, "Race, Marital History, and Risks for Stroke in US Older Adults," *Social Forces* 95, no. 1 (2016): 439–68. doi:10.1093/sf/sow040; Karen C. Holden and Hsiang-Hui Daphne Kuo, "Complex Marital Histories and Economic Well-Being: The Continuing Legacy of Divorce and Widowhood as the HRS Cohort Approaches Retirement," *The Gerontologist* 36, no. 3 (1996): 383–90. doi:10.1093/geront/36.3.383.

6. Matthew R. Wright and Susan L. Brown, "Psychological Well-Being among Older Adults: The Role of Partnership Status," *Journal of Marriage and Family* 79, no. 3 (2017): 833–49. doi:10.1111/jomf.12375.

7. W. Bradford Wilcox, "The Evolution of Divorce," *National Affairs* 1 (2009): 81.

8. James P. McHale and Kristin M. Lindahl, eds., *Coparenting: A Conceptual and Clinical Examination of Family Systems* (Washington, DC: American Psychological Association, 2011).

9. Jeong-Kyun Choi, Gilbert Parra, and Qingyu Jiang, "The Longitudinal and Bidirectional Relationships between Cooperative Coparenting and Child Behavioral Problems in Low-Income, Unmarried Families," *Journal of Family Psychology* 33, no. 2 (2019): 203–14. doi:10.1037/fam0000498; Julia S. Goldberg and Marcia J. Carlson, "Patterns and Predictors of Coparenting After Unmarried Parents Part," *Journal of Family Psychology* 29, no. 3 (2015): 416–26. doi:10.1037/fam0000078.

10. Mikko Myrskylä and Rachel Margolis, "Happiness: Before and After the Kids," Demography 51, no. 5 (2014): 1843–66. doi:10.1007/s13524-014-0321-x; Kelly Musick and Katherine Michelmore, "Change in the Stability of Marital and Cohabiting Unions Following the Birth of a Child," *Demography* 52, no. 5 (2015): 1463–85. doi:10.1007/s13524-015-0425-y.

11. Judith S. Wallerstein, *Surviving the Breakup: How Children and Parents Cope with Divorce* (New York: Basic Books, 1980).

12. Judith S. Wallerstein, Julia Lewis, and Sherrin Packer Rosenthal, "Mothers and Their Children after Divorce: Report from a 25-Year Longitudinal Study," *Psychoanalytic Psychology* 30, no. 2 (2013): 176. doi:10.1037/a0032511.

13. Colleen Leahy Johnson, "Active and Latent Functions of Grandparenting during the Divorce Process," *Gerontologist* 28, no. 2 (1988): 185–91. doi:10.1093/geront/28.2.185.

14. Denis A. Thomas and Marianne Woodside, "Resilience in Adult Children of Divorce: A Multiple Case Study," *Marriage & Family Review* 47, no. 4 (2011): 213–34. doi:10.1080/01494929.2011.586300.

15. Suniya S. Luthar, "Resilience in Development: A Synthesis of Research across Five Decades," in *Developmental Psychopathology*, 2nd ed., eds. Dante Cicchetti and Donald J. Cohen (Hoboken, NJ: Wiley, 2016); Michael Rutter, "Resilience as a Dynamic Concept," *Development and Psychopathology* 24, no. 2 (2012): 335–44. doi:10.1017/S0954579412000028.

16. Ann S. Masten, *Ordinary Magic: Resilience in Development* (New York: Guilford Press, 2014), 14.

17. Remarriage is especially difficult if children are adolescents because their own adjustment to body changes and social relationships occur at the same time. Julie Gosselin, Lyzon Babchishin, and Elisa Romano, "Family Transitions and Children's Well-Being During Adolescence," *Journal of Divorce & Remarriage* 56, no. 7 (2015): 569–89. doi:10.1080/10502556.2015.1080094.

18. Sarah Halpern-Meekin and Kristin Turney, "Relationship Churning and Parenting Stress among Mothers and Fathers," *Journal of Marriage and Family* 78, no. 3 (2016): 715–29. doi:10.1111/jomf.12297; Caitlin Cross-Barnet, Andrew Cherlin, and Linda Burton, "Bound by Children: Intermittent Cohabitation and Living Together Apart," *Family Relations* 60, no. 5 (2011): 633–47. doi:10.1111/j.1741-3729.2011.00664.x.

19. Edward R. Anderson and Shannon M. Greene, "Beyond Divorce: Research on Children in Repartnered and Remarried Families," *Family Court Review* 51, no. 1 (2013): 119–30. doi:10.1111/fcre.12013.

20. Neil Ferguson, "Children's Contact with Grandparents after Divorce," *Family Matters*, no. 67 (2004): 36–41; Sarah Katharina Westphal, Anne-Rigt Poortman, and Tanja Van Der Lippe, "What About the Grandparents? Children's Postdivorce Residence Arrangements and Contact with Grandparents," *Journal of Marriage and Family* 77, no. 2 (2015): 424–40. doi:10.1111/jomf.12173.

21. Amandine Baude, Jessica Pearson, and Sylvie Drapeau, "Child Adjustment in Joint Physical Custody Versus Sole Custody: A Meta-Analytic Review," *Journal of Divorce & Remarriage* 57, no. 5 (2016): 338–60. doi:10

.1080/10502556.2016.1185203; Sanford L. Braver and Ashley M. Votruba, "Does Joint Physical Custody 'Cause' Children's Better Outcomes?" *Journal of Divorce & Remarriage* 59, no. 5 (2018): 452–68. doi:10.1080/10502556.20 18.1454203.

22. William V. Fabricius, Michael Aaron, Faren R. Akins, John J. Assini, and Tracy McElroy, "What Happens When There Is Presumptive 50/50 Parenting Time? An Evaluation of Arizona's New Child Custody Statute," *Journal of Divorce & Remarriage* 59, no. 5 (2018): 414–28. doi:10.1080/10502556.201 8.1454196; Maaike Jappens and Jan Van Bavel, "Parental Divorce, Residence Arrangements, and Contact Between Grandchildren and Grandparents," *Journal of Marriage and Family* 78, no. 2 (2016): 451–67. doi:10.1111/jomf.12275.

23. Alexander Pashos, Sascha Schwarz, and David F. Bjorklund, "Kin Investment by Step-Grandparents—More Than Expected," *Evolutionary Psychology* 14, no. 1 (2016). doi:10.1177/1474704916631213.

24. Beverly Lowry, "What Counts," in *Eye of My Heart: 27 Writers Reveal the Hidden Pleasures and Perils of Being a Grandmother*, ed. Barbara Graham (New York: HarperCollins, 2010), 35–44.

25. David A. Coall, Sonja Hilbrand, and Ralph Hertwig, "Predictors of Grandparental Investment Decisions in Contemporary Europe: Biological Relatedness and Beyond," *PLoS ONE* 9, no. 1 (2014): e84082. doi:10.1371/journal.pone.0084082.

26. Ashton Chapman, Marilyn Coleman, and Lawrence Ganong, "'Like My Grandparent, But Not': A Qualitative Investigation of Skip-Generation Stepgrandchild–Stepgrandparent Relationships," *Journal of Marriage and Family* 78, no. 3 (2016): 639–40. doi:10.1111/jomf.12303.

CHAPTER 13: ADOLESCENTS

1. Marc H. Bornstein, "Positive Parenting and Positive Characteristics and Values in Children," in *What Can Parents Do? New Insights into the Role of Parents in Adolescent Problem Behavior*, eds. Margaret Kerr, Håkan Stattin, and Rutger C. M. E. Engels (Hoboken, NJ: Wiley, 2008).

2. Margaret Kerr, Håkan Stattin, and Rutger C. M. E. Engels, eds., *What Can Parents Do? New Insights into the Role of Parents in Adolescent Problem Behavior* (Hoboken, NJ: Wiley, 2008).

3. Wim Meeus, "Adolescent Psychosocial Development: A Review of Longitudinal Models and Research," *Developmental Psychology* 52, no. 12 (2016): 1969–93. doi:10.1037/dev0000243.

4. Judith Guest, "The Road to Imperfection," in *Eye of My Heart: 27 Writers Reveal the Hidden Pleasures and Perils of Being a Grandmother*, ed. Barbara Graham (New York: HarperCollins, 2010), 147–56.

5. Jeremy B. Yorgason, Laura Padilla-Walker, and Jami Jackson, "Nonresidential Grandparents' Emotional and Financial Involvement in Relation to Early Adolescent Grandchild Outcomes," *Journal of Research on Adolescence* 21, no. 3 (2011): 552. doi:10.1111/j.1532-7795.2010.00735.x.

6. Lauren R. Bangerter and Vincent R. Waldron, "Turning Points in Long Distance Grandparent–Grandchild Relationships," *Journal of Aging Studies* 29 (2014): 92. doi:10.1016/j.jaging.2014.01.004.

7. Claire Roberts, "When Things Go Tilt," in *Eye of My Heart: 27 Writers Reveal the Hidden Pleasures and Perils of Being a Grandmother*, ed. Barbara Graham (New York: HarperCollins, 2010), 135–46.

8. Lloyd D. Johnston, Richard A. Miech, Patrick M. O'Malley, Jerald G. Bachman, John E. Schulenberg, and Megan E. Patrick, *Monitoring the Future, National Survey Results on Drug Use, 1975–2018: 2018 Overview, Key Findings on Adolescent Drug Use* (Ann Arbor: Institute for Social Research, University of Michigan, 2019). *Monitoring the Future* is an annual report on adolescent and young-adult drug use. In 2017, among high school seniors who had tried e-cigarettes, 27 percent had smoked cigarettes, and 17 percent had swallowed a prescription drug not ordered by a doctor. Rates vary from year to year and by age, but over the past decades, almost every adolescent has tried a drug. Another report (Andrea S. Gentzke, MeLisa Creamer, Karen A. Cullen, Bridget K. Ambrose, Gordon Willis, Ahmed Jamal, and Brian A. King, "Vital Signs: Tobacco Product Use Among Middle and High School Students—United States, 2011–2018," *Morbidity and Mortality Weekly Report* 68, no. 6 [2019]: 157–64. doi:10.15585/mmwr.mm6806e1) finds that e-cigarette rates are continuing to escalate for both high school and middle school students. In 2018 in the United States, 28 percent of high school students and 5 percent of middle school students were frequent users. As best we know, rates are continuing to climb, with most adolescents at least experimenting.

9. Laura Kann et al., *Youth Risk Behavior Surveillance—United States, 2017* (Atlanta: Centers for Disease Control and Prevention, June 15, 2018). This is a biennial survey of more than 10,000 high school students, from every state

and every type of school. In 2017, 17 percent of high school students seriously considered suicide. Among ninth graders, almost 9 percent made a serious attempt, as did almost 6 percent of twelfth graders. Virtually none died.

10. Erik H. Erikson, *Identity: Youth and Crisis* (New York: Norton, 1994).

11. Steven Pinker, *Enlightenment Now: The Case for Reason, Science, Humanism, and Progress* (New York: Viking, 2018).

12. Jessica Portner, *One in Thirteen: The Silent Epidemic of Teen Suicide* (Beltsville, MD: Robins Lane Press of Gryphon House, 2001).

13. These statistics are from the United States. The United Nations reports higher rates in developing nations. The male/female ratio is similar in many nations, except China, where females of every age are more likely to kill themselves (usually by swallowing poison) than males are.

14. Daniela Barni, Sonia Ranieri, and Eugenia Scabini, "Value Similarity among Grandparents, Parents, and Adolescent Children: Unique or Stereotypical?" *Family Science* 3, no. 1 (2012): 46–54. doi:10.1080/19424620.2011.671499.

15. Jean Piaget, *The Psychology of Intelligence* (New York: Routledge, 2001), 163; Bärbel Inhelder and Jean Piaget, *The Growth of Logical Thinking from Childhood to Adolescence: An Essay on the Construction of Formal Operational Structures* (New York: Routledge, 2013), 251.

16. Karyn Moffatt, Jessica David, and Ronald M. Baecker, "Connecting Grandparents and Grandchildren," in *Connecting Families: The Impact of New Communication Technologies on Domestic Life*, eds. Carman Neustaedter, Steve Harrison, and Abigail Sellen (London: Springer-Verlag, 2013), 177.

17. Susan Moore and Doreen Rosenthal, *Grandparenting: Contemporary Perspectives* (New York: Routledge, 2017).

18. The birth rate per thousand U.S. fifteen- to nineteen-year-olds was 20.3 in 2016, compared to 62 in early 1991, when many grandmothers had babies. The peak was 96 in 1957, when some current grandmothers were young girls.

19. In 1955, half of all young women were married to a man by age twenty. Now the median age of marriage for women is twenty-eight.

20. Rachel Lynn Golden, Wyndol Furman, and Charlene Collibee, "The Risks and Rewards of Sexual Debut," *Developmental Psychology* 52, no. 11 (2016): 1913–25. doi:10.1037/dev0000206.

21. Bangerter and Waldron, "Turning Points in Long Distance Grandparent–Grandchild Relationships," 94.

22. Matthew Hill, "Perspective: Be Clear about the Real Risks," *Nature* 525, no. S14 (2015). doi:10.1038/525S14a.

23. Amy T. Schalet, *Not Under My Roof: Parents, Teens, and the Culture of Sex* (Chicago: University of Chicago Press, 2001), 115.

24. Alfgeir L. Kristjansson, Inga Dora Sigfusdottir, Thorolfur Thorlindsson, Michael J. Mann, Jon Sigfusson, and John P. Allegrante, "Population Trends in Smoking, Alcohol Use and Primary Prevention Variables among Adolescents in Iceland, 1997–2014," *Addiction* 111, no. 4 (2016): 645–52. doi:10.1111/add.13248.

25. Keith Humphreys, Robert C. Malenka, Brian Knutson, and Robert J. MacCoun, "Brains, Environments, and Policy Responses to Addiction," *Science* 356, no. 6344 (2017): 1238. doi:10.1126/science.aan0655.

26. Moffatt, David, and Baecker, "Connecting Grandparents and Grandchildren."

27. Alison Gopnik, *The Gardener and the Carpenter: What the New Science of Child Development Tells Us about the Relationship between Parents and Children* (New York: Farrar, Strauss and Giroux, 2016), 125.

28. Bangerter and Waldron, "Turning Points in Long Distance Grandparent–Grandchild Relationships," 93.

29. Azadeh Forghani and Carman Neustaedter, "The Routines and Needs of Grandparents and Parents for Grandparent-Grandchild Conversations over Distance" (paper presented at the ACM CHI Conference on Human Factors in Computing Systems, Toronto, Canada, 2014).

30. Monica Anderson, Andrew Perrin, and Jingjing Jiang, "11% of Americans Don't Use the Internet. Who Are They?" Pew Research Center, accessed January 23, 2019. https://pewrsr.ch/2oJDZst.

31. danah boyd, *It's Complicated: The Social Lives of Networked Teens* (New Haven, CT: Yale University Press, 2014).

32. Kimberly J. Mitchell, Lisa M. Jones, David Finkelhor, and Janis Wolak, "Understanding the Decline in Unwanted Online Sexual Solicitations for U.S. Youth 2000–2010: Findings from Three Youth Internet Safety Surveys," *Child Abuse & Neglect* 37, no. 12 (2013): 1225–36. doi:10.1016/j.chiabu.2013.07.002.

33. Jenna L. Clark, Sara B. Algoe, and Melanie C. Green, "Social Network Sites and Well-Being: The Role of Social Connection," *Current Directions in Psychological Science* 27, no. 1 (2018): 32–37. doi:10.1177/0963721417730833.

CHAPTER 14: EMERGING ADULTS

1. The average age of a first birth of all ethnic groups in the United States was 22.7 in 1980 and 26.6 in 2018. Minority groups are not much different from U.S.-born European Americans, with 25 the average for African American and Latina women. The outlier is Asian American, at age 30 on average. This data does not reflect the growing number of men and women who never have a baby. Joyce A. Martin, Brady E. Hamilton, Michelle J. K. Osterman, Anne K. Driscoll, and Patrick Drake, *Births: Final Data for 2016* (Hyattsville, MD: National Center for Health Statistics, January 31, 2018).

2. Taichi Sakai, Yumi Sugawara, Ikue Watanabe, Takashi Watanabe, Yasutake Tomata, Naoki Nakaya, and Ichiro Tsuji, "Age at First Birth and Long-Term Mortality for Mothers: The Ohsaki Cohort Study," *Environmental Health and Preventive Medicine* 22, no. 1 (2017): 1–14. doi:10.1186/s12199-017-0631-x.

3. Laura M. Padilla-Walker and Larry J. Nelson, eds., *Flourishing in Emerging Adulthood: Positive Development during the Third Decade of Life* (New York: Oxford University Press, 2017).

4. Wiebke Bleidorn, Theo A. Klimstra, Jaap J. A. Denissen, Peter J. Rentfrow, Jeff Potter, and Samuel D. Gosling, "Personality Maturation around the World: A Cross-Cultural Examination of Social-Investment Theory," *Psychological Science* 24, no. 12 (2013): 2530–40. doi:10.1177/0956797613498396.

5. Miri Scharf, "Maturing and Aging Together: Emerging Adult Grandchildren–Grandparents Relationships," in *The Oxford Handbook of Emerging Adulthood*, ed. Jeffrey Jensen Arnett (New York: Oxford University Press, 2015), 207–8.

6. Teun Geurts, Anne-Rigt Poortman, Theo van Tilburg, and Pearl A. Dykstra, "Contact between Grandchildren and Their Grandparents in Early Adulthood," *Journal of Family Issues* 30, no. 12 (2009): 1698–713. doi:10.1177/0192513X09336340.

7. This is from the 2012 AARP survey, *Family Today*, of a cross-section of 1,884 grandparents who did not live with their grandchild. AARP, *Family Today: A Study of U.S. Families* (Washington, DC: AARP, 2012).

8. Jeff Galak, Julian Givi, and Elanor F. Williams, "Why Certain Gifts Are Great to Give But Not to Get: A Framework for Understanding Errors in Gift Giving," *Current Directions in Psychological Science* 25, no. 6 (2016): 380. doi:10.1177/0963721416656937.

9. Gloria Luong and Susan T. Charles, "Age Differences in Affective and Cardiovascular Responses to a Negative Social Interaction: The Role of Goals, Appraisals, and Emotion Regulation," *Developmental Psychology* 50, no. 7 (2014): 1919–30. doi:10.1037/a0036621; Gloria Luong, Susan T. Charles, and Karen L. Fingerman, "Better with Age: Social Relationships across Adulthood," *Journal of Social and Personal Relationships* 28, no. 1 (2011): 9–23. doi:10.1177/0265407510391362.

10. Dara H. Sorkin and Karen S. Rook, "Dealing with Negative Social Exchanges in Later Life: Coping Responses, Goals, and Effectiveness," *Psychology and Aging* 21, no. 4 (2006): 715–25. doi:10.1037/0882-7974.21.4.715.

11. Andrew Mienaltowski, "Everyday Problem Solving across the Adult Life Span: Solution Diversity and Efficacy," *Annals of the New York Academy of Sciences* 1235, no. 1 (2011): 81. doi:10.1111/j.1749-6632.2011.06207.x.

12. An AARP survey asked grandparents what they thought their role was: 83 percent replied, "teaching values," and 86 percent said, "teaching family history."

13. Jean M. Twenge, Ryne A. Sherman, and Brooke E. Wells, "Changes in American Adults' Sexual Behavior and Attitudes, 1972–2012," *Archives of Sexual Behavior* 44, no. 8 (2015): 2273–85. doi:10.1007/s10508-015-0540-2.

14. Shalom H. Schwartz, "Basic Individual Values: Sources and Consequences," in *Handbook of Value: Perspectives from Economics, Neuroscience, Philosophy, Psychology and Sociology*, eds. Tobias Brosch and David Sander (New York: Oxford University Press, 2015); Shalom H. Schwartz et al., "Refining the Theory of Basic Individual Values," *Journal of Personality and Social Psychology* 103, no. 4 (2012): 663–88. doi:10.1037/a0029393.

15. Shalom H. Schwartz, "Individual Values across Cultures," in *The Praeger Handbook of Personality across Cultures*, ed. A. Timothy Church (Santa Barbara, CA: Praeger, 2017).

16. Armen E. Allahverdyan and Aram Galstyan, "Opinion Dynamics with Confirmation Bias," *PLoS ONE* 9, no. 7 (2014): e99557. doi:10.1371/journal.pone.0099557.

17. Ingrid Arnet Connidis, "Age Relations and Family Ties Over the Life Course: Spanning the Macro–Micro Divide," *Research in Human Development* 11, no. 4 (2014): 291–308. doi:10.1080/15427609.2014.967050.

18. Joan C. Chrisler, Angela Barney, and Brigida Palatino, "Ageism Can Be Hazardous to Women's Health: Ageism, Sexism, and Stereotypes of Older

Women in the Healthcare System," *Journal of Social Issues* 72, no. 1 (2016): 86–104. doi:10.1111/josi.12157.

19. Carroll L. Estes, "Crises and Old Age Policy," in *Handbook of Sociology of Aging*, eds. Richard A. Settersten and Jacqueline L. Angel (New York: Springer, 2011), 300.

20. Reports and details vary by definition and year. U.S. data sources include the U.S. Census Bureau's American Community Survey and Current Population. Age differences are always evident. For example, in 2015, the annual income of those aged eighteen to twenty-four was $17,659 (mostly wages), and for someone aged sixty-five to one hundred, it was $38,685 (mostly Social Security). The 2015 median wealth of households headed by someone age fifteen to twenty-five was $36,000 (usually with two wage earners in the household) and of households headed by someone aged 45 to 64, $68,000.

21. National Center for Health Statistics, *Health, United States, 2017: With Special Feature on Mortality* (Hyattsville, MD: U.S. Department of Health and Human Services, 2018).

22. Stipica Mudrazija, "The Balance of Intergenerational Family Transfers: A Life-Cycle Perspective," *European Journal of Ageing* 11, no. 3 (2014): 249–59. doi:10.1007/s10433-013-0302-8; Luc Arrondel and André Masson, "Altruism, Exchange or Indirect Reciprocity: What Do the Data on Family Transfers Show?" in *Handbook of the Economics of Giving, Altruism and Reciprocity*, eds. Serge-Christophe Kolm and Jean Mercier Ythier (Amsterdam: Elsevier, 2006).

23. Madonna Harrington Meyer, "Grandmother's Financial Contributions and the Impact on Grandmothers," in *Grandparenting in the United States*, eds. Madonna Harrington Meyer and Ynesse Abdul-Malak (Amityville, NY: Baywood, 2016).

24. Louis Hyman, *Borrow: The American Way of Debt* (New York: Vintage, 2012).

25. Again, numbers vary by cohort and culture. A million dollars over a lifetime is a low estimate based on the difference in annual salary over thirty-five years. Some calculations say two million.

26. Rachel E. Dwyer, Laura McCloud, and Randy Hodson, "Debt and Graduation from American Universities," *Social Forces* 90, no. 4 (2012): 1133–55. doi:10.1093/sf/sos072.

27. Quoted in Alexander Coggin, "Debt Dodgers: Meet the Americans Who Moved to Europe and Went AWOL on Their Student Loans," *Vice*, January 17, 2016.

28. Christian Deindl and Nicole Tieben, "Resources of Grandparents: Educational Outcomes Across Three Generations in Europe and Israel," *Journal of Marriage and Family* 79, no. 3 (2017): 769–83. doi:10.1111/jomf.12382.

29. National Center for Health Statistics, *Health, United States, 2016: With Chartbook on Long-Term Trends in Health* (Hyattsville, MD: U.S. Department of Health and Human Services, 2017).

30. Steven M. Kogan, Leslie G. Simons, Yi-Fu Chen, Stephanie Burwell, and Gene H. Brody, "Protective Parenting, Relationship Power Equity, and Condom Use Among Rural African American Emerging Adult Women," *Family Relations* 62, no. 2 (2013): 341–53.

31. Jeff Greenberg, "Terror Management Theory: From Genesis to Revelations," in *Meaning, Mortality, and Choice: The Social Psychology of Existential Concerns*, eds. Phillip R. Shaver and Mario Mikulincer (Washington, DC: American Psychological Association, 2012); Gurit Birnbaum, Gilad Hirschberger, and Jamie Goldenberg, "Desire in the Face of Death: Terror Management, Attachment, and Sexual Motivation," *Personal Relationships* 18, no. 1 (2011): 1–19. doi:10.1111/j.1475-6811.2010.01298.x.

32. Steven Pinker, *Enlightenment Now: The Case for Reason, Science, Humanism, and Progress* (New York: Viking, 2018).

33. Maike Luhmann, "The Development of Subjective Well-Being," in *Personality Development across the Lifespan*, ed. Jule Specht (San Diego, CA: Academic Press, 2017), 209.

34. Sara M. Moorman and Jeffrey E. Stokes, "Solidarity in the Grandparent–Adult Grandchild Relationship and Trajectories of Depressive Symptoms," *Gerontologist* 56, no. 3 (2016): 408–20. doi:10.1093/geront/gnu056.

35. Geneviève Gariépy, Helena Honkaniemi, and Amélie Quesnel-Vallée, "Social Support and Protection from Depression: Systematic Review of Current Findings in Western Countries," *British Journal of Psychiatry* 209, no. 4 (2016): 284–93. doi:10.1192/bjp.bp.115.169094.

Index

abduction, 174

ability, preserving, 235–40

abortion, 107, 215

accidents, 28; death by, 204*f*

achievement, as value, 228

activities: with adolescents, 217–18; with emerging adults, 226; with school children, 169–70

addiction, 190, 207, 237; babies and, 122

ADHD (attention-deficit/hyperactivity disorder), 70

admiration: and discipline, 166–67; for infant care, 132–38

adolescents, 203–21; causes of death in, 204–5, 204*f*; and stepfamilies, 279n17; and three-generation households, 79

adoption, 119–20

advice. *See* restraining comments

Africa, 27, 120

African Americans: and age at first birth, 284n1; and birth rates, 9; and custodial grandmothers, 67–68, 256n8; and racial socialization, 180; and stress, 155; and three-generation households, 77*f*

age: and causes of death, 204, 204*f*; change in approaches to, 12; evolution and, 17; and fatherhood, 21–22; at first birth, 284n1; and grandmothering, 6; of grandmothers, 91; and marriage, 87, 90, 190, 215, 282n18; of maturity, changes in, 99, 99*f*; and money, 231–33, 286n20; and pregnancy, 106; and stepfamilies, 201; of weaning, 146

ageism, 98; and death rates, 12; and grandmother role, 12–15

aging: attitudes toward, 240; effects of, 47, 230, 235–37

Ainsworth, Mary, 139

allomothers, 22–23, 120

altruism, 42

American Society of Pediatricians, 172

amniocentesis, 107–8

anchor role, in divorce, 193–98

Andersen, Hans Christian, 181

About the Author

Kathleen Stassen Berger is professor at Bronx Community College, City University of New York, where she has taught psychology for forty years. She is the author of the leading textbooks in human development used by college students in all fifty states and in twelve nations, in five languages. She is also the mother of four and the grandmother of three.